OXFORD HISTORIC.

Edito

P. CLAVIN, R. J. W. EVANS, L. GOLDMAN, J. ROBERTSON,
R. SERVICE, P. A. SLACK, B. WARD-PERKINS, J. WATTS

Writing the Holocaust

Identity, Testimony, Representation

ZOË VANIA WAXMAN

OXFORD
UNIVERSITY PRESS

OXFORD

UNIVERSITY PRESS

Great Clarendon Street, Oxford OX2 6DP

Oxford University Press is a department of the University of Oxford.
It furthers the University's objective of excellence in research, scholarship,
and education by publishing worldwide in

Oxford New York

Auckland Cape Town Dar es Salaam Hong Kong Karachi
Kuala Lumpur Madrid Melbourne Mexico City Nairobi
New Delhi Shanghai Taipei Toronto

With offices in

Argentina Austria Brazil Chile Czech Republic France Greece
Guatemala Hungary Italy Japan Poland Portugal Singapore
South Korea Switzerland Thailand Turkey Ukraine Vietnam

Oxford is a registered trade mark of Oxford University Press
in the UK and in certain other countries

Published in the United States
by Oxford University Press Inc., New York

British Library Cataloguing in Publication Data

Data available

Library of Congress Cataloging in Publication Data

Data available

Typeset by Laserwords Private Limited Chennai, India.
Printed in Great Britain
on acid-free paper by
Biddles Ltd., King's Lynn, Norfolk

ISBN 978–0–19–920638–4 (Hbk.) 978–0–19–954154–6 (Pbk.)

1 3 5 7 9 10 8 6 4 2

For Sharon Hannah Levine

Acknowledgements

This book arises from my doctoral thesis. I am extremely grateful to the Faculty of History, Oxford University, and St Antony's College, Oxford, for providing me with an Oxford University Graduate Studentship, and also to the managers of the Arnold, Bryce, and Read Funds for awarding me the 1999–2000 Lothian Studentship in Modern History. My thesis could not have been written without the expertise of my supervisor, Jonathan Webber. His extraordinary knowledge of the Holocaust and Jewish history were invaluable. I would also like to thank Connie Webber for her generous hospitality. Nick Stargardt and Isabel Wollaston examined my thesis. Their insightful suggestions instructed the writing of this book, and I am indebted to Nick Stargardt for his time and patience in seeing it through to publication.

I benefited from innumerable inspiring and challenging conversations with Mark Greenaway. We discussed many ideas over the course of days, if not months, and without him a very different book would have been written. He also provided friendship and support at a time when it was greatly needed. I hope he knows how much I appreciate it.

I would also like to thank my colleagues at Mansfield College, Oxford, for providing me with a supportive environment in which to finish the project, especially Michael Freeden, Kathryn Gleadle, David Leopold, Ron Nettler, Lucinda Rumsey, Prince Saprai, and my constantly stimulating tutees. Particular thanks go to Paul Lodge for being such a loyal and thoughtful friend. The Oxford Centre for Hebrew and Jewish Studies has been similarly encouraging of both my research and my teaching. I would particularly like to thank the many graduate students who have developed my thinking on the Holocaust, and also David Rechter, for his kindness and advice.

Acknowledgements

Josie McClellan and William Whyte have been generous not only with their considerable intellects but also with their friendship. A big thank you to you both. I am also greatly appreciative of the many others who have read and commented on the different parts of this book in its various stages. Particular thanks to Susannah Heschel, Esther Jilovsky, Matthew Reisz, David Rundle, Dan Stone, and Jean van Altena for her much needed help in preparing the manuscript for publication. Finally, I would like to thank my family for their love and the constant distractions.

Contents

Note on Foreign Language Names and Terms

To honour the original intentions of the authors, when using testimonies and other primary documents, or when citing historians and other theorists, original names and spellings have been retained. When referring to places that now have accepted English names, such as Warsaw, names are given in that form. However, to preserve accuracy and authenticity, and in line with current English trends, pre-war names with their original spellings are used in other cases. Many places in countries that were occupied were re-named by the Germans. However, with the exception of the German-named Auschwitz (for the Polish Oświęcim) and Theresienstadt (for Terezín), the original native names are given. For example, the Polish 'Chełmno' is used rather than the German 'Kulmnof'. Except in direct quotations, diacritics are used for all Latin-alphabet languages. For example, Bełżec not Belzec, and Łódź not Lodz. For the non-Latin-alphabet languages of Hebrew and Yiddish, non-scholarly transliteration systems are used. In the case of books with foreign-language titles I have included an English translation in parentheses at the first mention, and, where appropriate, other foreign-language terms are treated in the same way.

Introduction

Show an interest in this document. It contains rich material for
the historian.

Załman Gradowski

There is now an enormous literature attesting to the magnitude of the
Holocaust. From the beleaguered witnesses writing in the ghettos and
the concentration camps, to the émigré survivors committed to
remembering the dead, countless attempts have been made not only
to document the atrocities but to retrieve some meaning from what
the Jews were forced to endure. Increasingly, historians, philosophers,
and theologians are being left to confront this daunting task. As they
inherit the diaries and other documents written by those who knew
they would not survive, or the memoirs produced by those who have
dedicated their lives to educating future generations, they have to
decide how these testimonies should be comprehended and represented. For example: as testaments to the strength of the human
spirit; as historical documents; as attempts to describe the ineffable.
To answer such questions, it is necessary to resist the tendency of
recent Holocaust scholarship to universalize or collectivize Holocaust
testimony, and instead to revive the particular by uncovering the mul-
tiple layers within testimony. It is only by exploring the social and historical context of Holocaust testimony that we can appreciate the
sheer diversity of witnesses' experiences.

Three main theses emerge during the course of the present study.
First, Holocaust testimony has a history—a history that has been
largely ignored because testimony is usually treated as a separate,
homogenized, self-contained canon. Secondly, Holocaust testimony

not only has a history, one that goes back to the events of the Holocaust, it is also contingent upon and mediated by this history. Bearing witness is inextricably entwined with the social and historical conditions in which it is done; it is dependent on contemporary conceptions of identity, memory, and representation. Many witnesses were fully aware of both their role as documenters and of the historical importance of their experiences as they unfolded, and this guided their writing. Finally, Holocaust testimony attests to the heterogeneity of Holocaust experiences. The Holocaust was not just one event, but many different events, witnessed by many different people, over a time span of several years and covering an expansive geographical area. The following chapters will look at testimony written both during and after the Holocaust, including the testimonies of its first chroniclers, confined to the Nazi-enforced ghettos; the rare testimony constructed in the concentration camps; and post-war testimony, including today's survivors, writing as part of a 'collective memory'.[1]

While no study of testimony can be comprehensive, as the vast majority of victims perished without ever writing down their experiences, the testimonies featured are written by a wide variety of authors from both Eastern and Western Europe. They come from both men and women, the old, and from those who were children during the war. Some were educated, some religious, some both, and some neither. The primary focus is on post-war English-language materials readily accessible to the general reader. This allows us to look at the construction of testimony within the context of its publication and reception, and thus reassess the manner in which we

---

[1] In contrast to Sigmund Freud's conception of memory as essentially imposed, the French sociologist Maurice Halbwachs, a student of Émile Durkheim who made the original contribution that memory is necessarily socially constructed, proposed that 'collective memory' be understood as the 'social frameworks' on to which individual memories are woven. In other words, while remembering may be done individually, it is social groups that determine the form that the remembering takes. See Maurice Halbwachs, *On Collective Memory*, trans. Lewis A. Coser (Chicago, 1992). Peter Novick further elaborates that collective memory should not be understood as the past living on in the present, but rather how present and future concerns dictate which bits of the past we remember (Peter Novick, *The Holocaust and Collective Memory: The American Experience* (London, 2000), 3; for the American publication, see Peter Novick, *The Holocaust in American Life* (New York, 1999)).

approach the reading of testimony. Published testimonies not only relate witnesses' experiences, but also tell us something about collective understandings of the Holocaust. Although considerable weight is given to witnessing as a specifically Jewish response to the events of the Holocaust, also included are testimonies of non-Jewish victims, including the Polish poet Tadeusz Borowksi and Charlotte Delbo, a member of the French Resistance Movement. However, because this work is primarily concerned with Jewish experiences, the testimonies of other groups singled out for persecution under the Nazi regime, such as the Sinti (German Gypsies), the Roma (Gypsies of Eastern Europe), and Jehovah's Witnesses are not covered.

The first chapter looks at the testimony written during the events of the Holocaust, while the following chapters focus predominantly on survivors' testimonies written after the war. Along the way it will be seen how the conditions and motivations for bearing witness changed. Chapter 1 examines the work of Emmanuel Ringelblum, a trained social historian and teacher, who initiated the Warsaw-based secret archives of *Oneg Shabbat* (Sabbath Delight—a code-name for the clandestine Sabbath afternoon gatherings). These archives, which represent the most systematic attempt to record Jewish suffering during the Holocaust, were dedicated to finding the best way to record the uprooting of communities, and the suffering and destruction of Polish Jewry.[2] Ringelblum and his colleagues in the Warsaw ghetto

---

[2] The *Łódź Ghetto Chronicle*, compiled by the Department of the Archives of the Jewish Council in Łódź (German: Litzmanstadt) in south-west Warsaw, documents the life of the Jews of Łódź from January 1941 to July 1944. See Lucjan Dobroszycki (ed.), *The Chronicle of the Łódź Ghetto, 1941–44*, trans. Richard Lourie, Joachim Neugroschel, *et al.* (New Haven, 1984). Photographs taken by Mendel Grossman have also survived as part of the archive; see Mendel Grossman, *With a Camera in the Ghetto*, ed. Zvi Szner and Alexander Sened (New York, 1977). In Kovno (Lithuanian: Kaunas) in central Lithuania, the *Judenrat* (Jewish Council) commissioned artists to make a visual record of Jewish life. An engineer by the name of Hirsh Kadushin became the photographic chronicler of the ghetto. Using a small camera concealed in his clothing, he managed to film many aspects of ghetto life. He obtained the film from a nurse who worked with him in the ghetto hospital. Kadushin's buried photographs were discovered after the war, and can now be viewed in the United States Holocaust Memorial Museum in Washington. Archives were also set up in Białystok in north-east Poland; Vilna (Lithuanian: Vilnius), the capital of Lithuania; Kraków, in southern Poland; and Lvov (Polish: Lwów, German: Lemberg) in eastern Galicia.

were able to amass a considerable amount of information; he noted:
'The drive to write down one's memories is powerful . . . even young
people in labour camps do it.'[3] By secretly recording Jewish life in
Poland during the German occupation, and continuing the Jewish
tradition of witnessing, the Warsaw ghetto chroniclers, both individually and collectively, performed important acts of resistance. They
were able to foresee that what they were experiencing would one day
be studied as important historically, and this awareness shaped their
writing.[4] Chaim Kaplan, a committed diarist of the Warsaw ghetto,
even went so far as to anticipate the publication of his memoir: 'The
time may come when these words will be published. At all events they
will furnish historiographic material from the chronicle of our
agony.'[5]

Considerably fewer testimonies were written in the concentration
camps, or survived them. Chapter 2 highlights how the conditions of
the concentration camps largely militated against the writing of testimony, and looks at the few important exceptions, including the writings of the *Sonderkommando* (special detachment) prisoners forced to
work in the crematoria of Auschwitz-Birkenau,[6] who consciously
resisted the Nazis not only by leaving documentation of their existence, but also by bearing witness to the destruction of the European
Jews. The testimonies of survivors reveal how the concentration
camps disconnected prisoners from their previous identities. They

[3] Emmanuel Ringelblum, *Notes from the Warsaw Ghetto: The Journal of Emmanuel
Ringelblum*, trans. Jacob Sloan (New York, 1958), 31; originally published in Yiddish as
Notitsen fun Varshever geto (Warsaw, 1952).

[4] There are 272 diaries, written in Polish and Yiddish, held at the ŻIH (*Żydowski
Instytut Historyczny* (Jewish Historical Institute)) in Warsaw. Sixty-five of the diaries are
concerned with the Warsaw ghetto. Not all the diaries have been published.

[5] Chaim A. Kaplan, *Scroll of Agony: The Warsaw Diary of Chaim A. Kaplan*, trans.
Abraham I. Katsh (Bloomington, Ind., 1999), 121; originally published in Hebrew as
Megilat yishurin: yoman geto Varshah, ed. Abraham I. Katsh (Tel Aviv, 1966).

[6] What is commonly referred to as 'Auschwitz' was a conglomerate of two main camps
and some fifty subcamps and purpose-built factory compounds situated to the west and
south-west of the town of Oświęcim (renamed Auschwitz by the Germans), in eastern
Upper Silesia, 50 km south-west of Kraków. The name 'Auschwitz' will be used to refer to
the general collectivity of the camp when distinctions between its various components
are not relevant, or when referring to more than one of the camps. The two largest camps
were Auschwitz I (the *Stammlager*, or base camp), established by Heinrich Himmler,

also show that it was essential to regain a part of the past in order to find some meaning that would allow them to carry on the struggle to survive; for many, it was the desire to bear witness, and hence the post-war memoir became a vehicle for the resurrection of identity.

Chapter 3 charts the path of the 'liberated prisoners' and their gradual re-categorization over time, first as 'Displaced Persons', and eventually as 'survivors'. It shows how the post-war introduction of the concept 'the Holocaust' to describe survivors' experiences and the adoption of the post-war identity of the survivor as witness acted as organizational frameworks for survivors' experiences, enabling personal experiences of suffering to be viewed as essential components of a collective historical event. To illustrate the hegemony of collective memory, Chapter 4 looks at the representation of women's Holocaust testimonies, to show how studies of women's lives during the Holocaust, in attempting to portray women in a specific manner, seek a homogeneity of experience that did not exist, overlooking testimonies that do not fit with preconceived gender roles. These studies often project their own concerns, selecting testimonies that reinforce their pre-existing ideals and ignoring 'difficult' testimonies that reveal experiences outside the dictates of collective memory—such as the female Jewish *Kapos* (heads of work commandos) who came to mimic the behaviour of their SS (*Schutzstaffel* (Protection Squad)) captors.

The concluding chapter argues that while the role of the witness has given survivors a sense of purpose, their bearing of witness is

Reichsführer (Reich Leader) of the SS in April 1940, as a concentration camp for Polish political prisoners, but which operated a gas chamber and crematorium I from September 1940 until July 1943, and Auschwitz-Birkenau (Auschwitz II), hereafter referred to simply as Birkenau (Polish: Brzezinka). Birkenau, an extension camp built less than 3 km to the north-west of the original camp in October 1941, was originally intended for Soviet prisoners of war. Approximately five times the size of Auschwitz I, it later became a death camp housing the principal gas chambers and crematoria (crematoria II, III, IV, and V). Prisoners not murdered on arrival were housed in the Gypsy family camp, the Czech family camp, the *Frauenabteilung* (women's section), or one of the many men's barracks. Auschwitz-Monowitz (Auschwitz III), hereafter referred to as Monowitz (Polish: Monowice), became a slave labour camp in 1941, and included Buna Werke, a synthetic-rubber works erected by I. G. Farben. See Jonathan Webber, *The Future of Auschwitz: Some Personal Reflections* (Oxford, 1992), 4 n. 3, and Yisrael Gutman and Michael Berenbaum (eds.), *Anatomy of the Auschwitz Death Camp* (Bloomington, Ind., 1994).

inextricably mediated by the post-war concept of the Holocaust and by collective memory, both of which determine the parameters of Holocaust representation. It can be seen that the function of collective memory is not to focus on the past in order to find out more about the Holocaust, but to use the past to inform and address present concerns. Also, it shows how the role of the witness has expanded, so that survivors—who are considered unique—now inform us not just about the Holocaust, but provide universal lessons regarding morality and the human condition. As the historian Christopher Browning has observed, 'perhaps the most serious challenge in the use of survivor testimony as historical evidence is posed not by those who are inherently hostile to it but by those who embrace it too uncritically and emotionally.'[7] The sanctification of testimony further serves to entrench and concretize the position of accepted Holocaust narratives and forms of representation. Inevitably, this leaves the difficult testimonies that stand outside official narratives in an awkward position; it also sets the agenda for the representation of further testimonies that have to negotiate the political and ideological concerns of collective memory.

[7] Christopher R. Browning, *Collected Memories: Holocaust History and Postwar Testimony* (Madison, 2003), 40.

1

Writing as Resistance? Bearing Witness in the Warsaw Ghetto

> My utmost concern is for hiding my diary so that it will be preserved for future generations.
>
> Kaplan, *Scroll of Agony*

Jews writing in the ghettos consciously defied the Nazis' intention to leave no trace of Jewish existence. By secretly recording Jewish life in Poland during the German occupation, the Warsaw ghetto chroniclers—both on an individual and a collective level, and mediated by their Jewish identity—performed an important act of resistance. This chapter documents the various motivations for their writing, including personal confession, the need to produce historical testimony, to resist, to assert individual agency, to continue the Jewish tradition of witnessing, and to provide a memorial.

The writings cited in this chapter—the journal of Emmanuel Ringelblum and the diaries of Chaim Kaplan, Janusz Korczak, and Mary Berg, among others—were written by those not only inextricably immersed in the events they describe, but also inextricably linked to their historically contingent Jewish identities. While memory and post-Holocaust identity are coming to be acknowledged as factors that mediate the memories of survivors, the observations of the ghetto diarists are treated almost reverentially, as if providing snapshots of history, unaffected by the social, economic, and political

circumstances in which they were written. However, this chapter
demonstrates that the ghetto diaries cannot be read as accounts of
pure, unmediated experiences, for they are subject to the negotiation
of particular identities—predominantly a shared sense of Jewish
identity and the need to bear witness.

Emmanuel Ringelblum's journal indicates that he, like many other
ghetto diarists, saw himself as writing from within and for a specific
community, rather than as an isolated individual. Chaim Kaplan
describes the suffering experienced daily in the Warsaw ghetto, in
particular the hunger and frustration of the Jews; he saw it as his
duty to describe the suffering, and suggests that the recording of it
instilled in him a sense of purpose. Even personal accounts like Janusz
Korczak's, which make little reference to the growing turmoil in the
ghetto and the deportations, are concerned with the transmitting of
experience from the realization of its cultural, religious, and historical
importance.

A further important category of testimony included in this chapter
is the testimony of the escapees. For example, Yakov Grojanowski,
who managed to escape from the Chełmno (Kulmhof during the
German occupation) death camp and reach Warsaw to recount his
experiences. His testimony shows that during the war testimony had
a very concrete function: to warn the Jews of their impending fate and
to inform the free world of the tragedy befalling the Jews.[1] It also
demonstrates that bearing witness can be regarded as resistance not
just in a spiritual or emotional sense, but also in practical terms. In
Chapter 5 it will be seen how the concept of resistance has continued
to occupy a central place in the comprehension of Holocaust testimony, not only when looking at writings produced during the war,
but also when considering the post-war recollections of survivors. In
particular, the idea of testimony as collective Jewish resistance against
the Nazi attempt to erase any trace of the Jews of German-occupied

---

[1] The testimony of Yakov Grojanowski has been published in full in Martin Gilbert,
The Holocaust: The Jewish Tragedy (London, 1987), 252–79.

Europe continued to be a substantial part of the motivation for survivors to come forward to tell their stories.

However, not all the ghetto diarists were concerned with collective
resistance. For example, the diaries of Adam Czerniaków, head of
the Warsaw *Judenrat*, and Calel Perechodnik, a member of the
Ordnungsdienst (Order Service—the official name for the German-
organized Jewish police), elude the rhetoric of resistance. Their
morally ambiguous position within the structure of ghetto life is mir-
rored in their writings. Czerniaków and Perechodnik write not of a
shared sense of suffering, but of isolation and disconnection. While
Czerniaków's rather emotionless diary is widely cited as an important
source for exploring the role of the *Judenrat* in the fate of Polish Jewry,
Perechodnik's moral indictment of himself has been largely overlooked. Arguably, despite the many errors of judgement with which
he is charged, Czerniaków was still trying to work for the Jewish
community, whereas Perechodnik admits that he joined the
Ordnungsdienst in a desperate attempt to save himself and his family.
Their writings, like those cited above, offer important insights into
how these men perceived their position in the ghetto and what
prompted them to act the way they did. Also, they attest to the
heterogeneous nature of Holocaust testimony.

The mass deportations from the Warsaw ghetto, which began on
22 July 1942, brought renewed urgency to the matter of resistance.
They showed that cultural resistance in the form of the continuation
of intellectual and spiritual life was no longer enough to sustain the
survival of the Jews. Jewish leaders instead called for armed resistance.
The Warsaw Ghetto Uprising, although an extraordinary act, was
limited in scope. However, its significance for Jewish self-identity is
clear; as Mordecai Anielewicz wrote shortly before his death, 'The last
desire of my life has been fulfilled. Jewish self-defence is a fact.'[2]

[2] 'The Last Letter from Mordecai Anielewicz, Warsaw Ghetto Revolt Commander,
April 23, 1943', in Yitzhak Arad, Yisrael Gutman, and Abraham Margaliot (eds.),
*Documents on the Holocaust: Selected Sources on the Destruction of the Jews of Germany and
Austria, Poland, and the Soviet Union*, 4th edn. (Jerusalem, 1981), 315–16.

THE ESTABLISHMENT OF THE
WARSAW GHETTO

German troops invaded Poland on 1 September 1939, and Warsaw surrendered on 27 September 1939. In the pre-war period the Jewish community in Poland had represented the largest community of European Jewry; by 1939 there were around 3.3 million Jews living in Poland, and 375,000 in Warsaw, which was a major centre of Jewish cultural and political life.[3] On 21 September 1939, Reinhard Heydrich, head of the Security Police, sent a letter to the commanders of the *Einsatzgruppen* (mobile killing units) setting out instructions regarding Jews in the occupied territories and specifying the concentration of Jews in large cities and the introduction of the *Judenräte*.[4] Around 90,000 more Jews came to Warsaw from Łódź, Włocławek, Kalisz, and other cities and towns in the Western District of Poland—either as refugees or because they were deported by the Germans. On 26 October 1939, the *Generalgouvernement* was established to administer the central section of Poland covering Kraków, Lublin, Warsaw, and Radom. It was ruled from Kraków by the German governor-general, Hans Frank.[5] The Warsaw *Judenrat* was ordered to produce lists of all Jews living in their vicinity; all Jewish bank accounts and deposit accounts were blocked, and Jews were forbidden to have more than 2,000 *złotys* in cash.[6] On 17 October 1939, Ludwig Fischer, the governor of the Warsaw district, had issued a decree for the 'disposal

[3] On the history of Jews in Poland, see Joseph Marcus, *Social and Political History of the Jews in Poland, 1919–1939* (Berlin, 1983). For an account of the worsening situation of European Jewry, see Lucy S. Dawidowicz, *The War against the Jews, 1933–1945* (New York, 1975). For a study of Warsaw Jewry during the Holocaust, see Israel Gutman, *The Jews of Warsaw, 1939–1943: Ghetto, Underground, Revolt*, trans. Ina Friedman (Brighton, 1982). Gutman himself participated in the Warsaw Ghetto Uprising.

[4] See Document 73, in Arad *et al.* (eds.), *Documents on the Holocaust*, 173–8.

[5] After the German invasion of the Soviet Union, the province of Galicia, made up of parts of the pre-war Polish provinces of Lwów, Stanisłów, and Tarnapol, was added to the *Generalgouvernement*.

[6] Cited in Barbara Engelking, *Holocaust and Memory: The Experience of the Holocaust and its Consequences. An Investigation Based on Personal Narratives*, trans. Emma Harris, ed. Gunnar S. Paulsson (London, 2001), 21. In 1939, 1 US dollar was worth approximately 2.6 Polish *złotys* (ibid. 73).

and leasing of Jewish enterprises', and on 30 November 1939, a further decree ordered Jews to wear a white armband imprinted with a blue Star of David on the sleeve of their outer clothing. On the same day it was ordered that Jewish shops be marked with the Jewish star, and on 18 December, all Jewish property had to be registered.[7] By 2 October 1940, Fischer drafted an order for the establishment of a ghetto in Warsaw.[8] The decree was announced on 12 October 1940, which coincided with Yom Kippur (the Day of Atonement). On that day, Chaim Kaplan, a teacher and diarist of the Warsaw ghetto, noted:

The Jewish community of Warsaw left nothing out in its prayers, but poured its supplications before its Father in Heaven in accordance with the ancient custom of Israel. To our greatest sorrow, as the day drew to a close, at a time when the gates of tears were still open, we learned that a new edict had been issued for us, a barbaric edict which by its weight and results is greater than all the other edicts made against us up to now, to which we have become accustomed. At last the ghetto edict has gone into effect. For the time being it will be an open ghetto, but there is no doubt that in short order it will be closed.[9]

Kaplan was right: on 16 November 1940, the ghetto was declared a *Seuchensperrgebiet* (quarantine area) and was sealed with a 10-foot wall, imprisoning 138,000 Jews (the 113,000 non-Jewish Poles living in the area were forced to leave). It was soon supplemented by the arrival of numerous refugees. Around 30 per cent of the population of Warsaw was forced into 2.4 per cent of the city's area, and it became the largest ghetto in European history. At its height, more than 400,000 people were imprisoned there.

EMMANUEL RINGELBLUM AND *ONEG SHABBAT*

When the war began, Emmanuel Ringelblum was in Geneva, serving as a delegate to the Twenty-first World Zionist Congress. He returned

[7] Ibid. These are only a sample of the anti-Jewish decrees issued; they give a succinct insight into the social and economic conditions to which the Jews of Warsaw were subjected.
[8] See Document 100, in Arad *et al.* (eds.), *Documents on the Holocaust*, 220–1.
[9] Chaim A. Kaplan, *Scroll of Agony,* 207–8.

in order to continue his work for the Warsaw office of the American-based Jewish Joint Distribution Committee (the 'Joint'), which distributed funds to local Jewish agencies, including the network of orphanages CENTOS (*Centrala Opieki nad Sierotami* (National [Jewish] Society for the Care of Orphans)). Ringelblum's involvement in relief activities put him in an important position. He explains:

I had daily lively contact with everything that was happening . . . News came to me of every event affecting Jews in Warsaw and its suburbs. Almost every day I saw delegations from the Polish provinces. . . . At night, when my work with the committee was done, I made notes of what I had heard during the day.[10]

Within a month of the German invasion, Ringelblum was beginning to form the secret *Oneg Shabbat* archives in Warsaw. He started with just one senior assistant—the young historian Rabbi Shimon Huberband—but, in May 1940, employed several other helpers, including Hirsch Wasser, the secretary of the archives, and journalists Peretz Opoczynski and Rachel Auerbach.[11] With the sealing of the ghetto, Ringelblum and the staff of *Oneg Shabbat* (coded O.S. in Ringelblum's journal)—including Menahem Kon, a social worker who directed the finances of the O.S. (most of their funding came from the Joint Distribution Committee) and who also wrote a diary[12]—transformed the archive into an organized underground operation dedicated to finding the best way to record the uprooting of communities and the suffering and destruction of Polish Jewry. They decided to collect diaries and eyewitness accounts, which were mostly written in either Yiddish or Polish (Ringelblum himself wrote in Yiddish). Those involved in collecting the material were very much aware that it would provide vital information for future historians. They understood that the suffering they observed and experienced

---

[10] Ringelblum, *Notes from the Warsaw Ghetto*, p. xviii.

[11] See her monograph, Rachel Auerbach, *Varshever tsavoes: bagegenishn, aktivitetn, goy-roles 1933–1943* (Warsaw Testaments: Encounters, Activities, Fates) (Tel Aviv, 1974).

[12] See Menahem Kon, 'Fragments of a Diary (August 6, 1942–October 1, 1942)', trans. M. Z. Prives, in Joseph Kermish (ed.), *To Live with Honor and Die with Honor! Selected Documents from the Warsaw Ghetto Underground Archives 'O.S.' ['Oneg Shabbath']* (Jerusalem, 1986), 80–6.

was part of something very significant. Two days after the sealing of the ghetto, Chaim Kaplan wrote:

What we dreaded most had come to us. We had a premonition that a ghetto life awaited us, a life of sorrow and poverty, of shame and degradation, but no one believed that the fateful hour would come so soon. And suddenly—a frightful surprise! On the eve of the Sabbath of Parashat Vayera, the fourteenth of Marheshvan, 5701 [the Sabbath when the biblical portion—*parasha*—of Gen. 18: 1–22: 2 is read], we went to bed in the Jewish quarter, and the next morning we woke up in the closed ghetto, a ghetto in every detail.[13]

Emmanuel Ringelblum observed:

The war produced rapid changes in Jewish life in the towns of Poland. Each day was different from the next. The scene changed as quickly as in a movie. . . . Every month brought profound changes which fundamentally altered Jewish life. It was therefore important to capture every event in Jewish life in the heat of the moment, when it was still fresh and pulsating.[14]

Before the war Ringelblum had worked for the ŻIH in Warsaw and was an affiliate of YIVO (*Yidisher Vissenshaftlecher Institut* (Jewish Scientific Institute)), an institution which encouraged the collection of primary source material—especially autobiographies. He was born in Buczacz in eastern Galicia, educated at the University of Warsaw, and went on to teach history at a high school. In 1927 he was awarded a doctorate for a dissertation on the history of Warsaw Jewry in the Middle Ages. In 1928 he helped found the 'Circle of Young Historians' in Warsaw, which published the periodical *Der Yunger Historiker* (The Young Historian). He also published articles on the history of Warsaw Jewry, paying particular attention to social and economic problems. However, his perilous return to Poland points to something more than just a desire to produce historical records. Ringelblum and his colleagues envisaged the possibility of using their documentation to persuade the free world to intervene in order to save the Jews. In December 1942, Ringelblum wrote that they 'understood how important it was for

[13] Kaplan, *Scroll of Agony*, 225.
[14] Emmanuel Ringelblum, 'O.S.', in Kermish (ed.), *To Live with Honor and Die with Honor!*, 10.

future generations that evidence remain of the tragedy of Polish Jewry. Some also understood that the collected material served the present as well, informing the world of the horrors perpetrated against the Jews.'[15] The material was used as a source of information for bulletins mimeographed and sent to the communal leaders and editors of the Polish underground press. The Polish underground then sent reports alerting the free world to the atrocities and mass murders being committed on Polish soil, to the exiled Polish government in London, and through them, to the Allied governments. Information was based on documents, official instructions, oral testimonies, and the written reports of those who managed to escape from the camps. The first of these reports was sent in October 1941 recounting the mass murder of Jews in the territories of Eastern Europe, including occupied Poland, the Baltic States, Belorussia, and western Ukraine.

In March 1942, Ringelblum provided the Polish underground with a report citing the murder of 180,000 Jews (mostly from the Łódź ghetto and other towns of the Warthegau, an area of Poland annexed by Germany in October 1939) and Gypsies in gas-vans at the Chełmno death camp situated 60 km west of Łódź. On 6 January 1942, Mordechai Podchlebnik was among thirty men brought to Chełmno to dig pits in the nearby woods for the dead bodies; the previous diggers had all been shot. In the cellar where the men lived, Podchlebnik found various inscriptions on the wall stating: 'No one leaves this place alive'; 'Whoever can, should save himself'; 'Every day, two or three of us are being taken away and they do not return'; 'No one survives this place very long'; and 'When people are taken to work, they are being shot'.[16] The following day Podchlebnik was present at the arrival of a truckload of deportees. He observed their relief at being told they were going to the bath-house for a shower and new clothes, and then witnessed them being forced through a corridor and into a truck on the other side. He records:

The next day we continued to work, and more people were brought in—we heard the screams from the trucks as the engine began working and the gas

15 Ringelblum, 'O.S.', 7–8.   16 See M. Gilbert, *The Holocaust*, 246–8.

flowed in; then the screams died down, and we—five of us—were taken from a cellar and we had to take the clothes and shoes left behind and put them in a room which was already full of shoes and clothing. And in the evening people came back from working in the woods. They returned from work, but two or three were already missing—these people had grown weak and could no longer work: they were shot and left behind. The next day I didn't want to stay where I was. I was among the first five who were taken out to work in the forest. That's where they dug the trenches: there were twenty-five people and they were all digging trenches. . .

They were all completely dead. No one was alive any more. These people who were taken from the trucks were dead. But I remember that there was one in all that period, a man of my town, a healthy and strong man who still showed signs of life, and then someone approached him and shot him dead. But this was the only time. The man's name was Jakobowitz. When the trucks arrived we were still not permitted to go near them; we had to wait until they had stopped for two or three minutes and the fumes had dispersed. Then five or six people would open the doors and take out the corpses and place them right near the trenches.[17]

A few days later Podchlebnik managed to jump out of the vehicle taking him and the other grave-diggers to work in the woods. After the war, when testifying at the trial of Adolf Eichmann in Jerusalem, he recalled: 'By the time they turned round and started shooting, I was already in the forest.'[18] At the time, Ringelblum and the members of *Oneg Shabbat*, like the other Jews in the ghettos of Eastern Europe, were unaware of the gassings at Chełmno. However, on 19 January 1942, Yakov Grojanowski also escaped the grave-diggers' squad; he managed to reach the Warsaw ghetto, where he informed Ringelblum of the details of his fourteen days at the death camp and the mass killing of the Jews and the Gypsies.[19] Ringelblum realized the importance of Grojanowski as an eyewitness to the mass murder which was taking place in a death camp in occupied Poland—indeed, he was the first such eyewitness from what would later be known as

---

[17] Ibid. 247.   [18] Ibid. 248.
[19] This account of Yakov Grojanowski's escape and the full publication of his testimony can be found in ibid. 252–79. Cf. Shmuel Krakowski and Ilya Altman (eds.), 'The Testament of the Last Prisoners of the Chełmno Death Camp', *Yad Vashem Studies*, 21 (1991), 105–23.

16   *Writing as Resistance?*

one of the major death camps and of which fewer than ten prisoners are thought to have survived.[20]

On Friday, 26 June 1942, Ringelblum described the feelings of the members of the O.S. on hearing a broadcast by British radio consisting of information that he believed had been smuggled to London by the Polish underground:

It is not important whether or not the revelation of the incredible slaughter of Jews will have the desired effect—whether or not the methodical liquidation of entire Jewish communities will stop. One thing we know—we have fulfilled our duty. We have overcome every obstacle to achieve our end. Nor will our deaths be meaningless like the deaths of tens of thousands of Jews. We have struck the enemy a hard blow. We have revealed his Satanic plan to annihilate Polish Jewry, a plan which he meant to complete in silence.[21]

Although, by early 1942, reports were reaching England detailing the massacres of Jews in Poland and the Soviet Union, Ringelblum believed that London did not know of the atrocities being carried out against the Jews. Therefore for him and his staff, witnessing had a very concrete function. Using testimony to break the silence of both the British and the Germans by letting the world know what was going on gave them a sense of purpose and allowed them a moral victory. Even if it did not stop the killing, they had done their best to defy their German oppressors. However, attempts to influence Allied policy were soon to be seen to be in vain as the rate of destruction increased.[22] By 30 June 1942, Ringelblum began to ponder the world's silence:

During the last days the Jewish population has been living under the impact of news from London. The news that the world has not been stirred by the reports of the slaughter in Poland has aroused the deepest emotions in all of us. For many, many months we endured the most terrible suffering and we

[20] Simon Srebnik, who survived Chełmno, was interviewed by Claude Lanzmann in his documentary film *Shoah* (1985). For the full text of the film, see Claude Lanzmann, *Shoah: An Oral History of the Holocaust. The Complete Text of the Film* (New York, 1985).

[21] Ringelblum, *Notes from the Warsaw Ghetto*, 295–6.

[22] See Walter Laqueur, *The Terrible Secret: An Investigation into the Suppression of Information about Hitler's 'Final Solution'* (London, 1980). Cf. Martin Gilbert, *Auschwitz and the Allies* (London, 1981), and David Wyman, *The Abandonment of the Jews: America and the Holocaust, 1941–1945* (New York, 1984).

kept asking ourselves: Does the world know about our sufferings, and if it knows, why is it silent? Why was the world not outraged by the fact that tens of thousands of Jews were shot to death at Ponary. Why was the world silent when tens of thousands of Jews were poisoned in Chełmno? . . . Only now have we come to understand the cause of this silence: London just did not know anything about all that was happening here, and that was the reason for this silence . . . Now we ask: if London knew, the next day, that one hundred people [Poles] were shot in the Pawiak prison,[23] why then did it take many months before they learned in London of the hundreds of thousands of murdered Jews?[24]

Ringelblum and his colleagues, realizing the futility of their efforts to gain Allied intervention, redirected their energy into retaining physical evidence of the nature and existence of Jewish life in the Warsaw ghetto. They started to gather material for those who might one day want to research the destruction of Polish Jewry. They collected diaries, letters, medical prescriptions, wrapping papers from sweets produced in the ghetto, children's school reports and essays, invitations to literary events and concerts, documents from Jewish institutions and the German administration, publications of the Jewish underground press,[25] and notes on Allied radio broadcasts. In particular, it is the acquisition of items such as sweet wrappers and children's school reports that most speaks of their disillusionment in attempting to ward off an increasingly inevitable fate. Mounting awareness of the fragility of Jewish existence meant that Ringelblum and the O.S. were intent on documenting Jewish life and its destruction.

Although concerned with the Warsaw ghetto, they also sought material significant to the occupation of many other Jewish communities in Poland. The refugees living in the ghetto were looked after by ŻTOS (*Żydowskie Towarzystwo Opieki Społecznej* (Jewish Society for Social Welfare)), which provided the archives with dates and

[23] The nickname of the Warsaw prison at 24/26 Dzielna Street. When the ghetto was closed off, the prison was included.

[24] Cited in Nora Levin, *The Holocaust: The Destruction of European Jewry 1933–1945* (New York, 1973), 232.

[25] See Joseph Kermish and Yisrael Bialostocki (eds.), *Itonut-hamahteret hayehudit beVarshah* (Jewish Underground Press in Warsaw), 6 vols. (Jerusalem, 1979–97).

information regarding events in the different communities. The Warsaw archives of the O.S. represent the most systematic attempt to record Jewish suffering during the Holocaust. With the important exception of the Orthodox Rabbi Shimon Huberband,[26] it was staffed mostly by young Labour Zionists who were 'on the whole, grass-roots intelligentsia, mostly members of proletarian parties'.[27] In going about their work, the ghetto diarists had the same fear that many post-war witnesses developed about the aestheticization of the suffering of the Jewish people through the use of poetic or luxurious language. Ringelblum declared:

We intentionally avoided professional journalists because we did not want the writing to become hackneyed. We made a conscious effort that the course of events in every town, the experience of every Jew—and every Jew during the present War is a world in himself—would come across simply and faithfully. Every superfluous word, every literary turn of language or embellishment grates on the ear and evokes resentment. Wartime Jewish life is so rich in tragedy that it is unnecessary to enrich it with one superfluous line.[28]

The aim was to provide a simple and unambiguous account of the sufferings of the Jews: 'Comprehensiveness was the main principle of our work. Objectivity was the second. We endeavoured to convey the whole truth, no matter how bitter, and we presented faithful unadorned pictures.'[29] Ringelblum's description of the work of the O.S. shows how theories of testimony were already being formed while in the ghetto:

We tried to give an all-embracing picture of Jewish life during the war. Our aim was a presentation of a photographically true and detailed picture of what the Jewish population had to experience, to think and to suffer. We tried to have the same event, the history of a community for instance, described by both an adult and a young person; by a pious Jew who is conscious at all times of the rabbi, the synagogue, the cemetery and other

---

[26] See Shimon Huberband, *Kiddush Hashem: ktavim miymey hasho'ah* (Kiddush Hashem: Writings from the Holocaust), ed. Nachman Blumental and Joseph Kermish (Tel Aviv, 1969); published in English as *Kiddush Hashem: Jewish Religious and Cultural Life in Poland during the Holocaust*, trans. David E. Fishman, ed. Jeffrey S. Gurock and Robert S. Hirt (Hoboken, NJ, 1987).

[27] Ringelblum, 'O.S.', 7.   [28] Ibid.   [29] Ibid. 9.

religious institutions, and also by a secular Jew who stresses other moments of no less importance in his account.[30]

In the following chapters it will be seen how survivor witnesses have struggled to meet the ultimately impossible requirements of comprehensiveness and objectivity; as they learnt more about the many and varied events of the Holocaust, they were to realize the boundaries of their own, very subjective experiences. However, Ringelblum was not advocating that a single witness should meet the criteria of comprehensiveness and objectivity; rather, he saw the gathering of many different testimonies as a way to meet this aim. David Roskies points out that Ringelblum did not just want to provide his own account of events, but 'tried to have the same events described by as many people as possible'.[31] Although he was one of the leaders of the left-wing *Poalei Zion—Hitahdut* (Zionist Labour Movement) in the Warsaw ghetto, Ringelblum wanted to ensure that the O.S. did not record just one political perspective. The archives were, at least in theory, open to anyone who wanted to contribute. As Ringelblum explains: 'By comparing the different accounts, the historian will not find it difficult to reach the kernel of historical truth, the actual course of an event.'[32] The explicit purpose was to gain as much material as possible to help the future historian. A further unspoken reason might have been the belief that a multiplicity of voices would bear witness to the magnitude of the suffering of the Jews. Although Ringelblum wanted to leave behind a diversity of voices, they all shared a common theme: they were Jewish and described Jewish life.[33] Ringelblum and the staff of the O.S. were writing from within a Jewish discourse regarding catastrophe, persecution, and witnessing. From this perspective, it could be argued that the ghetto diarists were

---

[30] Ibid. 8–9.

[31] David G. Roskies, *The Jewish Search for a Usable Past* (Bloomington, Ind., 1999), 22.

[32] Ringelblum, 'O.S.', 8–9.

[33] Ringelblum also collected material on Jews who had converted to Christianity. The Nazi racial laws had consigned approximately 2,000 Jewish converts to Christianity to the Warsaw ghetto. Ringelblum noted the hostility directed at them by their Jewish neighbours, a hostility that some of them returned, and the relatively high rate of suicide among them.

not just bearing witness to their own destruction, but were placing it within a history of earlier acts of destruction.[34]

NEGOTIATING LIFE IN THE GHETTO

It is important to understand that many of Ringelblum's aims for the archives could never be realized fully. At first, Ringelblum thought that the Germans would not be interested in what went on behind the ghetto walls, but he soon saw that he was mistaken. In a climate of increasing hostility, the dangers of maintaining such an illegal activity amid a large Gestapo presence quickly became apparent, and large-scale recruiting was effectively abandoned. Furthermore, while theoretically the archives were open to anyone who wished to contribute (and Ringelblum believed that this was one way in which a stunned Jewish people could at least in part rebel against their predicament), its precarious nature meant that every new worker had to undergo certain tests before being admitted; even those involved in the archives could not be told who was in charge of the collection itself. Contact between the members was also limited. The very name *Oneg Shabbat* was intended to be vague so as to ensure secrecy. The slogan of the O.S. was 'We must work poorly', for, as Ringelblum explained, 'Everything must be done to avoid disclosing the rich O.S. treasure.'[35] Secrecy was not just an issue for Ringelblum and the staff of the O.S., but a necessity negotiated by many of the ghetto diarists. Ringelblum writes:

During the first months the public was fearfully terrorized and afraid of house-searches. At the time Jews burnt everything, even innocent books,

---

[34] For example, David Roskies writes that 'Ringelblum is to Oyneg Shabes as Rav Ashi was to the Babylonian Talmud' (Roskies, *Jewish Search for a Usable Past*, 25). The Talmud was collected and summarized by the Babylonian scholar Rav Ashi in response to the destruction of the Second Temple; written 300–400 years after the event, it records the rituals of the Temple service and creates a substitute to allow Judaism to continue. Roskies argues that the material collected by Ringelblum constitutes a similar response (see David G. Roskies, *Against the Apocalypse: Responses to Catastrophe in Modern Jewish Culture* (Cambridge, Mass., 1984)).   [35] Ringelblum, 'O.S.', 11.

which were not forbidden even under Hitler. . . . In time people calmed down. . . . And then Jews began to write. Everybody wrote: journalists, writers, teachers, social activists, youth and even children.[36]

However, the need for secrecy inevitably led to the omission of certain details, and these omissions resulted in unavoidable tensions which are expressed in the ghetto diaries. As James Young observes, 'Even though they may have been writing their journals explicitly for posterity's sake, the ghetto diarists remained ever aware that these works might be discovered prematurely.'[37]

Ghetto diarists had to be cautious about discussing plans for resistance: they had to balance carefully the need to inform future historians against their own need to survive. Ringelblum, although very much involved in plans for the Ghetto Uprising, made no mention of such activity in his journal. Nevertheless, he and his staff still managed to collect a significant amount of information on the wartime experiences of Jewish women, men, teenagers, children, the religious and the secular, and converts. In this sense, the work of the O.S. can be understood in terms of a particular approach to the recording of history—as *Alltagsgeschichte* (the study of everyday life), as it came to be called in the 1970s and 1980s. It significantly documents all of the following: the resistance movement, economic resistance, political parties, the *Judenrat*, the *Ordnungsdienst*, Jewish assimilationists and converts, independent social aid, welfare organizations, hospitals, deportations and transfers between towns, mass murders, cultural activities, literature, religion—including the 600 illegal *minyanim* (groups of Jews praying together, in which at least ten adult males need to be present) in Warsaw,[38] death rates, trade and contraband, craftsmen, the *Landmannschaften* organizations,[39] refugee concentrations, hunger, morality in the ghetto, and German workshops and legislation.

---

[36] Ringelblum, *Notes from the Warsaw Ghetto*, 318.

[37] James E. Young, *Writing and Rewriting the Holocaust: Narrative and the Consequences of Interpretation* (Bloomington, Ind., 1988), 26.

[38] See Ringelblum, *Notes from the Warsaw Ghetto*, 47.

[39] Social and philanthropic organizations formed by East European immigrants during the late nineteenth and early twentieth century, first in the United States, thereafter in Palestine, and later in Israel.

Following the great deportation—*Große Aktion* (Great Action)—beginning on 22 July 1942, Ringelblum and his staff became desperate to obtain any German document bearing witness to the mass destruction. Posters, copies of German letters, bulletins, and official forms were all collected. The archives also contain material on social class in the ghetto, and on the relations between Germans and Jews and between non-Jewish Poles and Jews. (Ringelblum wrote a volume on Polish–Jewish relations as part of his research project. He completed it after the liquidation of the ghetto when he was in hiding on the Aryan side of Warsaw in 1943.[40]) Sources for the archives include letters, newspapers from the Jewish and Polish undergrounds,[41] and German and Polish official newspapers. Another important means of information came from the couriers (usually Jewish girls able to pass as Aryan) who travelled illegally through occupied Poland.[42]

Ringelblum was particularly critical of the Warsaw *Judenrat*, chaired between October 1939 and July 1942 by Adam Czerniaków, who was appointed by the Gestapo. It had 7,000 employees in 1942, but the number was reduced to 3,000 after the deportations.[43] Most had served on Jewish community councils or had been leaders in the Jewish community before the war.[44] The staff of the O.S. sent requests to the *Judenrat* for copies or originals of important documents. Mostly they did not oblige. The *Judenrat* was ordered to provide the German

[40] See Emmanuel Ringelblum, *Polish–Jewish Relations during the Second World War*, ed. Joseph Kermish and Shmuel Krakowksi (Jerusalem, 1974).

[41] Yisrael Gutman has found forty-seven underground periodicals in Warsaw, written in Hebrew, Yiddish, and Polish. See Gutman, *Jews of Warsaw*, 144–54.

[42] See Lenore J. Weitzman, 'Living on the Aryan Side in Poland: Gender, Passing, and the Nature of Resistance', in Dalia Ofer and Lenore J. Weitzman (eds.), *Women in the Holocaust* (New Haven, 1998), 187–222.

[43] Abraham J. Edelheit and Hershel Edelheit, *History of the Holocaust: A Handbook and Dictionary* (Boulder, Colo., 1994), 88.

[44] See Isaiah Trunk, *Judenrat: The Jewish Councils in Eastern Europe under Nazi Occupation* (New York, 1972), 29–35. Trunk argues that understanding the role of the *Judenrat* provides 'the key to internal Jewish history under Nazi rule' (p. xviii). Cf. *idem*, 'The Organizational Structure of the Jewish Councils in Eastern Europe', *Yad Vashem Studies*, 7 (1968), 147–64. For an evaluation of Trunk's study, see Raul Hilberg, 'The Ghetto as a Form of Government: An Analysis of Isaiah Trunk's Judenrat', in Yehuda Bauer and Nathan Rotenstreich (eds.), *The Holocaust as Historical Experience* (New York, 1981), 293–305.

authorities with updated lists of Jews and their possessions, to pay levies and provide Jewish labour for German work projects, such as the slave labour factories producing goods for the German war effort.[45] The *Ordnungsdienst* had to ensure that German regulations were met, and also round up Jews for 'relocation'. Czerniaków was subordinate to the German authorities, but held significant responsibility for Jewish matters. Ringelblum criticized the *Judenrat* by suggesting that their actions were governed more by political considerations than by humanitarian concerns. However, he also realized that the *Judenrat* was faced with the impossible task of organizing ghetto life: control of the *Ordnungsdienst*, economic matters, education, and the provision of sustenance and health and welfare services.

The most difficult task that the *Judenrat* faced was the provision of lists of deportees to 'the East'—although some Jews, lured by false promises of bread, offered themselves voluntarily. On 20 July 1942, when deportations from the Warsaw ghetto were imminent, Czerniaków went to various members of the Gestapo asking about the validity of the rumours of 'resettlement'.[46] When he discovered that the final destination of these deportees was the gas chambers of Treblinka, he refused to sign the edict concerning the resettlement of children and instead took his own life. Before taking the cyanide tablet on 23 July 1942, he wrote two suicide notes, one to his wife and the other to a colleague: 'I am powerless. My heart trembles in sorrow and compassion. I can no longer bear all this. My act will prove to everyone what is the right thing to do.'[47] For Chaim Kaplan, this act served to exonerate Czerniaków from the mistakes he had made during his life: 'He perpetuated his name by his death more than his life.'[48] Others, such as Marek Edelman, a leader of the Ghetto Uprising who managed to survive, saw

[45] See Document 82, 'Establishment of Judenräte in the Occupied Territories, November 28, 1939', in Arad *et al.* (eds.), *Documents on the Holocaust*, 191–2. Cf. Trunk, *Judenrat*, chs. 1–2.

[46] See Adam Czerniaków, *The Warsaw Diary of Adam Czerniakow: Prelude to Doom*, ed. Raul Hilberg, Stanislaw Staron, and Josef Kermisz (New York, 1973).

[47] Joseph Kermish, 'Introduction', in *Adam Czerniaków, yoman geto Varsha: 6.9. 1939–23.7.1942* (Adam Czerniaków, Warsaw Ghetto Diary) (Jerusalem, 1968), p. xix.

[48] Cited in Dawidowicz, *War against the Jews*, 301.

the act as one of supreme selfishness. In his view, instead of killing himself, Czerniaków should have made the truth known: 'One should die only after having called other people into struggle.'[49] Edelman charged Czerniaków with 'having made his death his own private business'.[50] In other words, Czerniaków is condemned for deciding his fate from a personal rather than a collective perspective.

During his life, Czerniaków kept a carefully written diary, meticulously recording the date and time of each of his entries. He even recorded the criticism he received from Jews, Poles, and Germans. He made no mention of any underground activity, apart from stating that the Germans had asked him to stop it, and that they had threatened punishment, which possibly suggests that he was fearful of the diary falling into German hands. He wrote very little about his wife and about the loss of his son Jasz, who had vanished near Lvov (in the south-east of the country). Czerniaków's notebooks, which had been small enough to fit into his inside coat pocket, were discovered after the war hidden on the Aryan side of Warsaw. In August 1964, Yad Vashem acquired seven of the eight notebooks that make up the diary (the fifth notebook was lost). It is clearly not a finalized piece of work, for it is characterized by fragmentary sentences, abbreviations, and personal asides. One possibility is that Czerniaków might have planned to write a memoir once the war had ended; one day perhaps he intended to justify his position and his relationship to his fellow Jews, and place himself within the collective.

The *Ordnungsdienst* was also heavily criticized by Ringelblum; he said that its members' cruelty was 'at times greater than that of the Germans, the Ukrainians and the Latvians'.[51] However, they were also trying to negotiate survival within the difficult and uncertain terms of German occupation. For example, 27-year-old Calel

---

[49] Cited in Hanna Krall, *Shielding the Flame: An Intimate Conversation with Dr. Marek Edelman, the Last Surviving Leader of the Warsaw Ghetto Uprising*, trans. Joanna Stasinska and Lawrence Weschler (New York, 1977), 9. On the suicide of Czerniaków, see Aryeh Tartakower, 'Adam Czerniakow: The Man and his Supreme Sacrifice', *Yad Vashem Studies*, 6 (1967), 55–67, and Mendel Kohansky, 'The Last Days of Adam Czerniakow', *Midstream*, 15 (1969), 61–7.   [50] Cited in Krall, *Shielding the Flame*, 9.

[51] Cited in Israel Gutman, *Resistance: The Warsaw Ghetto Uprising* (Boston, 1994), 143.

Perechodnik, in the ghetto of Otwock, near Warsaw, decided to join the ghetto police to avoid deportation to the labour camps. He hoped that his decision would protect not only himself but also his wife Anka and their 2-year-old daughter Alúska. However, on 19 August 1942, when Perechodnik helped herd 8,000 Otwock Jews into cattle cars for deportation to Treblinka, he spotted his wife and daughter among them. In this event he became simultaneously a victim, a perpetrator, and a bystander. He spent the rest of his short life with his mother in a hiding place in Warsaw.[52] During those 105 days he wrote his story, but is thought to have taken a cyanide pill when his hiding place was discovered. He wrote:

To be exact, this is a confession about my lifetime, a sincere and true confession. Alas, I don't believe in divine absolution, and as far as others are concerned, only my wife could—although she shouldn't—absolve me. However, she is no longer among the living. She was killed as a result of German barbarity, and, to a considerable extent, on account of my recklessness. Please consider this memoir to be my deathbed confession.[53]

Determined that this confession would outlive him, shortly before his death in 1944, he gave it to his Polish friend 'Magister'. After the war, Magister's wife gave it to Perechodnik's older brother, Pesach, who had been in Russia during the war. The original text was given to the Yad Vashem archives in Jerusalem, and a further copy to the ŻIH. Its controversial nature (in particular, its condemnation of Jewish leaders and institutions) meant that it was not published until 1993; perhaps, in part, due to its differing so greatly from both Ringelblum's account and the collective response of other ghetto diarists. Perechodnik's concern was not the fate of the Jews, but the fate of himself and his family. Pawl Szapiro, who edited the Polish text, declared in his 'Afterword' that Perechodnik 'took part to a significant degree in its [the Holocaust's] implementation' and that he was also a 'collaborator in the crime'.[54] The title 'Am I a

[52] Frank Fox, 'Foreword', in Calel Perechodnik, *Am I a Murderer? Testament of a Jewish Ghetto Policeman*, ed. Frank Fox (New York, 1996), pp. ix–x; originally published in Polish as *Czy Ja Jestem Mordercą?*, ed. Pawl Szapiro (Warsaw, 1993).

[53] Perechodnik, 'Preface', in *Am I a Murderer?*, p. xxi.

[54] Fox, 'Foreword', p. xv.

Murderer?' comes from a quotation selected by Szapiro; Perechodnik's own title in the manuscript held at Yad Vashem is the rather less striking, but actually more revealing, 'A History of a Jewish Family During German Occupation'.[55] For Perechodnik, who had escorted his family to their deaths, only his wife could absolve him of his crimes.

SUFFERING IN THE GHETTO

For Lawrence Langer, author of numerous books on Holocaust literature, testimony, art, and film,[56] the significance of the Warsaw ghetto diaries is their ability to provide a glimpse into the daily struggle for survival. Jews in the ghettos of Eastern Europe were being purposefully starved to death. Whole families could be found in the streets begging for food. The inhabitants of the Warsaw ghetto were allocated just 300 calories per day (Poles had 634, and Germans 2,310). They were given half a pound of sugar and four pounds of bread per month[57]—although people in certain professions such as medics and firefighters received slightly larger rations. Other foodstuffs, such as potatoes, were allocated only sporadically, and in sparse quantities. Chaim Kaplan tells us how rampant hunger was in the ghetto: 'Our constant song—potatoes! This word is repeated a hundred and one times at every moment. It is our whole life. When I am alone in my room for a few moments of quiet, the echo of that word continues in my ears. Even in my dreams it visits me.'[58]

Also, it was impossible to keep kosher—*shehita* (Jewish ritual slaughter of animals for food) was forbidden, and for most, horsemeat

---

[55] Fox, 'Foreword', p. xvii.

[56] See Lawrence Langer, *Preempting the Holocaust* (New Haven, 1998); *idem*, *Admitting the Holocaust: Collected Essays* (Oxford, 1995); *idem*, *Art from the Ashes* (New York, 1991); *idem*, *Holocaust Testimonies: The Ruins of Memory* (New Haven, 1991); *idem*, *Versions of Survival: The Holocaust and the Human Spirit* (Albany, NY, 1982); *idem*, *The Age of Atrocity: Death in Modern Literature* (Boston, 1978); and *idem*, *The Holocaust and the Literary Imagination* (New Haven, 1975).

[57] Jeremy Noakes (ed.), *Nazism 1919–1945*, iv: *The German Home Front in World War II* (Exeter, 1998), 1067.   [58] Kaplan, *Scroll of Agony*, 226.

was the only meat to be obtained. Although it is not a permitted food, many observant Jews were driven by hunger to eat it. On 23 February 1941, rabbis in the Łódź ghetto ruled under the authority of the doctrine of *pikuakh nefesh* (saving an endangered life) that the consumption of non-kosher meat be permitted for pregnant women and those who were unwell.[59] As conditions worsened, horsemeat also became unavailable.

The lack of food deeply divided ghetto society. While people with limited financial resources were slowly starving to death, there were others who by purchasing foodstuffs on the black market could eat much better. Those who were affluent could even frequent the various cafés, restaurants, and nightclubs that sprang up in the ghetto. Stefan Ernest provides the following description of the situation:

There are twenty thousand, perhaps thirty thousand, people who really have enough to eat; they are the social elite. They contrast with the quarter-of-a-million-strong mass of beggars and paupers who are only struggling to postpone death by starvation. . . . And in between these two is a group of about two hundred thousand 'ordinary people' who more or less manage, and retain some sort of human face. They are still clean, dressed, their stomachs are not swollen from starvation.[60]

Among the social elite were Mary Berg and her family. Berg's was one of the first survivor accounts of life in the Warsaw ghetto to be published.[61] It is based on a diary—originally written in Polish—which Berg kept while in the ghetto, and which she took with her to the United States. Berg, who was 15 years old when she started her diary on 10 October 1939, tells how her family escaped from Łódź to Warsaw at the beginning of the German invasion, returned briefly to Łódź before returning to Warsaw—Mary and her sister in December 1939, and their parents slightly later—and then remained in the

---

[59] Dawidowicz, *War against the Jews*, 250.
[60] Cited in Engelking, *Holocaust and Memory*, 104.
[61] Mary Berg, *Dziennik z Getta Warszawkiego* (Warsaw, 1945); published in English as *Warsaw Ghetto: A Diary*, trans. Norbert Guterman and Sylvia Glass, ed. S. L. Shneiderman (New York, 1945).

ghetto from the time it was sealed off until a few days before the first major deportation began on 22 July 1942.[62] On 17 July 1942, the Bergs were interned in the Pawiak prison as American citizens: Berg's mother, Lena, was born in New York, and her status as an American citizen protected the family. On 18 January 1943, they were sent to an internment camp at Vittel in France, and one year later were selected for an exchange with German prisoners in the United States.[63] They arrived in the United States on 16 March 1944. Berg, who since the publication of her diary has attempted to deny her past, was clearly what people in the ghetto referred to as one of the 'golden youth'.[64] The Bergs had managed to hold on to some of their wealth in their flight from Łódź, and they were also able to receive packages from relatives in the United States. Furthermore, as an American citizen, Mrs Berg was allowed to leave the ghetto. Abraham Levin gives a glimpse of how the family might have been perceived in the ghetto:

The ghetto is most terrible to behold with its crowds of drawn faces with the colour drained out of them. Some of them have the look of corpses that have been in the ground a few weeks. They are so horrifying that they cause us to shudder instinctively. Against the background of these literally skeletal figures and against the all-embracing gloom and despair that stares from every pair of eyes, from the packed mass of passers-by, a certain type of girl or young woman, few in number it must be said, shocks with her over-elegant attire. . . . Walking down the streets I observe this sickly elegance and am shamed in my own eyes.[65]

While Mary Berg and her family might indeed have been privileged, they too suffered the misery of life behind the walls of the Warsaw

[62] This account of Mary Berg and her diary comes from Susan L. Pentlin, 'Holocaust Victims of Privilege', in Harry James Cargas (ed.), *Problems Unique to the Holocaust* (Lexington, Ky., 1999), 25–42.
[63] Vittel, a spa in the Vosges, near Nancy, was used to hold relatively protected persons, either those deemed suitable for exchange or holders of American documents.
[64] Pentlin, 'Holocaust Victims of Privilege', 30.
[65] Abraham Lewin [Levin], *A Cup of Tears: A Diary from the Warsaw Ghetto*, trans. Christopher Hutton, ed. Antony Polonsky (Oxford, 1988), 84. Cited in Pentlin, 'Holocaust Victims of Privilege', 33. Originally published in Hebrew as *Mipinkaso shel hamoreh miyehudia* (From the Notebook of the Teacher from Yehudia), ed. Zvi Szner (Tel Aviv, 1969).

ghetto. Moreover, Berg's diary shows that she was aware of the suffering around her. She writes: 'I have become really selfish. For the time being I am still warm and have food, but all around me there is so much misery and starvation that I am beginning to be very unhappy.'[66] As well as hunger, the majority of the ghetto inhabitants also endured a shortage of heating materials—in the Warsaw ghetto coal was so scarce that it was referred to as 'black pearls'.[67] Moreover, terrible overcrowding made the maintenance of basic hygiene standards extremely difficult. Living in close quarters to people dying from starvation, coupled with the presence of rotting corpses, encouraged typhus and tuberculosis. While a clandestine medical school was in operation between May 1941 and July 1942, as well as a professional school of nursing which was permitted by the SS, the ghetto's medical facilities were inadequate to curtail such diseases, or appease suffering.[68] An unknown nurse in a hospital in the Warsaw ghetto recorded:

In the entrance hall lies a boy of five, swollen with hunger. He is in the last stage, his life ending because of hunger. He came to the hospital yesterday. Eyes swollen, hands and feet puffed up like balloons. Every possible analysis is being made; maybe kidneys, perhaps heart. No, neither this nor that. The child still moves his lips, he begs for some bread. I try to feed him something, hoping he could take something down. Alas, the throat is swollen shut, nothing passes down, too late. The doctor asks him 'did you get anything to eat at home?' 'No.' 'Would you like to eat now?' 'Yes!' Some few minutes later he utters for the last time 'a piece of bread,' and with this expression he sinks into sleep. Dead for a piece of bread.[69]

During certain periods the Joint-sponsored ŻTOS catered for as many as 100,000 people—about 25 per cent of Jews living in

---

[66] Berg, *Warsaw Ghetto*, 57.   [67] Dawidowicz, *War against the Jews*, 209.

[68] See Charles G. Roland, *Courage under Siege: Starvation, Disease and Death in the Warsaw Ghetto* (Oxford, 1992), and *idem*, 'An Underground Medical School in the Warsaw Ghetto', *Medical History*, 33 (1989), 399–419.

[69] Anonymous, 'Scenes from a Children's Hospital', in Kermish (ed.), *To Live with Honor and Die with Honor!*, 405.

Warsaw. However, this did little to appease the hunger. On the dilemma of Jewish self-help, Ringelblum wrote:

The well-established fact is that people who are fed in the public kitchens are all dying out, subsisting as they do only on soup and dry rationed bread. So the question arises whether it might not be more rational to set aside the money that is available for the sole use of certain select individuals, those who are socially productive, the intellectual elite and the like. However, the situation is that, in the first place, the elite themselves constitute a considerable group and there wouldn't be enough to go around even for them; and, in the second place, why should laborers and artisans, perfectly deserving people who were productive in their home towns, and whom only the war and the ghetto existence have deprived of their productive capacity—why should they be judged worthless, the dregs of society, candidates for mass graves? One is left with the tragic dilemma: being that no one will survive? Or are we to give full measure to a few, with only a handful having enough to survive?[70]

One response to this tragic dilemma was the act of smuggling, which became a primary means of survival. Adam Czerniaków suggested that as much as 80 per cent of food entering the ghetto was smuggled in.[71] Professional smugglers brought in large quantities and protected themselves by bribing German, Polish, and Jewish gate guards. Amateur smugglers—often very small children—crept through gaps in the ghetto wall. A third group—Christian Poles—provided food to the Jews, mostly at black market prices.[72] The head of the *Judenrat's* Department of Hospitals, Dr Israel Milejkowski, wrote a tribute to smugglers in a preface to his medical study on hunger in the Warsaw ghetto (carried out under the auspices of the O.S.). He observed that the smuggler 'with his blood and sweat, gave us the possibility of existence and work in the ghetto'.[73] From this perspective, smuggling emerges as an important form of resistance. It is perhaps this type of activity—often overlooked in favour of more confrontational forms

[70] Ringelblum, *Notes from the Warsaw Ghetto*, 181–2.
[71] Cited in Gutman, *Jews of Warsaw*, 67.
[72] See Roland, *Courage under Siege*, 110–12.
[73] Cited in Dawidowicz, *War against the Jews*, 212–13.

of resistance—that informs us of the mundane nature of suffering in the ghetto.

WRITING AS RESISTANCE?

Although witnesses such as Mordecai Anielewicz wanted to promote Jewish resistance, Lawrence Langer—a well-known critic of the increasing tendency to use the Holocaust to promote simplistic moral messages about the importance of heroism, or the triumph of good over evil—dismisses any notion that the act of writing under such difficult conditions might be regarded as resistance. He explains:

Although this assumption has nurtured an extensive commentary on the Holocaust, it is at odds, linguistically and ultimately factually, with the reality of the survivors' memory. In framing the Holocaust through the lens of heroic rhetoric, Holocaust chroniclers exhibit their own discomfort with the facts left to us by Holocaust victims, dead and alive, and reveal the inadequacy of our language in the face of what there is to tell.[74]

Although 'framing the Holocaust through the lens of heroic rhetoric' might be 'factually' at odds with the grim reality of ghetto life, it does give voice to the concerns of many ghetto diarists, who needed to find something positive in their response to the catastrophe they were experiencing. Even so, it can be argued that Ringelblum and his staff—propelled by a strong sense of Jewish identity—shared a commitment to present Jewish responses to German persecution in the best possible light. This is illustrated by statements such as the following: 'The historian of the future will have to devote a fitting chapter to the role of the Jewish woman during the war. It is thanks to the courage and endurance of our women that thousands of families have been able to endure these bitter times.'[75]

Witnesses wanted to be remembered not just as passive victims, but also for their attempts to document their experiences. For men such as

---

[74] Langer, *Admitting the Holocaust*, 31.
[75] Ringelblum, *Notes from the Warsaw Ghetto*, 294.

Israel Lichtenstein, this desire also involved ensuring that their families would be remembered. Lichtenstein, a teacher of Yiddish and member of the O.S., made his last will and testament on the eleventh day of the 'resettlement' action in Warsaw. It expresses his pride for his work in the O.S. and his desire to be remembered for it:

With zeal and zest I threw myself into the work to help assemble archive materials. . . . I was entrusted to be the custodian; I hid the material. Besides me, no one knew. I confided only in my friend Hersh Wasser, my superior.

It is well hidden. Please God that it be preserved. That will be the finest and best that we achieved in the present gruesome time.

I know that we will not endure. To survive and remain [alive] after such horrible murders and massacres is impossible. Therefore I write this testament of mine. Perhaps I am not worthy of being remembered, but just for my grit in working with the society 'Oneg Shabbat' and for being the most endangered because I hid the entire material. It would be a small thing to give my own head. I risk the head of my dear wife Gela Seckstein and my treasure, my little daughter, Margalit.

I don't want any gratitude, any monument, any praise. I only want remembrance, so that my family, brother and sister abroad, may know what has become of my remains.

I want my wife to be remembered. Gela Seckstein, artist, dozens of works, talented, didn't manage to exhibit, did not show in public. During the three years of war worked among children as educator, teacher, made stage sets, costumes for the children's productions, received awards. Now together with me, we are preparing to receive death.

I want my little daughter to be remembered. Margalit, 20 months old today. Has mastered Yiddish perfectly, speaks a pure Yiddish. At 9 months began to speak Yiddish clearly. In intelligence is on par with 3- or 4-year-old children. I don't want to brag about her. Witnesses to this, who tell me about it, are the teaching staff at the school. . . .

I am not sorry about my life and that of my wife. But I am sorry for the gifted little girl. She deserves to be remembered also.

May we be the redeemers of all the rest of the Jews in the whole world. I believe in the survival of our people. Jews will not be annihilated. We, the Jews of Poland, Czechoslovakia, Lithuania, Latvia, are the scapegoats for all Israel in other lands.[76]

[76] Cited in Dawidowicz, *War against the Jews*, 296–7.

Lichtenstein saw his work for the O.S. as allowing him to speak to his relatives after his death; it also allowed him to shape their memories of his wife and daughter. He wanted his wife to be remembered as a talented artist, and his daughter, although only 20 months old, to be recognized as a gifted child. It was important for him that they did not become nameless victims.

Chaim Kaplan, another committed diarist of the Warsaw ghetto, was an Orthodox Jew and Hebrew educator who founded and directed a Hebrew elementary school in Warsaw. He published a book on Hebrew grammar and children's books on Jewish history and culture, and remained principal of the school until the outbreak of World War II, when the Jewish school system was abolished. He began a diary in 1933, and later recorded in detail all that he witnessed in the Warsaw ghetto. The diary is written in Hebrew, which was not common among the Jews of Warsaw (Hebrew remaining essentially a liturgical language at the time). For Kaplan, recording in his diary was not a release from reality, but an act of duty, which nurtured his will to survive. A diary entry written on 2 May 1940 states: 'In a spiritual state like the one in which I find myself at this time, it is difficult to hold a pen, to concentrate one's thoughts. But a strange idea has stuck in my head since the war broke out—that it is a duty I must perform. Record! Perhaps I am the only one engaged in this work, and that strengthens and encourages me.'[77] Before he was deported to Treblinka in late 1942, Kaplan gave his diary, recorded in a child's copybook, to a friend to smuggle out of the ghetto. The diary was discovered after the war almost totally intact in a kerosene can. He had written on 31 July 1942: 'My utmost concern is for hiding my diary so that it will be preserved for future generations.'[78]

At this time, Kaplan still held on to the belief '[that] our existence as a people will not be destroyed. Individuals will be destroyed, but the Jewish community will live on.'[79] Abraham Levin, who also kept a diary in the Warsaw ghetto, and who like Kaplan was to perish in Treblinka, similarly wanted to make the historian of the future aware

---

[77] Kaplan, *Scroll of Agony*, 144.   [78] Ibid. 395.   [79] Ibid. 30.

of the resilience of the Jews; he cites as evidence the fact that there had been so few suicides.

One of the most surprising side-effects of this war is the clinging to life, the almost total absence of suicides. People die in great numbers of starvation, the typhus epidemic or dysentery, they are tortured and murdered by the Germans in great numbers, but they do not escape from life by their own desire. On the contrary, they are tied to life by all their senses, they want to live at any price and to survive the war. The tensions of this historic world conflict are so great that they all wish to see the outcome of the gigantic struggle and the new regime in the world, the small and the great, old men and boys. The old have just one wish: the privilege of seeing the end and surviving Hitler.

I know a Jew who is all old age. He is certainly about 80. Last winter a great tragedy befell the old man. He had an only son who was about 52. The son died of typhus. He had no other children. And the son died. . . . A few days ago I visited the old man. When I left—his mind is still entirely clear— he burst out crying and said: 'I want to see the end of the war, even if I live only another half hour!'

Why should the old man wish so much to stay alive? There it is: even he wants to live, 'if only for half an hour' after the last shot is fired. That is the burning desire of all the Jews.[80]

Levin's diary, written in Yiddish and Hebrew, is not restricted to the Warsaw ghetto, but records everything he heard about other cities in occupied Poland. Levin was particularly interested in the collective responsibility of the German people, not just for the suffering inflicted upon the Jews but also for the loss to world Jewry. He wanted to ensure that one day the Germans would be punished for their crimes. An important unifying feature of Jewish identity in the Warsaw ghetto was the awareness that it was German policy that ultimately controlled life in the ghetto and was responsible for their misery. Diarists such as Levin used their writing to express thoughts of future retribution. Others turned to literature as a source of vicarious revenge. For example, the novels of World War I and Lloyd George's

---

[80] Document 89, 'Extracts from the Warsaw Ghetto Diary of Avraham Levin, 1942', in Arad *et al.* (eds.), *Documents on the Holocaust*, 204–5.

memoirs were popular because they dealt with Germany's defeat.[81] Ringelblum himself observed: 'People particularly enjoy descriptions of the year 1918 and the downfall of the Germans.'[82] He explained: 'being unable to take revenge on the enemy in reality, we are seeking it in fantasy, in literature.'[83]

The writings of the Yiddish poet Yitzhak Katznelson are also concerned with the problem of Jewish self-identity during the Holocaust, as well as his own impotence in the event of the deportation of his family. He wrote about thirty works between June 1940 and the beginning of 1942, and about ten works from the beginning of 1942 until the liquidation of the ghetto.[84] Some of these writings were hidden in a cellar by Mordechai Tenenbaum on 20 July 1942 (two days before the start of the *Große Aktion* in the ghetto). The material was discovered under the ruins of the house in the spring of 1945. Those written in the period between the liquidation of the ghetto and 1943 were discovered along with the second part of the archives of the O.S. in 1950. They included 'Job', a biblical play; 'The Ball', a poem describing the social differences in ghetto society; and a long poem of 1,200 lines entitled 'The Song of the Radiziner Rebbe'. This last, based on a true story, was written between December 1942 and January 1943, after the major liquidation of the ghetto in which more than 300,000 Jews were sent to their deaths at Treblinka. Among the condemned were Katznelson's wife and two children. Needing to find an antidote to his feelings of unease at what he perceived as the passivity of the Jews towards their fate, Katznelson discovered the heroic figure of Rabbi Samuel Solomon Leiner. He tells the story of the young Hasidic rabbi, who escapes German-occupied Radzyń and spends nearly two years in hiding in the small town of Vlodavi. During this time the rabbi struggles with the God who has abandoned his people, and pleads with him to go to Lublin to rescue the

---

[81] See N. Levin, *The Holocaust*, 226.
[82] Ringelblum, *Notes from the Warsaw Ghetto*, 300.   [83] Ibid.
[84] See Yitzhak Katznelson, *Yidishe ksovim fun Varshe, 1940–1943* (Jewish Writings from Warsaw, 1940–1943), ed. Yechiel Szeintuch (Tel Aviv, 1980); *idem, Ketavim aharonim, 1940–1944* (Last Writings, 1940–1944), ed. Yitzhak Zuckerman and Shlomo Even-Shoshan (Tel Aviv, 1956); and *idem, Vittel Diary*, trans. Myer Cohen (Tel Aviv, 1972).

Jews. In his place, the rabbi decides to go himself. He adopts the guise of a Gentile and goes to the death train carrying a sack of money, where he states that he will give money for every dead Jew, and twice as much for every Jew who lives. The inhabitants of the village storm the train in order to get the money. The rabbi manages to bury the dead, reciting Kaddish, the prayer for the dead. When the rabbi returns to Radzyń, he is warned that the Germans are searching for him with renewed vigour. However, the rabbi refuses offers to be taken to Warsaw and stays to meet the Germans, sacrificing himself to share the same fate as his fellow Jews.

It is through the story of the rabbi of Radzyń that Katznelson comes to see that a seemingly passive acceptance of death can also be a heroic act. In the Jewish tradition, a Jew who is killed for his or her faith is believed to have achieved *kiddush hashem* (sanctification of the name of God). Subsequently, Katznelson's poem serves as a memorial to his wife Hannah, the ordinary Jew, and the 'Assembly of Israel', which 'is more than any single Jew, even the sainted rebbe himself!'[85] It is important to note that 'The Song of the Radiziner Rebbe' was written before the author became acquainted with the more secular fighting heroism of the ghetto. After witnessing the first steps of the ŻOB (*Żydowska Organiżacja Bojowa* (Jewish Combat Organization)) in Kraków and Warsaw, he wrote two Hebrew poems: 'Jacob and Laban',[86] dealing with the events of Kraków, and another one on the armed resistance in the Warsaw ghetto between 18 and 21 January 1943, in which he participated. Unfortunately, these poems have not survived.

It can be argued that the need to find something redemptive in Jewish responses to the Holocaust is not just a post-war phenomenon, but was going on at the time of the Warsaw ghetto. The words of Israel Lichtenstein indicate that he used his writing as a way to deal

---

[85] Kermish (ed.), 'Introduction', in *To Live with Honor and Die with Honor!*, p. xiv.

[86] One of the first references to witnessing in the Torah is the figurative witness ascribed to a pile of stones erected by Jacob and Laban to symbolize their agreement (Gen. 31: 44–9). Cited in Young, *Writing and Rewriting the Holocaust*, 19. In Laban's words: 'This mound (*gal*) is a witness (*ed*) between you and me this day' (Gen. 31: 48).

with the loss of his loved ones. Katznelson's heroicizing of the life of the Radiziner rebbe acted both as a memorial to his wife and as a means of expressing his grief at witnessing the destruction of the Jewish people. Therefore, as well as providing historical documentation, diary writing can be seen to have been used both as an assertion of individual identity and as a more collective continuation of cultural life as a form of resistance.

Even before the establishment of the Warsaw ghetto, Polish Jews had been subjected to various abuses: they were excluded from mainstream Polish life, deprived of their livelihoods, had their food rations cut, were rounded up for forced labour, and suffered violence from both Christian Poles and Germans. However, even in the ghetto, Polish Jews were able to maintain some semblance of their pre-war lives. The continuation of cultural and religious life did continue to some degree.[87] School classes were held for children, and reading circles met to discuss Yiddish and Hebrew writers. A semi-clandestine organization by the name of YIKOR (*Yidishe Kultur-Organizatsye* (Jewish Cultural Organization)) organized lectures and literary, dramatic, and musical activities.[88] Zionist youth movements issued illegal publications in Hebrew, Yiddish, and Polish (in typed form, stencilled, or handwritten) addressed to the general public as well as to the youth groups. They included information, revolving to a great extent around news from the *Yishuv*,[89] regarding the progression of the war, party news, and various other articles, poems, and illustrations. Publications were also issued by anti-Zionist groups committed to non-territorial Jewish autonomy. For example, the Bundist *Yugend Shtimme* (Voice of Youth) wrote:

The very expression of apathy indicates submission to the enemy, which can cause our collapse morally and root out of our hearts our hatred for the

---

[87] See Huberband, *Kiddush Hashem*.

[88] For an excellent discussion of the role of music in the Warsaw ghetto, see Shirli Gilbert, *Music in the Holocaust: Confronting Life in the Nazi Ghettos and Camps* (Oxford, 2005), ch. 1.

[89] This is the Hebrew word for 'settlement', and refers to Jewish settlement in Palestine before the establishment of the state of Israel.

invader. It can destroy the will to fight; it can undermine our resolution. . . .
And because our position is so bitterly desperate our will to give up our lives
for a purpose more sublime than our daily existence must be reinforced. . . .
Our young people must walk with heads erect.[90]

Although many of the Warsaw ghetto diarists seem determined to
document Jewish resistance to adversity, others describe their disap-
pointment at the lack of resistance. Calel Perechodnik, for example,
devotes considerable time to describing his dismay both at his own
behaviour and that of others. Perhaps a further factor for the delay
in publishing Perechodnik's diary might be that it draws attention
away from the comforting rhetoric of heroism. The example of
Perechodnik shows that in times of extremity, resistance often
becomes reduced to the battle for individual survival. The diary of
Mary Berg also shows that writing is not just about resistance but can
be used as a means to express moral uncertainties. As noted above,
since the publication of her diary Berg has tried to distance herself
from the past. Whether, as Susan Pentlin suggests, out of 'shame that
privilege, position, wealth, and bribes earned her the right to life'[91] or
for some entirely different reason, it is difficult to know. However, her
diary clearly shows her guilt at being spared the fate of so many Jews.
While in the camp at Vittel, she wrote: '[W]e, who have been rescued
from the ghetto, are ashamed to look at each other. Had we the right
to save ourselves? . . . I am ashamed. Here I am, breathing fresh air,
and there my people are suffocating in gas and perishing in flames,
burned alive. Why?'[92]

While historians have rightly been expanding their understanding
of Jewish resistance during the Holocaust to incorporate activities
that do not fall into the categories of political or armed opposition— for
example, writing as resistance, the education of children,[93] the

---

[90] Cited in Joseph Kermish, 'The Underground Press in the Warsaw Ghetto', *Yad
Vashem Studies*, 1 (1957), 104–5.   [91] Pentlin, 'Holocaust Victims of Privilege', 37.
[92] Berg, *Warsaw Ghetto*, 227.
[93] On the dedication of teachers in the ghetto, see Emmanuel Ringelblum, *Ketavim
aharonim: Yanuar 1943–April 1944* (Last Writings: January 1943–April 1944)
(Jerusalem, 1994), 133–47.

continuation of cultural and spiritual life—this should not prevent us from acknowledging the limited possibilities for resistance. In a sense, it is not just Perechodnik, but the continuation of writing in the ghetto, that also informs us of the limits to active resistance. In a similar manner, the words of Mary Berg cited above, suggest that even as a young girl, she was only too aware that writing of her pain and guilt changes nothing.

THE MASS DEPORTATIONS

On 20 January 1942, the Wannsee Conference, chaired by Reinhard Heydrich, adopted the 'Final Solution'.[94] In Warsaw, the mass deportations began on 22 July 1942, and between then and 21 September 1942 around 265,000 Jews were herded into sealed, overcrowded cattle trucks and sent to the Treblinka death camp, about 60 km away. The number of deportees averaged 5,000–7,000 daily, and sometimes as many as 13,000. In addition, about 11,580 Jews were sent to forced-labour camps, and more than 10,000 were murdered in the streets. Approximately 8,000 Jews managed to escape to the Aryan side.[95] Among those deported to Treblinka were Dr Janusz Korczak (born Henryk Goldschmidt) and 190 orphaned children. Korczak, a paediatrician and educator, who had written more than twenty books and had introduced progressive orphanages for Jewish and Catholic children, wrote a diary each night after the children in his care were asleep. (After the establishment of the Warsaw ghetto, Korczak, the entire personnel of the Jewish orphanage and the children were moved to a building within the ghetto

---

[94] Minutes of the conference, prepared by Adolf Eichmann and edited by Reinhard Heydrich, have survived. They suggest that by the beginning of 1942 the Nazis were intent on eliminating the Jews of Europe. See Document 117, 'Protocol of the Wannsee Conference, January 20, 1942', in Arad *et al.* (eds.), *Documents on the Holocaust*, 249–61. For a discussion of the Protocol, see Mark Roseman, *The Villa, the Lake, the Meeting: Wannsee and the Final Solution* (London, 2002).
[95] Gutman, *Resistance*, 133. Cf. Gunnar S. Paulsson, *Secret City: The Hidden Jews of Warsaw 1940–1945* (New Haven, 2002), chs. 5–6.

walls.[96]) The diary covers only a very short period: from May until August 1942. Although Korczak describes the people he witnessed dying on the streets of the ghetto, his diary is not really intended as a historical chronicle. Unlike the other ghetto writers cited in this chapter, Korczak writes mainly of his memories of his family, and of the sick and orphaned children he looks after: 'The city is casting children my way, like little seashells. . . . I ask neither where they come from nor for how long or where they are going, for good or evil.'[97] He also writes of moral dilemmas, such as whether or not to use euthanasia on the orphans—something he rejected as 'the murder of the sick and feeble, as the assassination of innocents'.[98] His diary almost takes the form of a confession.[99] For example, Korczak writes of the guilt he feels at having given up medical work in the children's hospital—he calls it 'an ugly desertion'.[100] It also bears witness to Korczak's physical suffering: he dreams of food and sometimes conjures up imaginary menus. He is so overcome by starvation and illness that he is unable to believe 'his weighing machine and thermometer . . . they too tell lies'.[101]

At the end of June 1942, Korczak read the first part of his diary and found it lacked coherence. He was very much aware of the inherent difficulties in transmitting experiences, asking himself: 'Is it possible to comprehend someone else's memoirs, someone else's life? For that matter, is it possible to understand one's own remembrances?'[102] Korczak's diary makes no mention of the deportation notices appearing throughout the ghetto, or of the cattle cars, which carried the first deportees away.[103] Although Ringelblum spoke of the need for 'a photographically true and detailed picture',[104] Korczak's diary departed from this model and, in doing so, shows how an alternative

---

[96] See Yisrael Gutman, 'Janusz Korczak—Kavim Lidmuto' (Janusz Korczak's Personality), *Yalkut Moreshet*, 25 (1978), 7–20 [Hebrew].

[97] Janusz Korczak, *The Ghetto Years: 1939–1942*, trans. Jerzy Bachrach and Barbara Krzywicka (New York, 1978), 138.

[98] Cited in Betty Jean Lifton, *The King of Children: The Life and Death of Janusz Korczak* (New York, 1988), 321.   [99] Ibid., see 300–1.

[100] Ibid. 301.   [101] Korczak, *Ghetto Years*, 171.   [102] Ibid. 314.

[103] Ibid., see 327.   [104] Ringelblum, 'O.S.', 9.

approach can also provide the reader with important insights into Jewish life in the ghetto. While the diary gives little factual information, it is the form and presentation of Korczak's diary that informs us of his suffering; the lack of structure and rambling quality of much of the writing bears witness to Korczak's hunger and fatigue. On 5 August 1942 the Germans ordered the orphanage to be liquidated, and the children were sentenced to die in the gas chambers of Treblinka. Refusing offers by his Christian friends to go into hiding, Korczak accompanied the children to the *Umschlagplatz* (assembly point), and went to Treblinka with them. His last diary entry had been recorded four days before, after which Korczak gave the diary to his personal secretary from before the war, the writer Igor Newerly, who hid the diary on the Aryan side, where it was later uncovered. It was published for the first time in 1958, in the original Polish. The life of Janusz Korczak has since become legendary—a dominant image of nobility and sacrifice during the Holocaust.

After the mass deportations, about 60,000 Jews were left in the ghetto. It was converted into a series of labour camps, or 'shops' (code-name for German enterprises) controlled by the SS. The Nazi *Transferstelle* (Transport Authority), the office which had until this point controlled all official economic transactions between the ghetto and the outside world, ceased to exist, and the ration cards distributed by the *Judenrat* became mostly redundant. The leaders of the O.S. began to make plans to protect the archives. They decided to seal the materials in milk churns and metal boxes and then bury them. This was done on 3 August 1942 by Israel Lichtenstein, responsible for the preservation of the archive, and assistants 18-year-old Nachum Grzywacz and 19-year-old Dawid Graber, who buried their own last testaments along with the archives. Grzywacz wrote:

We have decided to describe the present time. Yesterday we sat up till late in the night, since we did not know whether we would survive till today. Now I am in the midst of writing, while in the streets the terrible shooting is going on. . . . Of one thing I am proud: that in these grave and fateful days, I was one of those who buried the treasure . . . in order that you should know the tortures and murders of the Nazi tyranny. . . . We must hurry, because we are not sure of the next hour. . . . I want the coming generations to remember our times. . . . With what ardour we dug the holes for the boxes . . . with what joy we received every bit of material. . . . How I would like to live to the moment when the treasure is dug out and the whole truth proclaimed. . . . But we certainly will not live to see it.[105]

The first part of the archives, together with Ringelblum's diary, was discovered in September 1946, in ten metal containers under the ruins of a house in the former Jewish quarter of Warsaw; the second part of the collection (including two of the milk churns[106]) was found there in December 1950.[107] Unfortunately, the third part remains lost. A few of the deported managed to escape from Treblinka and find their way back to the ghetto. Among the escapees was David Nowodworski, an older member of the youth movement and underground. Abraham Levin described his meeting with Nowodworski on 28 August 1942:

Today we had a long talk with David Nowodworski, who returned from Treblinka. He told us in detail the whole story of his ordeal, from the moment he was taken until he managed to escape from the slaughter site and reach Warsaw. From his account, it is once again confirmed in no uncertain terms that all the transports, whether they were made up of people who were snatched or whether they went of their own accord, are all put to death and no one is saved. This is the naked truth and it is terrible to think that during the last few weeks, at least some 300,000 individuals from Warsaw and the other cities such as Radom, Siedlce, and others have been murdered.

The written evidence recorded from his words is so painful that it cannot be grasped in so many words. This is undoubtedly the greatest crime in the history of mankind.[108]

---

[105] Cited in N. Levin, *The Holocaust*, 324–5.

[106] One of the two milk churns is on display at the ŻIH; the other is now on permanent loan to the United States Holocaust Memorial Museum.

[107] The originals of the recovered archives are held at the ŻIH, Yad Vashem in Jerusalem, and the Archives of the YIVO Institute for Jewish Research in New York. They consist of nearly 6,000 documents, some in two or three parts, and cover an estimated 40,000 pages. Many of the pages had been used previously, and therefore the writing is restricted to one side.   [108] Cited in Gutman, *Resistance*, 141.

Unsurprisingly, Ringelblum and the surviving members of the O.S. had by this time started to give considerable thought to Jewish reactions to the deportations and the fate of the remaining Jews. Ringelblum was clearly in favour of Jewish armed resistance and was troubled by its absence. On 15 October 1942, he asked: 'Why didn't we resist when they began to resettle 300,000 Jews from Warsaw? Why did we allow ourselves to be led like sheep to the slaughter?'[109] A possible answer is supplied by Levin who, despite the strength of the statement cited above, recorded the following diary entry the very next day:

Moshe Lewite or Levitas, of 40 Twarda Sreet, went to look for his wife three weeks ago [who was taken] to the *Umschlag[platz]*. He was caught and sent to Kosow. Two days ago, he returned, for the Germans had released him because he was a carpenter. He says that Kosow had been emptied and all its Jews expelled. People with money buy food from the farmers and share it with those who have no money. At any rate, this must be investigated. This was a sign that not all the expelled were slaughtered.[110]

It was clearly difficult to accept the enormity of the destruction which was unfolding. Alarmed by the mass deportations, the leaders of the underground movement decided to create the ŻOB. It comprised a coalition of fighting units from left-wing socialist Zionist youth movements—Hashomer Hat'sa'ir, Poalei Zion, Dror, He'halutz— and later from the non-Zionist Bund and the Communists, and was led by (Antek) Yitzhak Zuckerman.[111] Hashomer Hat'sa'ir activist Mordecai Anielewicz was named commander-in-chief in October 1942. The movement's aim was to use armed resistance to stop the slaughter of the Jews. In a leaflet dated January 1943, and distributed throughout the ghetto, it declared:

Jews in your masses, the hour is near. You must be prepared to resist, not give yourselves up like sheep to the slaughter. *Not even one Jew must go to the train.*

[109] Ringelblum, *Notes from the Warsaw Ghetto*, 310. The term 'sheep to the slaughter' comes from Ps. 44: 22.   [110] Cited in Gutman, *Resistance*, 142.

[111] See Yitzhak Zuckerman, *A Surplus of Memory: Chronicle of the Warsaw Ghetto Uprising*, trans. Barbara Harshav (Berkeley, 1993); originally published in Hebrew as *Sheva hashanim hahen: 1939–1946* (Those Seven Years: 1939–1946) (Tel Aviv,

People who cannot resist actively must offer passive resistance, that is, by hiding.
We have now received information from Lvov that the Jewish Police there
itself carried out the deportation of 3,000 Jews. Such things will not happen
again in Warsaw. The killing of Lejkin proves it. Now our slogan must be:
Let everyone be ready to die like a human being![112]

Although the primary aim of this leaflet was to encourage armed
resistance, it also recognized that for many this would not be possible,
and presented hiding as an alternative.[113] The aim was to make
'Jewish self-defence . . . a fact'.[114]

THE GHETTO UPRISING

When the second wave of deportations began on 18 January 1943, the
Germans were met with armed resistance. The Warsaw Ghetto
Uprising began on 18 January 1943, when 8,000 Latvians and 200 SS
went into the ghetto with the aim of rounding up the remaining Jews.
Although the Jews managed in the three-day battle to resist the liquidation of the ghetto, about 1,000 were killed in the fighting (nearly four-
fifths of the ŻOB), and 5,500 were deported.[115] However, more than
50,000 Jews remained. The final liquidation began on 19 April 1943,
the eve of Passover. Having been warned of what lay ahead, they were
prepared. The resistance movement consisted of approximately 750

1990). Zuckerman was one of the founder members of Beit Lohamei Hagheta'ot (Ghetto
Fighter's House), the Ghetto Uprising and Holocaust remembrance authority established
on 19 April 1950 at Kibbutz Lohamei Hagheta'ot in the western Galilee of Israel.

[112] Cited in Paul Mendes-Flohr and Jehuda Reinharz (eds.), *The Jew in the Modern
World* (Oxford, 1995), 674. Yaakov Lejkin, the head of the Jewish police in the Warsaw
ghetto, was assassinated by the ŻOB on 29 Oct. 1942 because of his collaboration with
the German occupation forces.

[113] On hiding and passing in Warsaw during the Holocaust, see Paulsson, *Secret City*.

[114] Document 138, 'Call to Resistance by the Jewish Fighting Organization in the
Warsaw Ghetto', in Arad *et al.* (eds.), *Documents on the Holocaust*, 301–2.

[115] For varying accounts of the January uprising, see Reuben Ainsztein, *The Warsaw
Ghetto Revolt* (New York, 1979); Meyer Barkai (ed.), *The Fighting Ghettos* (Philadelphia,
1962); Philip Friedman (ed.), *Martyrs and Fighters: The Epic of the Warsaw Ghetto*
(London, 1954); Yuri Suhl (ed.), *They Fought Back: The Story of Jewish Resistance in Nazi
Europe* (New York, 1967); and Zuckerman, *Surplus of Memory*, 263–347.

minimally armed young people (mostly aged between 18 and 21), and 40,000 unarmed Jews (engaged in more 'passive' resistance). The few pistols, rifles, hand grenades, and rounds of ammunition used by the Jews had been given to them by the underground movements. The uprising lasted about a month;[116] during this time there were also organized escapes from the ghettos, from freight cars, and from concentration and death camps. Some of those who managed to escape formed Jewish partisan units or joined the Russian and Polish groups in the Polish forests. Others attempted to pass as Aryan in the cities and countryside of Poland, about two-thirds of them women. An organization named *Żegota* (*Rada Pomocy Żydom* (Council to Aid Jews)), operating under the control of the Polish underground, helped to save Jews in hiding. German troops led by General Jürgen Stroop retaliated by burning down the ghetto, block by block. They also blew up the Great Synagogue in Warsaw. It is thought that about 150,000 civilians were killed, including several thousand Jews.[117] The majority of the fighters who survived were concentrated in the command bunker at 18 Miła Steet. On 8 May 1943, the Germans surrounded the bunker, and more than 100 fighters, including Mordecai Anielewicz, died. A group of fighters did manage to escape through the sewers to the Aryan side of the city.[118] Among them was Marek Edelman, an active member of the Bund and a member of the ŻOB command staff. After escaping to Aryan Warsaw, he fought in the Polish Uprising with about 1,000 other Jews.

Members of the ŻOB felt that they might be the last Jews able to tell their story, and as such were committed to documenting the 'days of destruction and revolt'.[119] Those reluctant to do so were reminded

[116] See Shmuel Krakowski, *The War of the Doomed: Jewish Armed Resistance in Poland 1942–1944*, trans. O. Blaustein (New York, 1984), and Gutman, *Jews of Warsaw*.

[117] Zuckerman, *Surplus of Memory*, 525.

[118] Simcha Rotem [Kazik], *Memoirs of a Warsaw Ghetto Fighter: The Past within Me*, trans. Barbara Harshav (New Haven, 1994), p. viii.

[119] The title of Zivia Lubetkin's memoir: *idem*, *In the Days of Destruction and Revolt*, trans. Ishai Tubbin (Tel Aviv, 1981); first published in German as *Die Letzen Tage des Warschauer Ghetto* (The Last Days of the Warsaw Ghetto) (Berlin, 1949). Lubetkin was active in Dror (led by Yitzhak Zuckerman/Antek), and also took a leading role in the

of their duty by the other members. During the uprising, the archives of the ŻOB, which had been based at 5 Panska Street and 18 Leszno Street (on the Aryan side of Warsaw) were lost. They had included the correspondence of the Polish underground with official representatives of the Polish government-in-exile, letters of prisoners of concentration and labour camps, memoranda, records, and approximately 2,000 testimonies of Jews living on the Aryan side.[120] However, copies of reports, publications, and propaganda leaflets collected by Adolf Berman, the archivist of the ŻKN (*Żydowski Komitet Narodowy* (Jewish National Committee)) and the political wing of the ŻOB, survived and are now kept at Beit Lohamei Hagheta'ot.

Although armed revolts against the Germans occurred in at least twenty ghettos in Eastern Europe, the Warsaw Ghetto Uprising, because it was led by Zionists, has become the model for heroic resistance during the Holocaust. This was the intention. In a letter written shortly before he died, Mordecai Anielewicz wrote: 'The dream of my life has risen to become a fact. Self-defence in the ghetto will have been a reality. Jewish armed resistance and revenge are facts. I have been a witness to the magnificent, heroic fighting of Jewish men of battle.'[121] However, the resistance must be put in context. As Lawrence Langer correctly points out, the resistance movement in the ghetto consisted of only several hundred (he suggests a figure of between 250 and 800) of the 50,000–60,000 Jews still living in Warsaw in April 1943. Apart from the lack of weapons, the majority of the Jews were too hungry, weakened, and demoralized to even consider active resistance.[122]

On 3 November 1943, the SS launched *Aktion Erntefest* (Operation Harvest Festival) to liquidate any remaining Polish Jews. During the mass deportations in the summer of 1942, and the destruction of the ghetto following the Uprising, it is likely that many

ŻOB. Married to Zuckerman, she too emigrated to Israel in 1946, where she published her first memoir, *The Last on the Wall* (Tel Aviv, 1947) [Hebrew].

[120] Kermish (ed.), 'Introduction', in *To Live with Honor and Die with Honor!*, pp. xiii–iv.

[121] Letter dated 23 April 1943, in Arad *et al.* (eds.), *Documents on the Holocaust*, 315–16.   [122] Langer, *Admitting the Holocaust*, 35.

other manuscripts were lost: for example, the second part of Calel Perechodnik's diary, Ringelblum's 200-page monograph on the camp of Trawniki, and the diary of Josef Kaplan. Kaplan, who was one of the leaders of Hashomer Hat'sa'ir, had collected data on the movement's activities in Warsaw and other cities in occupied Poland.[123] The secretive nature of this research made him reluctant to allow the O.S. to copy his diary, and by the time he consented, it was too late. As Ringelblum lamented in January 1943, 'A great deal was written, but the largest part was destroyed along with the end of Warsaw Jewry in the Deportation. All that remained was the material preserved in O.S.'[124] Together with his wife Judyta and 14-year-old son Uriel, Ringelblum left the ghetto in March 1943 to hide on the Aryan side. The notes he made at this time speak of his admiration for the Jewish youth movements who organized the armed revolt. On 18 April 1943 (the day before the last deportation and the eve of the uprising), he went back into the ghetto. While his exact motivation is unknown, it is likely that he either wished to be present during the uprising or, alternatively, wanted to spend what he realized would be his last Passover with his fellow Jews in the ghetto. He was captured in a round-up and sent to the Trawniki camp near Lublin. He was rescued in July by *Żegota*, and reunited with his wife and son in Warsaw. In March 1944, Ringelblum and his family were discovered with sixty other people, including the Christian Poles who were hiding them. They were all taken to the Pawiak prison and executed.

A CHALLENGE TO HISTORY

With the steady worsening of conditions in the ghetto and the Jews' increasing awareness of their fate came an increasing desperation. There is a sharp contrast between Chaim Kaplan's thoughts on 14 September 1939—'I will write a scroll of agony in order to remember

[123] Ibid. p. xv.
[124] Cited in David G. Roskies (ed.), *The Literature of Destruction: Jewish Responses to Catastrophe* (Philadelphia, 1989), 396.

the past in the future. For despite all the dangers I still have hopes of coming out of this alive'[125]—and his sorrow on 27 August 1940:

There is no end to our scroll of agony. I am afraid that the impressions of this terrible era will be lost because they have not been adequately recorded. I risk my life with my writing, but my abilities are limited; I don't know all the facts; those that I do know may not be sufficiently clear; and many of them I write on the basis of rumours whose accuracy I cannot guarantee. But for the sake of truth, I do not require individual facts, but rather the manifestations of the fruits of a great many facts that leave their impression on the people's opinion, on their mood and morale. And I can guarantee the factualness of these manifestations because I dwell among my people and behold their misery and their souls' torments.[126]

This powerful statement sets an important challenge to historians. First, it clearly states that Kaplan risked his life to document his experiences; and second, it informs future readers that despite not being able to give all the facts, his testimony 'can guarantee the factualness of these manifestations because *I dwell among my people*' (emphasis added). Stressing his position as an insider witness, Kaplan sets the fundamental challenge that testimony is not about objective facts, but about the supposed immediacy and misery of lived experience. The following chapters will explore whether or not later testimony fits this model or the challenges set by the Warsaw ghetto diarists: in particular, Ringelblum's call for 'comprehensiveness', 'objectivity', and 'a photographically true and detailed picture', or whether the existence of many different testimonies, written from a wide range of perspectives, can even begin to meet such criteria. As Kaplan's words suggest, even by the end of the Warsaw ghetto, diarists were beginning to rethink their conceptions of testimony, taking into account the emotive and subjective presentation of experience.

As we have seen, the ghetto diarists' writing, despite their overt intention to write objectively (or not), can be seen to document more than mere experience. The very process of bearing witness not only partook in long-established Jewish traditions and was an essential

---

[125] Kaplan, *Scroll of Agony*, 30.   [126] Ibid. 189.

part of Jewish identity, but also had very important practical consequences. For example, the ghetto diarists were not only able to foresee some of the concerns that would come to dominate historians studying this period—such as the issue of Jewish resistance—but also used their writing as a specific form of resistance. Those who participated in the armed resistance of the Warsaw Ghetto Uprising, as well as trying to halt the deportations, wanted to make Jewish armed resistance a fact in future history books. Although it is at first difficult to see the diaries of Adam Czerniaków and Calel Perechodnik, and even of Mary Berg, in terms of resistance, it is their positions in the ghetto's social and political structure that make their writing particularly significant. Whereas Czerniaków may have hoped to survive and use the notes he made during his life to write an explanation for his duties as head of the *Judenrat*, Perechodnik felt compelled to leave behind a confession of his role as a ghetto policeman. Perechodnik in particular must have been aware of the moral scrutiny to which his manuscript would be subjected. Their writings show that testimony is not uniform, but instead operates on many different levels: that there were different motivations behind the writing of testimony. The fact that not all Jews were concerned with resistance exposes as illusory the idea that there was a uniformity of experience in the ghettos.

Although the diarists paint vivid pictures of Jewish life in the Warsaw ghetto, it is important to realize that this ghetto was but one part of the Holocaust. Conditions varied between ghettos, and not all Jews experienced them. In the next chapter we will see that for those who did, the misery of the ghettos could not really prepare them for the horrors of the concentration camps. The camps broke down many of the notions of identity nurtured in the ghettos, and instead created an unbridgeable gulf whereby people became distanced from their previous lives and possible futures. However, it will be seen that for many the desire to bear witness persisted, and consequently, the Holocaust memoir emerges as an important vehicle for the resurrection of many of the identities and ambitions nurtured before and during life in the ghettos.

2

Writing to Survive: The Testimony of the Concentration Camps

My need to tell the story was so strong in the Camp that I had begun describing my experiences there, on the spot, in that German laboratory laden with freezing cold . . . yet I knew that I would not be able under any circumstances to hold on to those haphazardly scribbled notes, and that I must throw them away immediately because if they were found they . . . would cost me my life.

Primo Levi, 'Afterword'

Dear discoverer of these writings! I have a request of you: this is the real reason I write, that my doomed life may attain some meaning, that my hellish days and hopeless tomorrows may find a purpose in the future.

Załman Gradowski

Whereas many Jewish diaries and other documents were harboured in the Nazi-enforced ghettos, very few testimonies were written in the concentration camps, or survived them. This was due to the general lack of resources such as paper and writing equipment, the fear of punishment, lack of privacy in the barracks, and the German commitment to destroying evidence of their crimes. Aside from these practical considerations, few prisoners had the mental or physical energy to consider recording their experiences as they happened: each prisoner's capacities were stretched to the limit in an effort to survive. Important exceptions include the poetry written by children in the ghetto camp of Theresienstadt,[1] diaries written in the hundreds of labour camps in Poland and Germany, and the notes made in the transit camps. While imprisoned in Theresienstadt, Hans Günther Adler, a Prague-born academic, was able to make notes towards what he hoped would one day be published as a scholarly work.[2] However, in the concentration camps, where Jews found themselves not only separated from their families and communities, but set against each other in the battle for survival, few had the energy to write. The testimonies of the forced-labour workers murdered in Chełmno, discussed in the previous chapter, and the writings of the *Sonderkommando* prisoners forced to work in the crematoria of Auschwitz-Birkenau,[3] which will be examined presently, feature prominently among the rare exceptions.

Although eyewitness accounts written in the concentration camps are extremely scarce, this does not mean that those held captive did not have the desire to one day bear witness to their experiences. Informed by their captors that there would be no survivors, prisoners could only dream of one day telling the world of their suffering. As James Young asserts, 'When survival and the need to bear witness become one and the same longing, this desperate urge to testify in narrative cannot be underestimated.'[4] It can be seen that some prisoners in the camps always intended their experiences to be

[1] A teacher in one of the camp's children's homes encouraged the children to express themselves in poems and nursery rhymes, which she collected and saved. They have been translated and published in Hana Volavková (ed.), *I Never Saw Another Butterfly: Children's Drawings and Poems from Terezín Concentration Camp, 1942–44*, trans. Jeanne Nemcova (New York, 1964). For a discussion of children's art in Theresienstadt, see Nicholas Stargardt, 'Children's Art of the Holocaust', *Past and Present*, 161 (Nov. 1998), 192–235, and *idem*, *Witnesses of War: Children's Lives under the Nazis* (London, 2005), for an in-depth study of children's responses to German occupation.

[2] See Hans Günther Adler, *Theresienstadt 1941–1945: Das Antlitz einer Zwangsgemeinschaft—Geschichte, Soziologie, Psychologie* (Theresienstadt 1941–1945: The Face of an Involuntary Community—History, Sociology, Psychology) (Tübingen, 1955).

[3] For a history of the camp, see Deborah Dwórk and Robert Jan Van Pelt, *Auschwitz: 1270 to the Present* (London, 1996). For a detailed chronology, see Danuta Czech, *Auschwitz Chronicle, 1939–1945: From the Archives of the Auschwitz Memorial and the German Federal Archives* (New York, 1990).

[4] Young, *Writing and Rewriting the Holocaust*, 17.

known, and consciously preserved certain memories for this purpose. This chapter looks at testimonies of the concentration camps, to show, *contra* the prevalent idea, that Holocaust survivors have only recently come forward to tell their stories out of a new, flourishing culture of witnessing,[5] that the desire to bear witness did not always arise post-war, or more particularly during the latter part of survivors' lives, but was there during the events of the Holocaust, in the ghettos and camps. Just because many survivors have only recently started to write about their experiences does not mean that they did not want to do so all along.

It will be seen that with the move from the ghettos to the concentration camps, the nature and demands of bearing witness underwent significant changes. In the ghettos, the Jews, although suffering intensely, had many familiar points of reference: their names had not yet been replaced by anonymous numbers; they still had family and friends, and were not living in purpose-built camps but in familiar urban environments. Also, they were able to devote considerable time to documenting their experiences, and the many diaries and other projects carried out in the ghettos testify to this. Yet, while life in the concentration camps severely limited the ability to bear witness, and also introduced the Jews to a level of suffering hitherto unimaginable, writing still continued. Each camp gave rise to a different amount of documentation. Testimony from the death camps at Chełmno, Bełżec, Sobibór, and Treblinka is extremely limited, as very few prisoners survived, and most of the documentation was destroyed by the Nazis.[6] Most of the testimony discussed here comes from either

[5] A view espoused by Norman G. Finkelstein in his polemical attack on the so-called Holocaust industry. See Norman G. Finkelstein, *The Holocaust Industry: Reflections on the Exploitation of Jewish Suffering* (London, 2000). Finkelstein cites as his initial stimulus Novick's *The Holocaust in American Life*. Novick also critiques the centrality of Holocaust memory in American society.

[6] For a testimony of Sobibór, see Thomas Tovi Blatt, *From the Ashes of Sobibor: A Story of Survival* (Evanston, Ill., 1997). Rare testimonies of Treblinka include Richard Glazar, *Die Falle mit dem Grünen Zaun: Überleben in Treblinka* (Trap with a Green Fence: Survival in Treblinka) (Frankfurt, 1992); Yankel Wiernik, *A yor in Treblinke* (New York, 1944), published in English as *A Year in Treblinka* (New York, 1945); and Samuel Willenberg,

Auschwitz or Majdanek; not intended solely as death camps, they offered prisoners the slim possibility of survival if they were selected for labour. Although more people were killed at Auschwitz than at any other camp—at least 1.1 million men, women, and children perished, 90 per cent of them Jews[7]—there were more survivors than any other death camp. Testimony has also been written by survivors of Bergen-Belsen and other concentration camps, including Dachau, Buchenwald, and Ravensbrück.

It will never be known how many of the 6 million victims of the Nazi genocide wished to record their experiences. Those who did—either at the time of the events or after liberation—were not able to achieve the kind of comprehensive account that Emmanuel Ringelblum and members of *Oneg Shabbat* were able to produce. In terms of concrete historical information, what the testimony of a concentration camp witness can provide is extremely limited. As Primo Levi observed: 'For knowledge of the Lagers [camps],[8] the Lagers themselves were not always a good observation point. In the inhuman conditions to which they were subjected, the prisoners could barely acquire an overall picture of their universe.'[9] With the important exception of those connected with the network of underground resistance movements, concentration camp

Surviving Treblinka, trans. Naftali Greenwood, ed. Władysław Bartoszewski (Oxford, 1989). It is thought that only two people survived Bełżec: Rudolf Reder and Chaim Hirszman, who was murdered in Lublin in 1946 on the day he was going to testify to his experiences to the Lublin branch of the Jewish Historical Commission by two members of a Polish underground organization. In 1946, Reder, in collaboration with the editor Nella Rost, wrote a booklet entitled 'Bełżec', which was published in Kraków by the Jewish Regional Historical Commission. See M. M. Rubel, 'Translator's Note', in Antony Polonsky (ed.), *Polin. Studies in Polish Jewry,* xiii: *Focusing on the Holocaust and its Aftermath* (London, 2000), 268–9. For Reder's testimony, see Rudolf Reder, 'Bełżec', ibid. 270–89.

[7] This is the most recent figure provided by Franciszek Piper, head of the historical department of the Auschwitz State Museum, although 'approximately 1.5 million' appears on the monument at Birkenau. We shall of course never know the exact number. For a further discussion of this problem and for details of the numbers of Jews, Poles, Russians, Gypsies, and others murdered in Auschwitz, see Franciszek Piper, 'The Number of Victims', in Wacław Długoborski and Franciszek Piper (eds.), *Auschwitz 1940–1945: Central Issues in the History of the Camp*, trans. William Brand, iii (Oświęcm, 2000), 231.

[8] The term *Konzentrationslager* (concentration camp) was also abbreviated *KZ*.

[9] Primo Levi, *The Drowned and the Saved*, trans. Raymond Rosenthal (London, 1988), 6; originally published in Italian as *I sommersi è i salvati* (Turin, 1986).

witnesses had far less access to information outside their own particular experiences than was the case for Ringelblum and his colleagues. Even if interned in more than one concentration camp, witnesses would still have experienced only small parts of each one, and conditions within each camp were divergent and subject to constant modification. Even within a single concentration camp, things could change dramatically over the course of a few months. Furthermore, the specific nature of a particular work *Kommando* (labour detachment), or a prisoner's position within the social hierarchy of the camp, crucially affected not only a prisoner's experiences but also the possibility of bearing witness. Hence the men of the *Sonderkommando* were aware that they were in a unique position to witness the extent and nature of the crimes of the SS.

As if to illustrate the disjunction in experience between the ghettos and the arrival at the concentration camps, the vast majority of testimonies describing the descent into the concentration camps were written either after transferral to a labour camp or after liberation. Therefore, we have to rely on the testimonies of survivors to describe the initial adjustment to life in the concentration camps, and how the camps produced a rupture in the writing of testimony. Some experts on Holocaust testimony, such as David Roskies, might question the legitimacy of this approach, arguing that 'survival literature' is very different from 'real Holocaust literature' (testimony written during the Holocaust)[10] because it is not linked in time and place to the events it describes. Consequently, Roskies eschews the recollections of survivors in favour of what he refers to as the 'miracle' of Emmanuel Ringelblum and the staff of *Oneg Shabbat*. However, in order to illuminate writing *during* the Holocaust as a distinct literary genre, theorists of Holocaust literature often conflate writing in the ghettos, writing while in hiding, the testimony of escapees, and writing in the camps. Even David Patterson, who warns against 'dehistoricizing the [Holocaust] diary',[11] never really addresses the differences between

[10] David G. Roskies, 'The Holocaust According to the Literary Critics', *Prooftexts*, 1/2 (May 1981), 211.
[11] David Patterson, *Along the Edge of Annihilation: The Collapse and Recovery of Life in the Holocaust Diary* (Seattle, 1999), 6.

writing in the ghettos and writing in the concentration camps. In an attempt not to allow the efforts of ghetto diarists to obscure the fact that writing during the Holocaust was generally possible only in the ghettos and in hiding (and not in the concentration camps), survivor memoirs can be used to illustrate the differences between the ghetto and concentration camp testimonies. Furthermore, it can be seen that the desire to bear witness not only continued in the camps, but that this commitment also helped prisoners retain their will to survive.

DEPORTATION

The suffering in the ghettos had been so great that many Jews, particularly those who had lost loved ones, could not imagine that deportation could yield anything worse than what they had already been through. They had witnessed death on a daily basis, and had watched decomposing bodies pile up unburied in the streets and cemeteries. In her post-war memoir Sara Zyskind explains that she viewed deportation as a reprieve from the suffering of the Łódź ghetto:

Though fully aware that we were setting out for an unknown destination [Auschwitz], I couldn't disguise my excitement. I have nothing to be afraid of anymore, I thought, since I have already lost all those dearest to my heart. What else could happen to me? Was there anything worse than living in this ghetto? Worse than the hunger, sickness, and death?[12]

However, later she writes: 'Before long, I would discover that there were torments infinitely worse than these. . . . I had deluded myself, believing there could be nothing worse than the ghetto.'[13] This direct comparison has been made retrospectively, for Zyskind was only able to evaluate her experiences in the ghetto fully after experiencing Auschwitz. Emphasizing how testimony is mediated by different experiences, it is clear that the meanings Zyskind ascribes to different

---

[12] Sara Zyskind, *Stolen Years*, trans. Marganit Insar (New York, 1981), 135–6; originally published in Hebrew, as *Ha'atarah sh'avah* (The Release of the Captured) (Tel Aviv, 1978).   [13] Zyskind, *Stolen Years*, 136–48.

events are partly the result of knowledge gained after the war. For example, she now believes that it was the arrival of the freight cars that first informed her that something was wrong. Approaching the station with her uncle, aunt, and cousin, she remembers realizing:

It wasn't a passenger train puffing towards us but a long line of freight cars used for transporting cattle. Each car had only a small barred window at the top. A horrible fear took hold of me. I saw soldiers using brute force to shove the people onto the cars. Now, for the first time, the thought flashed through my mind that Salek [her cousin] may have been right: we ought not to have left the ghetto. Too late![14]

Zyskind uses the arrival of the freight cars to structure her narrative: to emphasize the severing of one world from another. Many other survivor-writers, regardless of their previous suffering, also state that it was the first experience of the freight cars that served to rupture them from their previous lives. However, as these testimonies were written after the war, it can be seen that accounts of ghetto life and subsequent deportation are mediated by the full knowledge of the horrors of the camps—conditions that were not known at the time.

Jews from Eastern Europe were transported to the camps in sealed cars, with at least 100 people forced into each car.[15] They were given no food or water, no toilet facilities, and no access to fresh air. Many people died in the cars, and the corpses were left to rot where they fell. Sometimes when the cars arrived at their destination, the dead outnumbered the living. Eugene Heimler, who was deported to Auschwitz at the age of 20, describes the experience as marking his entrance into another world:

As I recalled that nightmare three-day journey which bridged the abyss between two worlds, the horror of the past flooded back with renewed intensity, like the pain from a sudden blow that reopens a slowly healing

---

[14] Zyskind, *Stolen Years*, 139.

[15] Victims from parts of the *Großreich* (Greater Germany) and some Western European countries were often transported in regular trains, leaving them even less prepared for the horrors of the camps. See Edelheit and Edelheit, *History of the Holocaust*, 70.

wound. I had mounted the train of death wearing European clothes, a European man; I alighted at the other end a dazed creature of Auschwitz.[16]

While at the time of his journey the experience of the train ride was no doubt full of extreme suffering, the train now signals for Heimler, his transformation from European gentleman to concentration camp prisoner.

ARRIVAL AT THE CONCENTRATION CAMPS

Halina Birenbaum, a young girl who had endured years of suffering in the Warsaw ghetto and who had already lost her father and brother, also uses her memoir to evaluate the differences between life in the ghetto and life in the concentration camps. As well as describing the separation from her mother almost immediately upon arrival—part of the concentration camp system's aim was to dissolve any remaining family ties and strip prisoners of emotional and physical support— she draws particular attention to the surroundings of Majdanek, to emphasize how much worse life in the camp was to life in the Warsaw ghetto:

The camp—especially the watch towers bristling with machine-guns and the electrified barbed wire—horrified me. I was used to cellars, attics and other hiding-places in the ghetto, and feared open spaces, coming face to face with our executioners. The shock that followed the unexpected loss of my mother, my frantic terror at the sight of the watch-towers, the machine guns, the green uniforms of the SS, and finally the impossibility of escaping everything I had learned to run away from in the years in the ghetto— drove me almost to the point of insanity. . . . The reality of Majdanek weighed me down even more than that pile of bodies under which I almost stifled in the railroad car. The 'labor' camp proved entirely different from the picture my mother had drawn for me. It was not a question of work, cozy huts and rest after work—it was nothing but ceaseless fear, penal

16 Eugene Heimler, *Night of the Mist*, trans. André Ungar (New York, 1959), 21.

servitude and a bottomless pit of hell. How can anyone find words to describe it?[17]

Even the most sceptical survivors of the ghettos stress that the full horrors of the camps could not be imagined. Survivor-writer Kitty Hart, after serving what she describes as 'an apprenticeship in the Lublin ghetto, on the run, and in prison', and who writes, 'Nothing could ever again take us entirely by surprise',[18] could not fathom the peculiar smell (of the crematoria) that she met with on arrival at Birkenau—or what she called 'this bewildering place'.[19]

While on a factual level the new arrivals were at this stage now part of the camps, in writing about their experiences after liberation, survivors often situate themselves as incredulous observers, employing meanings and frameworks of reference from their previous lives. Many testimonies describe the horror of seeing the blank-eyed, bald-headed, genderless inmates. Never dreaming that this was the fate that awaited them, many quickly dismissed those whom they saw as insane. To indicate the distance they remember feeling between themselves and the unfortunate ones around them, witnesses have drawn on the imagery of popular science fiction novels, such as Aldous Huxley's *Brave New World* (1932) to describe their first impressions. On seeing two identical-looking male prisoners, dressed in striped uniforms, with numbers over their chests, Judith Magyar Isaacson remembers exclaiming: 'Bokanovsky twins. . . . Sprung from a test tube in the *Brave New World*.'[20] However, Livia Bitton-Jackson recalls that she was soon to realize:

The people we saw as we entered the camp [Birkenau], the shaved, grey-cloaked group which ran to stare at us through the barbed-wire fence, they were us! Same bodies, same dresses, same blank stares. We, too, look like an insane horde—soulless, misshapen figures. They, too, must have arrived

[17] Halina Birenbaum, *Hope is the Last to Die: A Personal Documentation of Nazi Terror*, trans. David Welsh (New York, 1971), 94–5; originally published in Polish as *Nadzieja Umiera Ostatnia* (Hope Dies Last) (Warsaw, 1967).

[18] Kitty Hart, *Return to Auschwitz: The Remarkable Story of a Girl who Survived the Holocaust* (London, 1983), 89. For her initial testimony see *idem, I Am Alive* (London, 1961).　　　　　　　　　　　　　　[19] Hart, *Return to Auschwitz*, 79.

[20] Judith Magyar Isaacson, *Seed of Sarah: Memoirs of a Survivor*, 2nd edn. (Urbana, Ill., 1991), 62.

from home quite recently: their heads were freshly shaven. They were women just like us. They, too, were ripe mothers and young girls, bewildered and bruised. They, too, longed for dignity and compassion: and they, too, were transformed into figures of contempt instead.[21]

Until May 1944, 'selection' took place on a temporary ramp just outside Birkenau, and then on a specially built *Judenrampe* (Jew-ramp) situated through the gate of the Birkenau guard building at the railway platform. SS personnel instructed the Jewish arrivals where to leave their luggage—in accordance with instructions, most Jews arrived with luggage weighing between 66 and 110 pounds, consisting of household articles, clothes, food, and personal items—which was collected by specifically designated prisoners.[22] The Jews were made to form two lines—men were separated from women—and an SS doctor (often the infamous Dr Josef Mengele, who between May 1943 and November 1944 took part in at least seventy-four such acts)[23] carried out selections. Transports of non-Jews did not go through the selection process, but were registered as prisoners. Those judged unfit to work—the elderly, the weak, children—were immediately sent to their deaths in the gas chambers after being made to leave their clothes, shoes, and other possessions outside in designated changing rooms, to be sorted later by the *Sonderkommando* prisoners. It is estimated that approximately 865,000 Jews were sent to the gas chambers on arrival without ever being registered.[24] The majority had no idea of the fate that awaited them until it was too late. Their bodies were either burned in the crematoria, or, if there were too many, in an open space. Those spared an immediate death were sent to the 'quarantine' area of Birkenau, where they were taken to the 'sauna' (bath), made to discard their clothes and hand over any last possessions, and have their heads, underarms, and pubic areas shaved before receiving an ice-cold shower. They were then given either blue-and-white striped prison

[21] Livia E. Bitton-Jackson, *Eli: Coming of Age in the Holocaust* (London, 1984), 80.

[22] See Andrzej Strzelecki, 'The Plunder of Victims and their Corpses', in Gutman and Berenbaum (eds.), *Anatomy of the Auschwitz Death Camp*, 249–50.

[23] Other doctors included Professor Carl Clauberg and, later, Dr Johann Kremer. See M. Gilbert, *The Holocaust*, 582.   [24] See Piper, 'Number of Victims', 230.

uniforms or the clothes of previous arrivals deemed not good enough to be distributed to Germans, and were either allowed to keep their own shoes or given ill-fitting wooden clogs. Alternatively, they were given the uniforms of Russian soldiers who had perished in Auschwitz or, occasionally, clothes of a mockingly unsuitable nature, such as ball gowns or flimsy evening dresses. Although the clothing often reeked of disinfectant, it was usually filthy. They re-emerged from the sauna as part of the monolithic mass they had previously dismissed as insane; they were no longer individuals but *Häftlinge* (prisoners). If a prisoner was not transferred out of quarantine to one of the forced-labour camps, soon, he or she would die of thirst and starvation within a few weeks. Those selected for forced labour either in Auschwitz I or II or in one of its subcamps were registered and given tattoos on their left fore-arms.[25] Prisoners sent to work in other concentration camps were not included in the registration process and did not receive tattoos.

The tattooing and shaving of new inmates served to dehumanize the victims. As David Patterson writes, 'Numbers . . . are opposed to being: they are the ciphers of nothingness and the spokesmen of indif-ference. . . . And numbers are precisely the language—or the anti-language—of weight, measurement, and enumeration.'[26] Patterson highlights the importance of the numbering process in Holocaust memoirs, pointing out that in his memoir *Survival in Auschwitz*,[27] Primo Levi devotes a lot of time to talking about the significance of the tattooing process and its ongoing effects: a prisoner may leave Auschwitz in the physical sense, but never really leaves it in his or her mind.[28] For Levi, the tattoo declares, 'you will never leave here'.[29] The removal of a person's name was also intended to deprive the prisoner of his or her past and all the memories associated with that identity.

[25] Prisoners were only tattooed at Auschwitz. The first prisoners to be tattooed were Soviet prisoners of war in the autumn of 1941. They were tattooed on the left side of the chest.

[26] David Patterson, *Sun Turned to Darkness: Memory and Recovery in the Holocaust Memoir* (New York, 1998), 164.

[27] See Primo Levi, *Survival in Auschwitz: The Nazi Assault on Humanity*, trans. Stuart Woolf (New York, 1961); originally published as *Se questo è un uomo* (If This is a Man) (Turin, 1947).   [28] Patterson, *Sun Turned to Darkness*, 165.

[29] Levi, *The Drowned and the Saved*, 165.

INITIATION

To describe their initiation into the camps, survivors select a vocabulary of meanings that stress the other-worldly quality of the experiences. Whereas Judith Magyar Isaacson seizes on the objectifying language of science fiction, Joseph Bau, who survived the Płaszów concentration camp, states: 'The story of the concentration camps is like the scenario of a horror movie directed by someone devoid of human emotions, whose purpose is to scare the audience and to set its nerves on edge.'[30] At this stage of the concentration camp experience, comparison with the creations of science fiction novels or horror movies is strangely apt. Many horror films begin with a portrait of an orderly society, which the audience can relate to, before introducing something to destroy that sense of stability and knowledge. This in many ways describes the concentration camp inmates' journey into the camps. For many, the transformation of their world was so acute that they appear to have felt that they were watching the movie described by Bau, rather than actually being a part of it. For example, Sara Selver-Urbach, writing of her first experience of '*Zähl-Appell*' (roll-call)[31] at Auschwitz, is unable to place herself within the scene she describes. She states: 'The first time, I *saw* an "Auschwitz roll-call"' rather than 'the first time I *took part* in an Auschwitz roll-call'. She continues: 'the whole thing looked like some grotesque stage-décor illuminated by the last rays of a setting sun' (italics added).[32] Of her one week at Auschwitz she recalls: 'Every minute that I spent in Auschwitz, I was unable to grasp that what I was undergoing and witnessing was real, that I was not trapped inside a horrible

[30] Joseph Bau, *Dear God, Have You Ever Gone Hungry?*, trans. Shlomo Yurman (New York, 1990), 110.

[31] There was a twice-daily roll-call in the concentration camps, when all inmates had to stand to attention. The purpose of the roll-calls was to account for all inmates, including those who had died during the night. They could last for hours, regardless of weather conditions.

[32] Sara Selver-Urbach, *Through the Window of My Home: Memories from the Ghetto Lodz*, trans. Siona Bodansky (Jerusalem, 1971), 127; originally published in Hebrew as *Mi-ba'ad le-ohalon beti* (Jerusalem, 1964).

nightmare from which I had to wake up.'[33] David Patterson draws attention to the human transformations that took place, citing Isabella Leitner's memory of herself and her sister Chicha in the de-lousing process: 'Some naked-headed monster is standing next to me. Some naked-headed monster is standing next to her.'[34]

It was not until she had been transferred from Auschwitz to the labour camp at Mittelsteine that Sara Selver-Urbach was able to make sense of her thoughts on paper, and to begin to connect herself with what she had experienced. While in the labour camps at Mittelsteine and Grafenort she wrote a diary on scraps of paper, which she hid in the sleeve of her coat and copied out after the war 'without changing a word'.[35] However, it is interesting that she presents her diary as an addendum to the main body of her book—a memoir of a Jewish family in the Łódź ghetto and their deportation to Auschwitz. She clearly views her post-war recollections as containing a more accurate reflection of her wartime experiences than what was written in her diary. Introducing her diary, she writes: 'I don't know if I managed to gleam more than a few crumbs or capture more than some frayed shreds of what we were undergoing. The conditions under which we lived in the camp prevented me from expressing adequately all that was going on there, because suffering often benumbed my ability to concentrate.'[36]

A further diary entry states:

After five years of suffering and deprivation in the Ghetto, after five years of incessant wrestling and contriving in order to stay alive, we were hurled into an abyss in which everything that ever was, crashed down and shattered and was buried under mounds of waste and ruins. All the ideals and ideas we had fought for, all our spiritual struggles to preserve the ultimate goal of our life in the face of a most cynical reality which proved to us every day and every moment that there was no purpose or point to our existence; all our desperate endeavour to safeguard one spark of faith in the meaningfulness of what

[33] Selver-Urbach, *Through the Window of My Home*, 125.

[34] Isabella Leitner, *Fragments of Isabella: A Memoir of Auschwitz* (New York, 1978), 26. Cited in Patterson, *Sun Turned to Darkness*, 171.

[35] Selver-Urbach, *Through the Window of My Home*, 133.   [36] Ibid.

was happening to us and around us—all that has now crashed down and turned to dust.[37]

David Patterson suggests that what the inmates of the concentration camps experienced was the death of the self. Beginning with the loss of a name, it 'proceeds to the breakdown of the body that is the image of the self. And it culminates in the decomposition of the soul that is the life of the self.'[38] Seweryna Szmaglewska writes:

> You lost the capacity of proving to yourself, in a moment of doubt, that you are still the same human being you were when you came here. That being is gone, and only a miserably wretched creature remains in her place. A naked creature deprived of everything and avidly covering her body with someone else's sweat-saturated garments in spite of keen disgust.[39]

As Patterson explains, 'the self here is invaded by the other, both in the form of blows received and in the form of the very skin and sweat of the other, resulting not only in disgust but in *disjuncture*.'[40] Charlotte Delbo, a member of the French Resistance Movement imprisoned in Auschwitz, also writes of the fragmentation of the self. For her, Auschwitz represented a premature death, as the soul— inseparable from the physical self—is slowly destroyed by cold, hunger, filth, and exhaustion.[41]

Initiation into the camps involved the realization that nothing was as it seemed; there were few reliable points of reference, and a sense of betrayal is a common theme in the concentration camp testimonies. As a new slave-labourer at the Auschwitz factory of I. G. Farben in Monowitz, Primo Levi, an Italian Jew, reached out of a window for an icicle to soothe his thirst. Immediately the icicle was snatched away by an SS guard. When Levi asked ' "*Warum?*" "Why?" ', he was told ' "*Hier*

---

[37] Ibid. 136.   [38] Patterson, *Sun Turned to Darkness*, 163.

[39] Seweryna Szmaglewska, *Smoke Over Birkenau*, trans. Jadwiga Rynas (New York, 1947), 78. Cited in Patterson, *Sun Turned to Darkness*, 161. Originally published in Polish as *Dymy nad Birkenau* (Warsaw, 1945).   [40] Patterson, *Sun Turned to Darkness*, 161.

[41] Cited in Lawrence Langer, 'The Literature of Auschwitz', in Gutman and Berenbaum (eds.), *Anatomy of the Auschwitz Death Camp*, 615. Langer cites Delbo's trilogy, *Auschwitz et après* (Auschwitz and After) (Paris, 1970).

ist kein warum!" "There is no why here" '.[42] Delbo has written of Auschwitz: 'one couldn't be sustained by one's past, draw on its resources. It had become unreal, unbelievable. Everything that had been our previous existence had unravelled.'[43] And Hanna Lévy-Haas wrote in her diary while in Bergen-Belsen: 'The spiritual damage runs so deep that your whole being runs away. You have the impression of meeting with a thick, massive wall that cuts you off from the normal world of before. It is as though all capacity for perception has been blunted or has disappeared. No longer do you remember yourself or your own past.'[44]

The words hanging above the gates to the main camp at Auschwitz I, '*Arbeit macht frei*' (work makes you free) promised not salvation through hard work, but *Vernichtung durch Arbeit* (destruction through work), and the Red Cross ambulances did not carry medical supplies but canisters of Zyklon-B gas. More experienced prisoners soon informed the new arrivals that, contrary to the promises of the SS, their children were not being looked after in special children's camps, nor their elderly parents in camps where they did not have to work. Olga Lengyel, a Jewish physician, asked the SS officer standing on the disembarking platform of Birkenau whether her 11-year-old son could join his little brother in the children's camp. Not thinking for one moment that the Germans would harm children, she was comforted when her mother was allowed to join her sons. A few days later she learnt that her mother and sons had been sent to the gas chamber.[45]

LEARNING TO SURVIVE

Those arriving at the camps observed a huge difference between themselves and the more experienced prisoners. The new arrivals (the

---

[42] Levi, *Survival in Auschwitz*, 25.

[43] Charlotte Delbo, *Days and Memory*, trans. Rosette C. Lamont (Marlboro, Vt., 1990), 168; originally published in French as *La Mémoire et les jours* (Paris, 1985).

[44] Hanna Lévy-Hass, *Vielleicht war das alles erst der Anfang: Tagebuch aus dem KZ Bergen Belsen 1944–1945* (Maybe All That Was Just the Beginning: Diary from Bergen Belsen), ed. E. Geisel (Berlin, 1969), 37.

[45] See Olga Lengyel, *Souvenirs de l'au-delà* (Memories from Beyond) (Paris, 1946); published in English as *Five Chimneys: The Story of Auschwitz*, trans. Clifford Coch and

Zugänge) still had 'the smell of home'[46] and were despised by many of the veteran prisoners, who, envious of the longer amount of time they had spent with their families, termed the newcomers 'millionaires with six-digit numbers'.[47] On occasion, it was this type of resentment that led the veteran prisoners to tell the new arrivals the true fate of their loved ones. However, the *Zugänge* had the highest death rates; Jean Améry writes how early on in Auschwitz, he 'had not yet adjusted to the terror of the camp. The suffering and dying of those others whom I ran into at every step still did not just roll off my back. I had not yet cast off the thin skin of the *zugang*. This came later. Unless you sloughed off that skin you would not survive in Auschwitz.'[48]

The first to perish were those who had not been in the ghettos, for while the ghettos might not have been able to prepare the Jews emotionally or intellectually for the shock of the camps, the material deprivation endured in the ghettos helped to prepare them physiologically. In particular, those arriving at Auschwitz from Mediterranean countries died in large numbers from the shock of not being protected from the extreme weather conditions of Eastern Europe; they had to adapt quickly to their new surroundings if they were to stand any chance of survival. They also had to learn to understand the German orders of the SS and the Polish spoken by many of the *Kapos*.[49] They needed to work out how to negotiate the soup queues in order to obtain 'thicker' soup, or an additional bowl, and to work out which was better: to eat their bread ration at once or to nibble it throughout the day. Prisoners

---

Paul P. Weiss (Chicago, 1947); repr. under the title *Five Chimneys: A Woman Survivor's True Story of Auschwitz* (Chicago, 1995). All quotations are taken from the 1995 reprint.

[46] Levi, *The Drowned and the Saved*, 39.

[47] Yisrael Gutman, 'Social Stratification in the Concentration Camps', in Gutman and Avital Saf (eds.), *The Nazi Concentration Camps: Proceedings of the Fourth Yad Vashem International Conference, January 1980* (Jerusalem, 1984), 167.

[48] Jean Améry, *At the Mind's Limits: Contemplations by a Survivor on Auschwitz and its Realities*, trans. Sidney Rosenfeld and Stella P. Rosenfeld (Bloomington, Ind., 1980), 39; originally published in German as *Jenseits von Schuld und Sühne: Bewältigungsversuche eines Überwältigten* (Beyond Guilt and Atonement: Attempting to Overcome the Overwhelming) (Munich, 1966).

[49] The term *Kapo* is derived from the Italian word *capo* (chief), and was used in the concentration camps to refer to a prisoner appointed by the SS to be in charge of a labour *Kommando* of other prisoners.

needed to realize that it was vital to try to keep clean: to wash with the morning's ersatz coffee, and, in the absence of any means of laundering their clothes, to at least remove the lice. The difference between the incredulous new arrivals and the emerging seasoned prisoners is exemplified in the way in which the distancing language of insanity, or science fiction, is abandoned. For Judith Magyar Isaacson, the imagery of Aldous Huxley soon became redundant, for 'The Brave New World is dwarfed by comparison—the same mad discipline, the same infernal crowding, but our world beastly, Huxley's overrefined'.[50] Prisoners even had to learn a new language: Primo Levi explains that the ' "*Lager* jargon" of the camps was a mixture of German, the remnants of the different languages of the victims, and words created within the camp itself'.[51] He believes: 'If the *Lagers* had lasted longer, a new, harsh language would have been born.'[52] In the meantime, familiar words had to be stretched to fit the dictates of the camps. For example, Kitty Hart states that 'organization' was 'the most important word in the Auschwitz language' and 'the key to survival'.[53] She explains: 'It meant to steal, buy, exchange, get hold of. Whatever you wanted, you had to have something to barter for it. Some people spent every waking minute "organizing": stealing from their fellow prisoners, bribing others, swapping a crust of bread for a can of water, a crumpled sheet of notepaper for a more comfortable corner of a bunk.'[54]

Sara Selver-Urbach sees this new language as expressing the difference between the ghetto and her new surroundings:

We were no longer the human society we'd been in the Ghetto. True, there, too, we'd given expression to human anger and hatred, but here in the concentration camp, feelings had undergone a transformation, the relationship between people was changed, as though people were total strangers who spoke different languages. And the words that people acquired here, a whole lexicon of expressions that they mastered right away! A special language reigned in the place, consisting of the rudest and most vulgar terms and

<hr/>

[50] Isaacson, *Seed of Sarah*, 84.   [51] Levi, *Survival in Auschwitz*, 135.
[52] Cited in Michael Tager, 'Primo Levi and the Language of Witness', *Criticism*, 35 (Spring 1993), 284.   [53] Hart, *Return to Auschwitz*, 83.
[54] Ibid.

definitions, stripped of every human feeling. It was another world, another planet, governed by different concepts and laws.[55]

To decide to go on living and not succumb to the fate of the '*Muselmann*' (Muslim),[56] or the 'temptation' of the electric wired fence, prisoners had to adapt themselves to this new way of life. Almost all those who survived describe this process; Livia Bitton-Jackson describes how it worked for her:

At first I was frightened of the latrine. The ditch was wide and very deep and I had a nightmarish fear of falling into it. Mummy was holding my two hands while I was crouching above the smelly abyss, and I held hers while she was. But after the first few times we learned to balance at the precarious edge of the ditch. The fear is gone. Amazing how fast one learns. Everything. Even swallowing the daily mush became easier. Lying on the hard floor is much easier now, and the *Zählappell* [Roll-call] quite bearable. Getting used to the thirst is the most difficult.[57]

Bitton-Jackson realizes that her mother played an important part in helping her adjust to concentration camp life. Many of those who survived did so because they were able to remain with a family member, and they recognize this as being an important contributing factor to their survival. Those who had lost family members sometimes formed close friendships in their place. However, some turned their back on family and friends and immersed themselves in the logistics of their own survival. Still others, who had been parted from their family, decided to shut themselves off from the horrors they were experiencing. Mordehay Klein remembers of his arrival at Auschwitz:

They sent me to the right and my little brother was separated from me and sent to the left. . . . He was crying, 'Why are you leaving me alone?' Even if

---

55 Selver-Urbach, *Through the Window of My Home*, 128–9.

56 This was the slang used in Auschwitz for prisoners who had abandoned the will to live and who were on the verge of death. In the women's camp at Ravensbrück it was *Muselweib* (a feminized version), in Majdanek, *Gamel* (based on *Kamel*, or camel), in Dachau a *Kretiner* (cretin), in Buchenwald a *müder Scheich* (tired sheik), in Mauthausen a *Krüppel* (cripple), and in Neuengamme a *Schwimmer* (swimmer). See Wolfgang Sofsky, *Die Ordnung des Terrors: Das Konzentrationslager* (The Order of Terror: The Concentration Camp) (Frankfurt, 1993), 152–68 and 363 n. 5.   57 Bitton-Jackson, *Eli*, 95.

I live for a thousand years in hell, this moment will still be the worst in my life. At that instant I knew that if I could not quickly blot out my feelings and thoughts, I would go crazy. From this period on I switched off my brain, and stopped thinking entirely, just like you would turn off an electric light. I shut off all feelings and memories of anything but the present moment. I was concerned only with 'today' and 'this moment'; there was no past or future.[58]

The above statement also shows how time itself was one of the modes in which survival was measured. For most, the battle for survival involved a changing notion of time, although this manifested itself in a multiplicity of ways. For Mordehay Klein, survival meant concentrating on each moment or day and avoiding any thoughts that might detract from such a focus. Similarly, Primo Levi asks: 'Do you know how one says "never" in camp slang? "*Morgen früh*, tomorrow morning".'[59] In the ghettos, the Jews had held on to the possibility of a reprieve from their plight, but in the camps that possibility was suspended. Prisoners had no way of knowing how long their ordeal would last. However, if they were to continue the battle for survival, they had to develop a heightened awareness of the present situation. While Primo Levi states that prisoners refused to speak of 'tomorrow', Mordehay Klein indicates that this was due to the need to monitor carefully their survival from one moment to the next. It also involved deciding which part of their past identity it was useful to retain, and what of the future they could afford to imagine. As Primo Levi writes:

Nothing belongs to us any more; they have taken away our clothes, our shoes, even our hair; if we speak, they will not listen to us, and if they listen, they will not understand. They will even take away our name: and if we want to keep it, we will have to find in ourselves the strength to do so, to manage somehow so that behind the name something of us, of us as we were, still remains.[60]

[58] Mordehay Klein, *My Life—Our History* (London, 1997), 23–4.
[59] Levi, *Survival in Auschwitz*, 133.
[60] Levi, *If This is a Man*, 33.

HOLDING ON TO THE PAST

Testimonies also describe how Orthodox Jews continued to find ways to practise their religion. Women's testimonies document how religious women would go to great lengths to observe the Sabbath, lighting candles made from bits of grease and oil saved from the factories where some of the prisoners worked.[61] In Birkenau, candles could also be obtained from the 'Kanada' *Kommando* (the labour detachment dealing with incoming possessions, named by Polish-Jewish prisoners after a country perceived to hold untold riches), where workers were often able to smuggle certain items. Hebrew prayerbooks, prayer shawls, and *tefillin* (phylacteries) were also obtained in this way.[62] However, for many it seemed incredible that the doomed continued to affirm God's presence. In Elie Wiesel's memoir *Night*, on seeing a group of men reciting Kaddish (the prayer for the dead) upon their arrival at Auschwitz, the young protagonist Eliezer asks: ' "Why should I bless His name?" ' However, he goes on, ' "in spite of myself, the words formed themselves and issued in a whisper from my lips: *Yitgadal veyitkadash shme raba* . . . [May His great name grow exalted and sanctified]".'[63]

In his essay 'Jewish Identities in the Holocaust: Martyrdom as a Representative Category', Jonathan Webber gives examples of how Jewish rituals provided religious Jews with the ability to retain important aspects of their pre-war identities. He makes the important observation—which he attributes to a personal correspondence with Rabbi Shlomo Zalman Lehrer, a former Auschwitz prisoner[64]—that

[61] See e.g. Bitton-Jackson, *Eli*, 166. Bitton-Jackson also describes the lighting of Hanukkah candles.

[62] See Jonathan Webber, 'Jewish Identities in the Holocaust: Martyrdom as a Representative Category', in Polonsky (ed.), *Polin. Studies in Polish Jewry*, xiii: *Focusing on the Holocaust and its Aftermath*, 139.

[63] Elie Wiesel, *Night*, trans. Stella Rodway (New York, 1960), 43; originally published in French as *La Nuit* (Paris, 1958).

[64] Cf. Shelomoh Zalman Lehrer and Leizer Strassman, *The Vanished City of Tsanz* (Southfield, Mich., 1997).

'[k]nowledge of the correct date in the Jewish calendar, regularly confirmed by newly arriving transports of deportees, constantly provided religious prisoners with an anchorage in their own cultural world'.[65]

In an attempt to similarly retain an aspect of pre-camp life, some inmates went to extreme measures to obtain books. Charlotte Delbo spent a full day's ration of bread on a paperback copy of Molière's *The Misanthrope*.[66] Delbo was a political prisoner, and was therefore relatively privileged in comparison to the less fortunate Jewish women. Others tried to remember poetry and songs. Ruth Elias writes in her memoir that in Auschwitz, remembering the lyrics of songs acted as 'spiritual and mental nourishment', since she and her friends 'knew intuitively that if we gave up spiritually and intellectually, we would be giving up all hope of survival'.[67] Primo Levi describes how he tried to recite passages from Dante's *Inferno* to his neighbour Jean. However, he is so overcome by hunger that he is unable to translate the passages into French.[68] Levi was not the only one to find that literature in general, and in this case Dante, was inadequate in the face of the concentration camps. While recognizing the extreme nature of the camps, prisoners still clutched at ways to connect with some previous fragment of knowledge. The Jewish religion has no notion of hell to draw on, so it is Dante's descriptions that many testimonies use as the benchmark of horror.[69] However, most found Dante's hell an insufficient comparison for what they wished to describe; survivor Alexander Donat (Michael Berg)[70] states: 'Maidanek was hell. Not the naïve inferno of Dante, but a twentieth-century hell where the art of cruelty was refined to perfection and every facility of modern technology and psychology was combined to destroy men physically and spiritually.'[71]

[65] Webber, 'Jewish Identities in the Holocaust', 139.

[66] Cited in Tzvetan Todorov, *Facing the Extreme: Moral Life in the Concentration Camp*, trans. Arthur Denner and Abigail Pollack (New York, 1996), 92.

[67] Ruth Elias, *Triumph of Hope: From Theresienstadt and Auschwitz to Israel*, trans. Margot Bettauer Dembo (New York, 1998), 123. For a discussion of music in Auschwitz, see S. Gilbert, *Music in the Holocaust*, ch. 4.   [68] Levi, *If This is a Man*, 118–21.

[69] See Stephen Eric Bronner, 'Making Sense of Hell: Three Meditations on the Holocaust', *Political Studies*, 47/2 (1999), 324. Cf. Rachel Falconer, *Hell in Contemporary Literature: Western Descent Narratives since 1945* (Edinburgh, 2005).

[70] For the origin of Michael Berg's pseudonym, see p. 160.

[71] Alexander Donat, *The Holocaust Kingdom: A Memoir* (London, 1967), 165.

While some sought to retain something of themselves through either religion, literature, relationships, or the rituals of survival, the brutal design of the concentration camps meant that the desire to hold on to some previous identity often had negative manifestations. Whereas Kitty Hart and her mother were able to realize the depravity of 'the system' and resist it, other prisoners retained the desire to 'do well'—to perform their jobs to the best of their abilities and to be seen doing so. Hart writes:

Most of the great complex of Auschwitz and Birkenau camps was in fact run by prisoners themselves, and it was hideous to see how readily one of your own people would turn against you in return for a few privileges and the chance of a few more months of life. Some were as proud of their armbands, which denoted their status, as of a military decoration, and appeared genuinely touched when they got a word of commendation from an S.S. officer. They set themselves to making careers within the camp, and were very conscious of their status.[72]

Filip Müller tells us that imitating, as far as was possible, the clothing of the SS allowed certain *Sonderkommando* prisoners to 'look more human' and was dubbed 'Auschwitz fashion'.[73] The Christian doctor Ella Lingens-Reiner also observed that many of her fellow inmates 'transferred their ambitions and emotions to the life inside the camp. Therefore they would fight for positions not only because they intended to survive, but also for their own sake, because it satisfied their need to win power, recognition. . . . Some of them invested their whole being in these matters, and so lost much of their intellectual and moral standards.'[74]

The desire for power was certainly exploited by the SS. The concentration camps were based on the co-operation of the prisoners in the

[72] Hart, *Return to Auschwitz*, 89.
[73] Filip Müller, *Eyewitness Auschwitz: Three Years in the Gas Chambers*, trans. Susanne Flatauer (Chicago, 1979), 62; published in the UK as *Auschwitz Inferno: The Testimony of a Sonderkommando*, trans. Susanne Flatauer (London, 1979); originally published in German as *Sonderbehandlung: Drei Jahre in den Krematorien und Gaskammern von Auschwitz* (Special Treatment: Three Years in the Crematoria and Gas Chambers of Auschwitz) (Munich, 1979).
[74] Ella Lingens-Reiner, *Prisoners of Fear* (London, 1948), 91.

administration of terror and death. As Kitty Hart points out, although the SS were responsible for the overall running of the camps, everything but the direct administration of camp affairs was placed in the hands of prisoners in positions of authority—*Lagerältesters* (camp elders), *Blockältesters* (block elders), and *Kapos*. These prisoners were responsible for enforcing discipline, carrying out punishments, supervising work, and other duties. It was not only the additional privileges that came with such positions that the prisoners responded to, but, as Hart illustrates, they desired commendation from those in authority. When Judith Magyar Isaacson was selected for the role of *Kapo*—which she later surrendered when she realized the brutality that the position involved—her mother could not help but proudly exclaim: 'To think she picked you out of a thousand. . . . Wait till I tell papa!'[75] Primo Levi noted that if a person in their pre-war life was used to carrying out a job to the best of their ability, it was hard to abandon this tendency even if the job in question was to benefit the enemy:

I frequently noticed in some of my companions (sometimes even in myself) a curious phenomenon: the ambition of a 'job well done' is so deeply rooted as to compel one 'to do well' even enemy jobs, harmful to your people and your side, so that a conscious effort is necessary to do them 'badly'. The sabotage of Nazi work, besides being dangerous, also meant overcoming atavistic inner resistance.[76]

The wish to do a job well often translated itself into violence. Many *Kapos*, both Jewish and non-Jewish, used extreme violence to ensure discipline. For many, the savagery of the Jewish *Kapos* acted as a particularly cruel form of betrayal. For Sara Zyskind, the Jewishness of a *Kapo* 'made their cruelty all the worse'. She asked one: 'If you're Jewish, why do you help the Germans torture us? Why do you beat your own sisters? Haven't you any feelings of pity? Haven't we all gone through enough, torn from our relatives, deprived of everything we possessed?'[77] The *Kapo*, not wanting to be reminded of who she was, or perhaps because she could not forget it, proceeded to punish

75 Isaacson, *Seed of Sarah*, 79.   76 Levi, *The Drowned and the Saved*, 98.
77 Zyskind, *Stolen Years*, 157.

Zyskind with ferocious zeal. It is these types of beatings and other acts of sadism that are the hardest to explain. Although many witnesses talk of beatings and whippings in their testimonies, they do so sparingly; physical pain is described much less than other forms of suffering. Jean Améry, who has provided one of the few detailed accounts of physical torture in the concentration camps, writes:

> Whoever has succumbed to torture can no longer feel at home in the world. The shame of destruction cannot be erased. Trust in the world, which already collapsed in part at the first blow, but in the end, under torture, fully, will not be regained. That one's fellow man was experienced as the antiman remains in the tortured person as accumulated horror. It blocks the view into a world in which the principle of hope rules.[78]

To feel excruciating pain meted out at the hands of another is to lose control over one's body, mind, and ultimately one's life. In her study of torture, which is clearly informed by her reading of Améry, Elaine Scarry explains: 'Physical pain does not simply resist language but actively destroys it, bringing about an immediate reversion to a state anterior to language, to the sounds and cries a human being makes before language is learned.'[79] To describe such pain, witnesses would have to abandon 'comprehensiveness' and 'objectivity'—the guiding principles of witnessing set out by Emmanuel Ringelblum[80]—and revert to the primordial vocabulary of acute and inexplicable suffering. Such a vocabulary does not speak of shared experiences, of being part of history, but of individual agony and humiliation.

Many lost the sense of purpose that had enabled them to survive the torments of the ghetto. This was the case for Alexander Donat, a journalist who had been in the Warsaw ghetto and who, on arriving at Majdanek, wrote that he 'still felt some of the exaltation of the last days of the Warsaw Ghetto', for 'that desperate fight still casts its

---

[78] Améry, *At the Mind's Limits*, 40.

[79] Elaine Scarry, *The Body in Pain: The Making and Unmaking of the World* (Oxford, 1985), 4.

[80] It should also be noted that Ringelblum, as a trained historian, would have had considerably more education than many of the concentration camp inmates, particularly those whose education had been cut short by the war.

retrospective glow'.[81] Echoing the sentiments of many of the Warsaw ghetto chroniclers, he continues: 'I felt I was a witness to disaster and charged with the sacred mission of carrying the Ghetto's history through the flames and barbed wire until such time as I could hurl it into the face of the world. It seemed to me that this sense of mission would give me the strength to endure everything.'[82] However, Donat was unable to retain his 'sense of mission' once he left the ghetto. He writes: 'But I was underestimating Maidanek. Hell has no bottom. During the first days there I felt so many blows upon my head that I was completely crushed.'[83] As Primo Levi has noted, 'the concentration camp system . . . had as its primary purpose shattering the adversaries' capacity to resist.'[84]

'I MUST SURVIVE AS A WITNESS'

For some of the inmates, what resurrected the desire to bear witness[85] was the fear that the SS's frequently repeated dictum, that they would ensure no witnesses would survive to tell the world about the destruction inflicted on the Jews, would come true. Szymon Laks recalls the words spoken by an SS officer in Auschwitz:

You see, . . . according to the instructions of the Führer himself, not even one Häftling [prisoner] should come out alive from any concentration camp. In other words, there will be no one who can tell the world what has happened here in the last few years. But even if such witnesses should be found—and this is the essence of the brilliant plan of our Führer—NOBODY WILL BELIEVE THEM. . . . Even if we lose the war . . . no one will present us with the reckoning.[86]

---

[81] Donat, *Holocaust Kingdom*, 180.　　　[82] Ibid.　　　[83] Ibid.

[84] Levi, *The Drowned and the Saved*, 38.

[85] See Frida Michelson, *I Survived Rumbuli*, trans. Wolf Goodman (New York, 1979), 42; originally published in Russian as *Ya perezhila Rumbulu* (Tel Aviv, 1973).

[86] Szymon Laks, *Music of Another World*, trans. Chester A. Kisiel (Evanston, Ill., 1989), 79. For the original French publication, see Szymon Laks and René Coudy, *Musique d'un autre monde* (Paris, 1948).

A key concern for all witnesses is the issue of credibility; aware of their own disbelief at encountering the hellish world of the concentration camps, they must have realized how difficult it would be to recount their experiences to the outside world. The SS clearly exploited this fear. However, for some prisoners, it also strengthened their resolve to let the world know of the horrors they had been forced to endure. Although the concentration camps did alter the inmates immeasurably, this does not mean that their individual personalities and psycho-social histories were irrelevant. For example, witnesses from a certain intellectual milieu, and particularly those who had taken part in the archival projects in the ghettos, were far more likely to dwell on the political or historical significance of their experiences. For example, Alexander Donat was instructed by the well-known Jewish historian Ignacy Schiper, whom he had known in the Warsaw ghetto:

History is usually written by the victor. What we know about murdered people is only what their murderers vaingloriously cared to say about them. Should our murderers be victorious, should *they* write the history of this war, our destruction will be presented as one of the most beautiful pages of world history, and future generations will pay tribute to them as dauntless crusaders. Their every word will be taken for gospel. Or they may wipe out our memory altogether, as if we had never existed, as if there had never been a Polish Jewry, a Ghetto in Warsaw, a Maidanek.[87]

Likewise, Primo Levi's friend Steinlauf tells him: 'even in this place one can survive, and therefore one must survive, to tell the story, to bear witness.'[88] In this way the commitment to bear witness can be seen as synonymous with survival. But, depending on the individual circumstances of the prisoner—for example, the conditions of the camps in which they were and his or her position within the camps— it meant different things for different witnesses.

While at Monowitz, Primo Levi, a trained chemist used to making observations with a scientist's precision, was able to make notes of

[87] See Donat, *Holocaust Kingdom*, 206.   [88] Levi, *Survival in Auschwitz*, 36.

things he planned to tell the world upon liberation.[89] Ana Novac, a
15-year-old Hungarian girl, somehow managed to keep a journal
while in Auschwitz and the Płaszów concentration camp in 1944. She
wrote with a pencil stub that she found in the ground on SS notices
ripped from the walls (carrying statements such as 'CLEANLINESS IS
HEALTH'), and hid the notes in her shoes; when too many accumulated,
she memorized them to reconstruct later.[90] She explains in her journal:
'I'm not writing for myself, that goes without saying. I hope that these
notes will be part of the evidence, on the day of reckoning! But even if
I knew that I would be my only reader, I would still write! I would
take the trouble to find the right word, the strongest word.'[91]

Renata Laqueur Weiss, a concentration camp diarist who went on
to make a study of concentration camp diaries, cites fourteen such
journals.[92] She agrees with Ana Novac, believing that the few concentration camp diarists were not only writing to one day bear witness,
but also 'to write themselves out of the concentration camp world'.[93]
It was a way of connecting themselves to life outside the camps. In her
own diary Laqueur Weiss writes: 'Father, Mother, I implore you,
think of me for a few intense seconds. I shall do the same for you, and
our thoughts will meet and merge.'[94] Although only a few were able
to find the resources or energy to write while in the camps, many still
intended to bear witness one day. Halina Birenbaum states: 'I decided
that if I lived to see liberation, I would write down everything I saw,
heard and experienced.'[95] For Kitty Hart, 'something inside kept

---

[89] Although the notes were never published in their original form, Levi published his
memoir, *Se questo è un uomo*, in Turin in 1947. For a discussion of this work, see Robert
Gordon, 'Holocaust Writing in Context: Italy 1945–47', in Andrew Leak and George
Paizis (eds.), *The Holocaust and the Text: Speaking the Unspeakable* (London, 2000),
32–50.

[90] Ana Novac, *The Beautiful Days of My Youth: My Six Months in Auschwitz and
Plaszow*, trans. George L. Newman (New York, 1997), 7–8; originally published in
German as *Die Schönen Tage meiner Jugend* (Hamburg, 1967).   [91] Ibid. 70.

[92] Renata Laqueur Weiss, *Schreiben im KZ: Tagebücher 1940–1945* (Writing in the
Camps: Diaries 1940–1945) (Bremen, 1991).

[93] Cited in Patterson, *Along the Edge of Annihilation*, 23.

[94] See Renata Laqueur Weiss, *Bergen-Belsen Tagebuch 1944/45* (Bergen-Belsen Diary
1944/45), trans. Peter Wiebke (Hannover, 1983), 45. Cited in Patterson, *Along the Edge
of Annihilation*, 24.   [95] Birenbaum, *Hope is the Last to Die*, 244.

telling me that I had to last out. Never obey. Never give in. Some of us had to live, to defy them all, and one day tell the truth.'[96]

Whereas the majority of prisoners had little opportunity to witness anything beyond their own predicament, Kitty Hart, as a member of the Kanada *Kommando*, was aware that she was in a position which allowed her more knowledge than the average prisoner of the destruction taking place. When Hart was a member of Kanada, *Kommando* workers were housed near the arrival ramp so that they could sort without delay the belongings of the hundreds of thousands of Hungarian Jews about to be murdered. She remembers a girl calling to her, ' "You must see this. Look!" '[97] Hart writes:

I didn't want to look. I was too afraid of what I might see. But I had to go and stand beside her. Not fifty yards away was an incredible sight. A column of people had been shuffling from the direction of the railway line into a long, low hall. When the place was full there was a delay; but I went on watching, hypnotized. What I was witnessing was murder, not of one person, but of hundreds of innocent people at a time. Of course we had known, had whispered about it, and been terrified of it from a distance; but now I was *seeing* it, right there in front of me.[98]

By directly witnessing the genocide, Kitty Hart realized that she was setting herself apart from the ordinary prisoners, who may have 'whispered about it, and been terrified of it from a distance' but had never actually seen it 'right there' in front of them. Hart herself realized the price she would have to pay: the SS would make particularly sure that no one who had witnessed the killing would survive to bear witness. However, Hart was able to escape the fate of her *Kommando* as a result of her mother's strangely successful plea to the commander of Auschwitz, Rudolf Höss, that her daughter join her on a transport out of Auschwitz.[99]

Others who might be regarded as having a particular motivation to bear witness include members of the medical profession. Miklos Nyiszli, a Jewish doctor who worked as Mengele's personal research

[96] Hart, *Return to Auschwitz*, 127.   [97] Ibid. 149.   [98] Ibid.
[99] Ibid. See pp. 173–4.

pathologist and also as a physician to the *Sonderkommando*, states: 'I felt it my duty to be able to give an accurate account of what I had seen if ever, by some miraculous whim of fate, I should escape.'[100] Nyiszli did survive and went on to produce a detailed account both of the medical experiments he participated in and also of what it was like to live day by day with the men of the *Sonderkommando*.

However, it is important that the desire to bear witness is not overstated, or seen as a reprieve from suffering. Prisoners were terrified that if they did get to tell their stories, no one would believe them. Primo Levi describes a recurring dream he had in Auschwitz. In the dream he leaves the camp and returns home to tell of the horrors which he had witnessed. While he is speaking, he realizes that no one is listening:

This is my sister here, with some unidentifiable friend and many other people. They are all listening to me and it is this very story that I am telling: the whistle of three notes, the hard bed, my neighbour whom I would like to move, but whom I am afraid to wake as he is stronger than me. I also speak diffusely of our hunger and of the lice control, and of the Kapo who hit me on the nose and then sent me to wash myself as I was bleeding. It is an intense pleasure, physical, inexpressible, to be at home, among friendly people, and to have so many things to recount: but I cannot help noticing that my listeners do not follow me. In fact, they are completely indifferent: they speak confusedly of other things among themselves, as if I were not there. My sister looks at me, gets up and goes away without a word.[101]

According to Levi, this type of dream was common among inmates, and subsequently the duty to bear witness was felt by many to be a burden. A statement by Gerda Klein is illustrative of this: 'I am haunted by the thought that I might be the only one left to tell the story.'[102] Furthermore, trying to remember the details of their suffering—the beatings, the work, the selection—was for many impossible. The battle

---

[100] Miklos Nyiszli, *Auschwitz: A Doctor's Eyewitness Account*, trans. Tibère Kremer and Richard Seaver (New York, 1960), 75; originally published in Hungarian as *Dr. Mengele boncolóorvosa voltam az Auschwitzi krematóriumban* (I was Dr Mengele's Pathologist in the Auschwitz Crematorium) (Nagyvarad, 1946).

[101] Levi, *Survival in Auschwitz*, 256.

[102] Gerda Weissman Klein, *All But My Life* (New York, 1997), p. vii.

to remember everything consumed energy that was badly needed for survival; thinking needed to be geared towards the procurement of additional food and the avoidance of selections. Even Ana Novac, who kept a diary while in the camps, writes: 'I'm hungry. Today all my thoughts take the shape of sausages . . . lethargy. . . . I'm not worrying my brain anymore.'[103] The effects of starvation on the brain must not be overlooked. For example, Olga Lengyel, who worked in the infirmary of Birkenau, observed: 'the inmates revealed signs of mental deterioration. They lost their memory and the ability to concentrate.'[104] Coupled with the effects of filth, lice, dysentery, selections, beatings, and all manner of other tortures, attempts to document camp experiences became an impossibly daunting task. Novac was aware of the impossibility of providing a detailed and comprehensive account. She writes from Płaszów: 'I admit it, I'm an incomplete witness, but otherwise how could I get through this experience without losing my mind? I observe in particular this crumb of the camp that is me, and the crumbs around me. No, how could I hope to give a complete view of the camp? (Like emptying the ocean with a ladle).'[105]

Similarly, Sara Selver-Urbach writes in the introduction to her diary: 'Like everybody else, I was a human wreck, and writing was a futile attempt to pick up the pieces of my shattered life and faith, and to glue them anew.'[106] Simone Veil speaks of the differences between her experiences of Birkenau and that of her sister deported to Ravensbrück:

Some women took notes in order to be able to give testimony later. I don't know anyone who was able to do so at Birkenau with the exception of those who worked in the offices. But most of us were assigned to land labour. We were so worn out, trying merely to survive, that we were incapable of procuring the necessary paper and pencil, even less of writing.[107]

[103] Novac, *Beautiful Days of My Youth*, 25.
[104] Lengyel, *Five Chimneys* (1995), 96.
[105] Novac, *Beautiful Days of My Youth*, 69.
[106] Selver-Urbach, *Through the Window of My Home*, 133.
[107] Interview with Simone Veil (June 1990), in Annette Wieviorka, 'On Testimony', trans. Kathy Aschheim in Geoffrey H. Hartman (ed.), *Holocaust Remembrance: The Shapes of Memory* (Oxford, 1994), 29. As an addendum, Wieviorka, a French historian,

THE AUSCHWITZ PROTOCOLS

At Auschwitz there were groups of prisoners who did not have to battle every day to survive; they were able to collect incriminating evidence against the SS and did not have to face the issue of whether or not they would be believed. They were the prisoners who held positions in the camp administration—in the prisoners' office, the infirmary, the Labour Deployment Department, the Political Department—and were able to make secret copies of letters, reports, and statistics to smuggle out of the camps and send to the Polish underground, who then published them in the underground press.[108] On 7 April 1944, two Slovak Jews, Walter Rosenberg (Rudolf Vrba), a clerk in the camp, and Alfred Wetzler, aided by the Auschwitz underground, started to plan their escape. For three days (and two nights) they concealed themselves in a hide-out in a gap of woodpile beyond the camp's inner perimeter. Strong Russian tobacco soaked in gasoline was spread around to confuse the dogs that were searching for them. Once the search ended, the two men escaped to Slovakia, where they were met by the remaining Jewish leadership. Rosenberg and Wetzler gave details of the camp and estimated the number of Jews that had been killed (1.75 million). They also warned that preparations were in place for the murder of nearly 800,000 Hungarian Jews and the 3,000 Czech Jews who had arrived from Theresienstadt in June. A thirty-page report was prepared that was later supplemented by a report from two other escapees: Czesław Mordowicz and Arnošt Rosin, who escaped from Auschwitz on 27 May and reached the Slovak border on 6 June 1944. They reported the arrival and murder of approximately 3,000 Greek Jews and the beginning of the murder of the Hungarian Jews—90 per cent of whom were killed on arrival. The report, which called for the Allies to bomb Auschwitz, finally reached the Czech

---

states that with the exception of physicians, the population of Birkenau was on the whole less educated than the prisoners at Ravensbrück (ibid.).

[108] Czech, *Auschwitz Chronicle*, p. xiii.

government-in-exile on 13 June 1944, and was subsequently dispatched to Washington on 16 June, broadcast by the BBC on 18 June, and received by the Swedes on 23 June 1944.[109]

THE TESTIMONY OF THE *SONDERKOMMANDO*

In another category were the mostly Jewish members of the *Sonderkommando* (some were Russian prisoners-of-war), who were told repeatedly that they would never live to see liberation. Not having even the barest hope of survival, they knew that anything they wanted to document had to be done immediately. Moreover, because they knew with complete certainty that as *Geheimnisträger* (secret bearers) they would be murdered, they were perhaps more willing to risk being caught in the act of writing.[110] Three men—Załman Gradowski, Załmen Lewental, and Leib Langfuss—united to document their experiences of the ghetto, deportation, arrival at Auschwitz, and their work in the *Sonderkommando*. Between 1945 and 1962, fragments of notes and six diaries written by the men were found buried near the crematoria at Birkenau. It is possible that there were more writings hidden by other members of the work force that deteriorated over time and were never found.[111] Gradowski urges the

---

[109] See Rudolf Vrba's post-war memoir (written with Alan Bestic), *I Cannot Forgive* (London, 1963). For a history of these first reports, see John S. Conway, 'The First Report about Auschwitz', *Simon Wiesenthal Center Annual*, 1 (1984), 133–51.

[110] However, some prisoners did survive to bear witness. These include Filip Müller, who, together with Dov Paisikovic and Milto Buki, testified at the Auschwitz trial in Frankfurt in 1964. For another account of an Auschwitz *Sonderkommando* prisoner, see Rebecca Camhi Fromer, *The Holocaust Odyssey of Daniel Bennahmias, Sonderkommando* (Tuscaloosa, Ala., 1993). For interviews with other survivors of the *Sonderkommando*, see Gideon Greif, *Wir weinten tränenlos . . . Augenzeugenberichte der jüdischen 'Sonderkommandos' in Auschwitz* (We Wept without Tears . . . Testimonies of the Jewish Sonderkommando from Auschwitz) (Cologne, 1995). Cf. *idem* and Andreas Kilian, 'Significance, Responsibility, Challenge: Interviewing the Sonderkommando Survivors', *Studies on the Audio-Visual Testimony of Victims of the Nazi Crimes and Genocides*, 9 (June 2003), 75–83.

[111] For a history of the manuscripts and their discovery, see Ber Mark (ed.), *The Scrolls of Auschwitz* (Tel Aviv, 1985). For the Yiddish publication, see *idem* (ed.), *Megilas Oyshvits*

finder of his writings to continue digging the area in the search for the many manuscripts buried there:

Dear finder, search everywhere, in every inch of soil. Tons of documents are buried under it, mine and those of other prisoners which will throw light on everything that was happening here. It was we, the Kommando workers, who expressly have strewn them all over the terrain, as many as we could, so that the world would find material traces of the millions of murdered people. We ourselves have lost hope of being able to live to see the moment of liberation.[112]

The writings, which have become known as the 'Auschwitz scrolls' (*Megilas Oyshvits* in Yiddish),[113] were written in Yiddish and Polish by the *Sonderkommando* prisoners; the scrolls were not only an attempt to let the world know of their experiences, but also serve as a reminder of the men's existence. The first manuscript of Załman Gradowski,[114] an observant Jew from Suwałki (on the border of Lithuania and Poland), explains: 'it may be that these, the lines that I am now writing, will be the sole witnesses to what was my life.'[115]

Gradowski began making notes soon after his deportation to Auschwitz in February 1943.[116] Although he soon realized that he would not live to see the world's reaction to his story, it became increasingly important to him that the world should know of the torture he had suffered. More than that, he was aware of his significance as a unique witness to the mass murder of European Jewry, and wanted to bear witness for the victims of the gas chambers. On 6 September

(Tel Aviv, 1977). Photographs taken by members of the *Sonderkommando* also survived the war. For a discussion of the photographs, see Dan Stone, 'The Sonderkommando Photographs', *Jewish Social Studies: History, Culture, and Society*, 7/3 (2001), 131–48.

112 Załman Gradowksi, 'Manuscript of a Sonderkommando Member', trans. Krystyna Michalik, in Jadwiga Bezwinska and Danuta Czech (eds.), *Amidst a Nightmare of Crime: Manuscripts of Members of Sonderkommando* (Kraków, 1973), 76. Cf. *idem, In harts fun gehenem* (In the Heart of Hell) (Jerusalem, 1944).

113 See Mark (ed.), *Scrolls of Auschwitz.*

114 See Nathan Cohen, 'Diaries of the Sonderkommando', in Gutman and Berenbaum (eds.), *Anatomy of the Auschwitz Death Camp*, 523. Cf. *idem*, 'Diaries of the Sonderkommando in Auschwitz: Coping with Fate and Reality', *Yad Vashem Studies*, 20 (1990), 273–312.   115 Cited in Roskies (ed.), *Literature of Destruction*, 548.

116 See M. Gilbert, *The Holocaust*, 730.

1944 Gradowski collected the notes he had made over the last nineteen months and buried them in one of the pits of human ashes.[117] He explains in a covering letter: 'I have buried this under the ashes, deeming it the safest place, where people will certainly find the traces of millions of men who were exterminated.'[118] The first page of his notebook, written in Russian, Polish, German, and French, clearly states: 'Show an interest in this document. It contains rich material for the historian.'[119] He invites his readers to join him on the November 1942 transport from the transit camp in Kalabosin, near Grodno, through Treblinka and Warsaw, and finally arrive with him at Auschwitz. They are then confronted with the final journey of the victims. Gradowski describes how he and the other members of the *Sonderkommando* were forced to lead the victims to the gas chambers, after the gassing drag out the corpses, wash away the cyanotic acid that had stained them pink and green, search the orifices of the bodies for hidden objects, extract gold teeth, cut the women's hair and wash it with ammonium chloride, place the bodies in the crematoria; oversee their incineration, and then remove the ash from the ovens.[120]

But Gradowski wanted to leave more than just an eyewitness account of the destruction he was forced to witness; he wanted to emphasize resistance, albeit a martyred one. His second manuscript, found among the ruins of the ovens in the summer of 1945, consists of three parts: 'A Moonlit Night', 'The Czech Transport', and 'The Parting'. 'The Czech Transport' recounts the murder of 5,000 Czech Jews in the gas chambers of Birkenau. The Jews were deported from Theresienstadt, where they had been mostly able to stay together as families. On arrival at Auschwitz, they were placed in the *Familienlager* (family camp) BIIb—a 'showpiece' built at Birkenau in September 1943 for the purpose of a Red Cross visit. On 7 March 1944, they were all sent to their deaths. Gradowski describes the death procession in terms of a martyred resistance. Rather than

[117] Ibid.   [118] Cited ibid.
[119] Cited in N. Cohen, 'Diaries of the Sonderkommando', 524.
[120] Giorgio Agamben, *Remnants of Auschwitz: The Witness and the Archive*, trans. Daniel Heller-Roazen (New York, 1999), 25.

focusing on his own helplessness in the face of such destruction, he chooses to focus on the defiance of the Czech Jews—in a sense, to bear witness for them. For example, he states: 'All glanced scornfully at the line of officers, not wishing to grace them with direct gazes. No one pleaded, no one sought mercy. . . . They didn't want to give them the pleasure of watching them beg for their lives in despair.'[121] He also recounts the words spoken to SS officers by a woman marching in a naked procession to her death with her 9-year-old daughter:

'Murderers, thieves, shameless criminals! Yes, now you kill innocent women and children. You blame us, helpless as we are, for the war. As if my child and I could have brought this war upon you. You think murderers, that with our blood you can hide your losses on the front. But the war is already lost. . . . You will be carved up alive. Our brothers all over the world will not rest until they have avenged our innocent blood. . . . You will pay for everything—the whole world will take revenge on you.' Then she spat in their faces and ran into the bunker with her child.[122]

Wanting 'to immortalize the dear, beloved names of those, for whom, at this moment, I cannot even expend a tear',[123] Gradowski and other members of the *Sonderkommando* buried with their writings a large number of teeth—as a means to trace the dead.[124]

Załmen Lewental's testimony was discovered in 1962, in a jar buried in the ground near Crematorium III.[125] It was written on a few sheets of paper and contains plans to blow up Crematorium IV, which took place on 7 October 1944; Lewental's documentation remains the primary source of information regarding the *Sonderkommando* uprising at Birkenau.[126] However, the notes do more than plan the uprising; like Gradowski, Lewental wanted to leave behind a record of Jewish resistance. By leaving behind their testimony, Lewental and Gradowski, like the ghetto diarists, have tried

---

[121] Cited in Roskies (ed.), *Literature of Destruction*, 558.   [122] Ibid.
[123] Ibid.   [124] See N. Cohen, 'Diaries of the Sonderkommando', 524–5.
[125] M. Gilbert, *The Holocaust*, 649. Cf. Salmen [Załmen] Lewental, 'Manuscript of Sonderkommando Member', trans. Krystyna Michalik, in Bezwinska and Czech (eds.), *Amidst a Nightmare of a Crime*, 130–78.
[126] See also Camhi Fromer, *Holocaust Odyssey of Daniel Bennahmias, Sonderkommando*, 63–81.

to find some meaning to their fate. Gradowski writes: 'Dear discoverer of these writings! I have a request of you: this is the real reason I write, that my doomed life may attain some meaning, that my hellish days and hopeless tomorrows may find a purpose in the future.'[127] Knowing that he could not wait until liberation to bear witness, Gradowski buried his work before taking part in his final act of resistance: the *Sonderkommando* revolt.

WILL THE WORLD EVER KNOW?

During the closing period of World War II, as the Soviet forces advanced in the East and the American, British, and French forces in the West, the Germans, in the summer of 1944, made preparations to evacuate prisoners from Auschwitz, and in October 1944 began the systematic attempt to destroy any evidence of the gas chambers and crematoria. Files concerning individual prisoners, death certificates, and charge sheets were taken to Crematorium II and burned.[128] Hundreds of thousands of prisoners were marched away from Auschwitz and the advancing Red Army, and sent to camps such as Belsen, Dachau, Buchenwald, Mauthausen, Sachsenhausen, Ravensbrück, and also to factories in central and western Germany. These marches, known as 'death marches', were to result in many more deaths. Prisoners died of the cold, exhaustion, and starvation, while the guards shot many others for failing to keep pace.

The destruction of the evidence of the SS crimes as part of their continued commitment to prevent witnessing, and the removal of the prisoners from the sites of their crimes, exemplified the fears of many prisoners that the free world would never get to learn of their suffering. Throughout their ordeal, despite pledges to bear witness and the attempts to do so, many prisoners were fearful that their captors would be proved right—that the world would never know how they had suffered and died. They had always been unsure about how the

---

127 Cited in Roskies (ed.), *Literature of Destruction*, 548.   128 Ibid. 757.

war would end and what their individual fates would be. A month before he died in the labour camp at Gross-Bressen, Günther Marcuse wrote: 'For us, the prospects of a prolonged stay are diminishing. Filled with apprehension, we await coming events.'[129] It was this awareness of mortality that led some to attempt to write their testimony while in the camps. Like the workers of *Oneg Shabbat*, the *Sonderkommando* prisoners—the ultimate witnesses to the destruction of the Jews—took pains to bury their writings to ensure that they would not be forgotten by historians of the future. For them, the writing and burying of their testimony served as the ultimate act of resistance. It is likely that there were many other prisoners who wrote testimonies which have either been lost or destroyed. Those that remain show both a desire to find some meaning to the suffering and, simultaneously, the need to find some form of resistance to it. The latter came through the writing of testimony itself, and also potentially provided a means for a person's identity to survive after their death.

The camps disrupted many of the beliefs and notions of identity and witnessing formulated in the ghettos, yet also fuelled the desire to resurrect them. While the rare surviving testimonies written in the concentration camps lack the additional thoughts and observations which serve to organize the experiences of survivors retrospectively—such as the post-war cultural identity of the 'survivor', Holocaust historiography, and other social phenomena that mediate and shape one's views of one's experiences—this does not mean that authors wrote with thoughts of objectivity and comprehensibility. The nature of the camps rendered these principles of witnessing obsolete. We have seen through a combination of survivor reflections and wartime testimony that the extreme suffering of the camps marked a significant departure from the model of bearing witness prescribed by Emmanuel Ringelblum and the staff of *Oneg Shabbat*. Whereas in the ghettos it was possible to document Jewish life under German occupation, concentration camp life militated against doing so. The

[129] Günther Marcuse, 'The Diary of Günther Marcuse (The Last Days of the Gross-Bressen Training Centre)', trans. Joseph Walk, *Yad Vashem Studies*, 8 (1970), 181.

desire to bear witness had to be subsidiary to the main goal, which was to survive. Only a few were able to make witnessing their primary aim. They were aware that while they had little chance of survival, their testimonies at least had the chance to outlive the Nazis. While it can be seen that the writing of testimony in the concentration camps expressed the twin need to inform the world of the horrors of the camps and to allow the person bearing witness to be remembered after their death, it should be noted that the *desire* to bear witness (regardless of the possibility of doing so) also gave prisoners an incentive which fuelled their instinct to survive.

The memoirs of survivors illustrate that testimony cannot be treated as a homogeneous entity. Life in the concentration camps was very different from that in the ghettos, and the horrors encountered presented a major obstacle to survivors writing their memoirs—particularly when conveying the death of the self, which they experienced on arrival at the camps. Also, the brutality of the few Jewish *Kapos* in the concentration camps attests to the heterogeneity of Holocaust experiences. The following chapters, beginning with the liberation of the camps, will show how survivors—using the concept of the Holocaust and the adoption of the post-war identity of the survivor as witness, as organizational frameworks for their experiences—seek to discover through the writing of memoirs a post-war identity that provides a means of reconciling their wartime experiences with the desire to create a new life after the Holocaust. Furthermore, the post-war identity and representation of the Holocaust also brings about further changes in the nature of bearing witness.

3

Writing to Remember: The Role of the Survivor

> Immediately after the war, we were 'liberated prisoners'; in sub-
> sequent years we were included in the term 'DPs' or 'displaced
> persons' . . . In the US we were sometimes generously called
> 'new Americans.' Then for a long time . . . there was a good
> chance that we, as a group, might go nameless. But one day I
> noticed that I had been reclassified as a 'survivor.'
>
> Weinberg, *Self-Portrait of a Holocaust Survivor*

Following the war, the position of the Holocaust witness entered a
phase very different from that of the ghetto inhabitants, escapees, and
concentration camp inmates who wrote of events as they happened.
Holocaust survivors, as they later became known, had to confront the
fact that whereas they survived, millions did not. This had a significant effect on the giving of testimony; many felt not only a moral
duty to testify, but also the need somehow to account for their own
survival. The introduction of a concept to describe survivors' experiences years after they occurred also had important consequences. The
post-war introduction of the term 'the Holocaust'[1] has meant that

---

[1] It was not until sometime between 1957 and 1959 that the English word 'holocaust'
was used to describe the murder of European Jewry during World War II. See Gerd
Korman, 'The Holocaust in American Historical Writing', *Societas—A Review of Social
History*, 2/3 (Winter 1972), 262–3. The term *holocaust* comes from the Septuagint, the
ancient Greek translation of the Hebrew Scriptures, starting in the third century
BCE, when the term *holokaustos* (translated as 'totally burnt') became—via the Latin

survivors' individual experiences have become part of a collective historical memory.

The concept of the Holocaust as an analytical tool, although one way of talking about a subject so vast, is, however, constricting. For example, it is unclear when the Holocaust begins. With the rise of the Nazi Party in 1933? With the *Kristallnacht* (Night of Broken Glass) pogrom conducted in Germany and Austria on 9 and 10 November 1938? With the *Einsatzgruppen* shootings in the summer of 1941? Or with the murder of Jews in the gas-vans of Chełmno in December 1941? Or, if the Holocaust is to include the mass murder of both Jews and non-Jews, does it begin with the euthanasia programme in 1939?[2] The Holocaust is not a unified event, but many different events. Also, defining it implies that it is an event with an end. However, as a result of the type of experiences described below, the term 'Holocaust survivor', although used originally to refer to a person who outlived persecution under the Nazi regime, has more recently been expanded to take into account the suffering many endured after the war. Furthermore, many survivors feel inextricably linked to their traumatic past. For them, as perhaps for their children and even their grandchildren, there will never be an end. Although the term 'Holocaust survivor' might therefore appear to be fairly malleable, like the concept of the Holocaust, it also conceals the diversity of the experiences it seeks to represent. There is no universal survivor experience. Many survivors never experienced a concentration camp or a labour camp but survived by hiding (some with false Aryan papers and some without), some alone, some with family members. The length of time spent in the ghettos and concentration camps also varies widely. Not even taking into account religious, cultural,

---

holocaustum—the Greek version of the Hebrew *olah*: a burnt sacrificial offering which can be made only to God. It was first used in the translation of 1 Sam. 7: 9, meaning 'a burnt offering to God', and was later expanded to refer to the mass murder of human beings. See Jon Petrie, 'The Secular Word HOLOCAUST: Scholarly Myths, History, and 20th Century Meanings', *Journal of Genocide Research*, 2/1 (March 2000), 63.

[2] Petrie, 'The Secular Word HOLOCAUST', 62. On non-Jewish experiences of Nazi persecution, see Michael Berenbaum (ed.), *A Mosaic of Victims: Non-Jews Persecuted and Murdered by the Nazis* (London, 1990).

economic, and gender differences, those who survived the concentration camps had quite different experiences, depending on the camps
they were sent to, the conditions within the camps while they were
there (conditions were divergent and subject to constant change), the
specific nature of a particular work *Kommando*, or their position
within the social hierarchy of the camp, and the support systems to
which they had access.[3] These factors not only crucially affected a
prisoner's experiences, but also critically affect how survivors
interpret the Holocaust in their post-war lives.

Despite the popular belief of an all-pervasive post-war silence, by
constructing a history of Holocaust testimony, two points can be
made: witnesses developed a desire to tell their stories not after liberation, but during the events of the Holocaust, and this desire persisted;
there was an interest in documenting and publishing survivors' experiences in the immediate post-war period. For example, the members
of *Oneg Shabbat* realized that their suffering was part of an important
historical event, and many Jews in the labour and concentration
camps vowed to make sure that one day the world would know of the
appalling crimes committed by the Nazis. In the immediate post-war
period, survivors bore witness to meet this promise.

IN THE AFTERMATH OF LIBERATION

When the war ended on 8 May 1945, it is estimated that there were
around 200,000 Jewish survivors of the forced-labour camps, concentration camps, death camps, and death marches. Thousands of other
survivors, who had been with the partisan groups, or in hiding, were
also freed from Nazi control. The majority of those who survived were
aged between 16 and 40 years old. The death toll continued to rise
after liberation, with tens of thousands dying of starvation, disease,
and the after-effects of malnutrition.[4] For many who survived this

---

[3] See Emanuel Tanay, 'On Being a Survivor', in Alan Berger (ed.), *Bearing Witness to
the Holocaust, 1939–1989* (Lewiston, Me., 1991), 17–31.

[4] Michael Marrus, *The Holocaust in History* (Harmondsworth, 1993), 195.

initial period, their suffering was to continue after liberation. In numerous cases, survivors had not realized the extent of the destruction they had experienced. Many hoped to be reunited with their loved ones, but in most cases this was not possible. Sara Nomberg-Przytyk remembers the loneliness of her first day of release from Auschwitz: 'I was alone, no one was waiting for me, there was no one to return to.'[5] A few were lucky, discovering surviving family members. Others found that they were the sole survivors of previously large families. But many never found out the exact fate of their loved ones. Many of those deported to death camps such as Chełmno and Treblinka were not recorded on lists or given prison numbers but were sent straight to the gas chambers. Six million is the figure named by the International Military Tribunal at Nuremberg in its final judgment, and is the estimated minimum number of Jews who were murdered—about two-thirds of European Jewry and one-third of the world's Jewish population at that time.[6] Approximately 4 million people died in the camps, and 2 million elsewhere, mainly by shooting in Belorussia, Ukraine, Latvia, Estonia, Lithuania, and Yugoslavia, or by starvation and disease in the ghettos of Eastern Europe.

After the war the Commander of the Allied Forces in Europe, General Dwight Eisenhower, implemented a policy of repatriation for Displaced Persons. Generally this was possible only for non-Jews and Jews from Western Europe. Eastern European Jews, as well as Jews from Germany and Austria, faced many obstacles. The re-division of Europe meant that German Jews from, for example, Breslau, found that their home town had been renamed Wrocław, and was now in Poland.[7] The rise of Communist regimes in Eastern Europe made the delicate process of rehabilitation especially difficult for Jews returning to homes in Poland, Hungary, Romania, Czechoslovakia, and Bulgaria. There are numerous testimonies of

[5] Sara Nomberg-Przytyk, *Auschwitz: True Tales from a Grotesque Land*, trans. Roslyn Hirsch, ed. Eli Pfefferkorn and David H. Hirsch (Chapel Hill, NC, 1985), 154.

[6] Marrus, *Holocaust in History*, 199.

[7] Anton Gill, *The Journey Back from Hell: Conversations with Concentration Camp Survivors* (London, 1994), 38.

Jews discovering Christian families living in their homes, and their former neighbours being both suspicious and unfriendly. This burden was often too much when combined with all they had been through. Survivor Etu Weisfried, together with her new husband, returned to her pre-war home in Hungary, but soon left. She found her old family home in shambles, with a Christian family living in it. The family reluctantly gave her and her husband a room to stay in, but made life very difficult for them. She wrote in a letter to her two surviving sisters: 'It was foolish for us to think that we could build new lives on top of smoldering ashes.'[8] Others were forced to leave to escape further pogroms.[9]

Those with nowhere to go, or who found themselves unable to return home—nearly 50,000 of the Jewish survivors—were gathered in Displaced Persons (DP) camps in the Allied zones of Austria and Germany, and in Italy.[10] In the immediate aftermath of the war the term 'survivor' was not yet in common usage, and instead 'Displaced Person' was used. Historian Leonard Dinnerstein explains that this meant anyone who had been uprooted as a result of the war and found themselves unable to return home, and not necessarily *only* Jews.[11] However, while around 6 million DPs were successfully repatriated, the non-repatriable Jewish DPs—most of whom were from Eastern Europe and referred to themselves as *she'erit hapletah* (the surviving remnant, a biblical term from Ezra 9: 14 and I Chron. 4: 43)[12]—remained a problem for the UNRRA (United Nations

[8] Quoted in Aranka Siegal, *Grace in the Wilderness: After the Liberation 1945–1948* (New York, 1986), 66.

[9] Michael Steinlauf estimates that 1,500–2,000 Jews were murdered by Poles between 1944 and 1947. See his *Bondage to the Dead: Poland and the Memory of the Holocaust* (Syracuse, NY, 1997), 52. Cf. Lucjan Dobroszycki, 'Restoring Jewish Life in Post-war Poland', *Soviet Jewish Affairs*, 3/2 (1973), 58–72.

[10] For details of the different types of DP camps, see Zorach Warhaftig, *Uprooted: Jewish Refugees and Displaced Persons after Liberation, from War to Peace* (New York, 1946).

[11] Leonard Dinnerstein, *America and the Survivors of the Holocaust* (New York, 1982), 9. Cited in Judith Tydor Baumel, *Double Jeopardy: Gender and the Holocaust* (London, 1998), 234.

[12] See Z'ev Mankowitz, 'The Formation of *She'erit Hapleita*: November 1944–July 1945', *Yad Vashem Studies*, 20 (1990), 337–70, and idem, 'The Affirmation of Life in *She'erit Hapleita*', *Holocaust and Genocide Studies*, 5 (1990), 13–21.

Relief and Rehabilitation Administration) and the occupying armies, particularly the American forces. The situation was precarious, with the Jewish DPs complaining that they were being treated like criminals with curfews and limited rations. Also they were often housed with non-Jews, including those who had collaborated with the Germans. The situation was deemed so serious that in the summer of 1945 President Harry S. Truman sent Earl G. Harrison, dean of the University of Pennsylvania Law School and American envoy to the Inter-Governmental Committee on Refugees, to investigate the situation of the Jews in the DP camps of the American zone in Germany. As a result, not only did living conditions improve, but a special American provision recognized the Jews in their zone as a particular ethnic group with distinct requirements. They were given exclusively Jewish camps, and a special adviser on Jewish affairs was appointed. Increasingly, Jewish voluntary agencies such as the American Jewish Joint Distribution Committee (JDC) took over the running of the camps' internal administration, including sanitation, education, and religious and cultural activities. Similarly, in the British zone, the Jewish Relief Unit (JRU) managed welfare activities. In both cases, by early 1946 the Jewish DPs themselves had become recognized authorities.

The Jewish DPs were desperate to regain control over their lives. As well as marrying and having children,[13] establishing historical committees to record testimonies and plan monuments to the dead, they revived many of the pre-war Zionist movements, such as the pioneering youth movement Dror, and demanded the establishment of a Jewish homeland. However, although there was emigration during the two years before the establishment of the State of Israel in 1948, it was an option only for those young and energetic enough to feel able to overcome the hardships and restrictions of British mandatory rule.[14]

[13] On childbearing in the DP camps, see Judith Tydor Baumel, 'DP's, Mothers and Pioneers: Women in the *She'erit Hapletah*', *Jewish History*, 11/2 (1997), 99–110.

[14] See Hanna Yablonka, 'The Formation of Holocaust Consciousness in the State of Israel: The Early Days', in Efraim Sicher (ed.), *Breaking Crystal: Writing and Memory After Auschwitz* (Urbana, Ill., 1998), 120, and *idem, Survivors of the Holocaust: Israel after the War* (London, 1999).

Many survivors decided to emigrate elsewhere. Unfortunately, to reach countries such as Britain, Canada, the USA, or Australia, they often had to wait several years. The experience of Kitty Hart and her mother clearly demonstrates that although many East European Jews had long dreamt of emigrating to these countries, they faced many hurdles. New immigrants had to adjust to a completely new way of life, learn a new language, and adapt to a new culture. Even Jewish communities in the receiving countries, while providing much needed material support, did not always want to listen to what the survivors had suffered. Hart and her mother were two of only 12,000 surviving Jews who managed to enter Britain (compared with 100,000 post-war Jewish refugees admitted into the United States).[15] This was largely due to the restrictions within the British 'Distressed Relatives Scheme', whereby a British subject with permanent residence in Britain could apply to bring over surviving relatives, providing that their only remaining family resided in Britain. If permission was granted, the ticket had to be bought in England, the exit permit and visa obtained from a special office, and transport had to be by sea from Hamburg to Tilbury.[16] For most, life in Britain rarely met the survivors' expectations.[17] After surviving Auschwitz, Kitty Hart and her mother reached England hoping to be able to start a new life, but were soon disappointed. Describing her first minutes in England, Hart writes: 'My uncle was waiting at Dover. The moment we got into his car he staggered us by saying firmly: "Before we go off to Birmingham there's one thing I must make quite clear. On no

[15] David Cesarani, *Justice Delayed: How Britain Became a Refuge for Nazi War Criminals* (London, 1992). Cited in Anne Karpf, *The War After: Living with the Holocaust* (London, 1996), 197.
[16] Norman Bentwich, *They Found Refuge: An Account of British Jewry's Work for the Victims of Nazi Oppression* (London, 1956). Cited in Karpf, *War After*, 197. On Britain and the Holocaust, see David Cesarani, *Britain and the Holocaust* (London, 1998); *idem, Justice Delayed*; M. Gilbert, *Auschwitz and the Allies*; Tony Kushner, *The Holocaust and the Liberal Imagination: A Social and Cultural History* (Oxford, 1994); *idem*, 'The British and the Shoah', *Patterns of Prejudice*, 23/3 (1989), 3–16; and *idem*, 'The Impact of the Holocaust on British Society and Culture', *Contemporary Record*, 5/2 (1991), 349–75.
[17] See Tony Kushner, 'Holocaust Survivors in Britain: An Overview and Research Agenda', *Journal of Holocaust Education*, 4/2 (1995), 147–66.

account are you to talk about any of the things that have happened to you. Not in my house. I don't want my girls upset. And *I* don't want to know." '[18] She continues:

I was soon to discover that everybody in England would be talking about personal war experiences for months, even years, after hostilities had ceased. But we, who had been pursued over Europe by the mutual enemy, and come close to extermination at the hands of the enemy, were not supposed to embarrass people by saying a word. . . . It may seem grotesque to say, after surviving the tortures and terrors of Auschwitz, that this was one of the unhappiest times of my life. But for such a long time I had been forcing myself to hold on, had refused to give in, had kept going in the assurance that there *had* to be light at the end of the tunnel. And still there was no light.[19]

Survivors such as Kitty Hart, whose original memoir *I am Alive* was first published in 1962, suggest that in the immediate post-war period little time was given to understanding, or even listening to, the experiences of the Jewish survivors of the Holocaust.[20] Historians such as Tony Kushner concur, arguing that, despite the immediate post-war newsreels of the liberation of the camps, the destruction of European Jewry was a relatively undiscussed topic for the first twenty years after the war. This is attributed in the international context to the looming spectre of the Cold War, and in the specifically British context to the failure of the public to understand the scale of the destruction and the inability to place what had happened to the Jews within the context of World War II. The British had been responsible for the liberation of just one concentration camp—Bergen-Belsen— and Belsen had not functioned solely as a death camp.[21]

---

[18] Hart, *Return to Auschwitz*, 14.   [19] Ibid. 14–17.

[20] The chapter on Hart's experiences in post-war England was added to the later reprinting of her memoir *Return to Auschwitz* (1983).

[21] Kushner, 'Impact of the Holocaust', 356. On the liberation of Bergen-Belsen, see Joanne Reilly, *Belsen: The Liberation of a Concentration Camp* (London, 1998). On American responses in the immediate aftermath of the war, see Deborah Lipstadt, *Beyond Belief: The American Press and the Coming of the Holocaust 1933–1945* (New York, 1986), and Henry L. Feingold, *Bearing Witness: How America and its Jews Responded to the Holocaust* (Syracuse, NY, 1995).

DOCUMENTING THE HOLOCAUST

While many survivors, who desperately needed people to be interested in what they had been through, unquestionably did not receive
the support they should have had after liberation, it would be wrong
to ignore the fact that very early on significant attempts were under
way to document the devastation of European Jewry. Centres such as
the Wiener Library in London (founded in 1939),[22] the Jewish
Historical Commission in Lublin (August 1944),[23] and the Centre
de Documentation Juive Contemporaine (Centre for Contemporary
Jewish Documentation) in Grenoble (1943)[24] had begun to interview the Jewish survivors even before the end of the war.[25] The aim
was to remember the dead and help bring those who perpetrated the
atrocities to trial. Immediately after the war, documentary projects
were undertaken in the DP camps to gather testimonies,[26] and by
1948 the Central Historical Commission of the Central Committee
of Liberated Jews, founded in the American sector of Munich in
December 1945, had, through historical committees established in
Poland, France, Hungary, Slovakia, Italy, Austria, and Germany,
collected 2,550 testimonies.[27] Training sessions were held for those

[22] The library was founded by Dutch scholars in Amsterdam in 1934 before being
transferred to London by its director Alfred Wiener. See Ben Barkow, *Alfred Wiener and
the Making of the Holocaust Library* (London, 1997).

[23] It was later moved to Warsaw and became the *Żydowski Instytut Historyczny* (Jewish
Historical Institute). By 1945 there were twenty-five branches in Poland. Between 1945
and 1948 more than 7,000 accounts of Jewish survivors were collected. They are housed at
the ŻIH in Warsaw.   [24] It continued in Paris after the liberation.

[25] See also the efforts of Jewish refugees to document the suffering of their people, such
as Jacob Apenszlak (ed.), *The Black Book of Polish Jewry: An Account of the Martyrdom of
Polish Jewry under the Nazi Occupation* (New York, 1943).

[26] For a summary of these projects, see Shmuel Krakowski, 'Memorial Projects and
Memorial Institutions Initiated by She'erit Hapletah', in Gutman and Saf (eds.), *She'erit
Hapletah, 1944–1948*, 388–98.

[27] For more information on these committees, see Philip Friedman, 'European Jewish
Research on the Recent Jewish Catastrophe in 1939–1945', *Proceedings of the American
Academy for Jewish Research*, 18 (1949), 179–211, and *idem*, 'Problems of Research on the
European Jewish Catastrophe', *Yad [V]ashem Studies*, 3 (1959), 25–40.

involved in gathering the testimonies, and initiatives such as the *Fun Letstn Khurbn: tsaytshrift far geshikhte fun yidishn lebn beysn natsi rezhim* (From the Recent Destruction: A Journal for the History of Jewish Life under Nazi Rule), published in 1946, further encouraged survivors to tell their stories.[28] Also in 1946, the American psychologist David Boder travelled to the DP camps of France, Italy, Switzerland, and Germany carrying out interviews with more than 100 survivors of the camps, the majority of whom were Jewish. His findings were published in 1949 in *I Did Not Interview the Dead*.[29]

While it is true that the most significant historians of Nazism, such as Alan Bullock, Hugh Trevor-Roper, and A. J. P. Taylor,[30] made only minimal references to the Jewish catastrophe, Jewish historians were writing about the devastation of European Jewry fairly early on, although the best-known accounts—Léon Poliakov's *Brévaire de la haine: la IIIe Reich et les juifs* (Harvest of Hate: The Third Reich and the Jews) (1951),[31] and Gerald Reitlinger's *The Final Solution: The Attempt to Exterminate the Jews of Europe 1939–1945* (1953)[32]— tended to avoid using the testimony of Jewish victims in an attempt to infuse their work with objectivity.[33] Other early accounts include

---

[28] See Zeev W. Mankowitz, *Life between Memory and Hope: The Survivors of the Holocaust in Occupied Germany* (Cambridge, 2002), 218–22. By 1948 ten volumes of the journal were published, reaching a distribution of 12,000 copies (ibid. 221). The material collected by the Commission is now housed at Yad Vashem.

[29] David Boder, *I Did Not Interview the Dead*, 16 vols. (Urbana, Ill., 1949). Thirty-six of the interviews have been reproduced in Donald Niewyk (ed.), *Fresh Wounds: Early Narratives of Holocaust Survival* (Chapel Hill, NC, 1998). Cf. Donald Bloxham and Tony Kushner, *The Holocaust: Critical Historical Approaches* (Manchester, 2005), 31.

[30] See Alan Bullock, *Hitler: A Study in Tyranny* (London, 1952); Hugh Trevor-Roper, *The Last Days of Hitler* (London, 1947); and A. J. P. Taylor, *The Course of German History: A Survey of the Development of Germany since 1815* (London, 1945).

[31] Léon Poliakov, *Brévaire de la haine: la IIIe Reich et les juifs* (Paris, 1951); published in English as *Harvest of Hate: The Nazi Program for the Destruction of the Jews of Europe*, trans. Albert J. George (Syracuse, NY, 1954). Poliakov was the head of the Centre de Documentation Juive Contemporaine.

[32] Gerald Reitlinger, *The Final Solution: The Attempt to Exterminate the Jews of Europe 1939–1945* (London, 1953).

[33] See Kushner, *The Holocaust and the Liberal Imagination*, 3. Kushner cites Poliakov's statement that 'wherever possible, to forestall objections, we have quoted the executioners rather than the victims' (ibid.).

Artur Eisenbach's *Hitlerowska Polityka Eksterminacji Żydów w Latach 1939–1945 Jako Jedenz Przejawów Imperializmu Niemieckiego* (Hitler's Policy of Extermination of the Jews during 1939–1945 as a Manifestation of German Imperialism) (1953);[34] Hans Günther Adler's *Theresienstadt 1941–1945* (1955), which Adler had begun while imprisoned in Theresienstadt; Joseph Tenenbaum's *Race and Reich: The Story of an Epoch* (1956);[35] and Raul Hilberg's *The Destruction of the European Jews* (1961),[36] which, in 1958, was rejected for publication by Yad Vashem for, amongst other things, not emphasizing Jewish acts of resistance.[37] Attempts were also made to analyse the specific phenomenon of the Nazi concentration camps— for example, Denise Dufurnier's *La Maison des mortes, Ravensbrück* (The House of the Dead, Ravensbrück) was published in 1945[38]— and articles appeared in both the Jewish press[39] and scholarly journals attempting to analyse the survivor experience from a psychological perspective.[40] However, there was a tendency to approach that

---

[34] Artur Eisenbach, *Hitlerowska Polityka Eksterminacji Żydów w Latach 1939–1945 Jako Jedenz Przejawów Imperializmu Niemieckiego* (Warsaw, 1953); published in Yiddish as *Di Hitleristishe politik fun yidn-farnikhtung in di yorn 1939–1945* (Hitler's Policies for Jewish Annihilation in the Years 1939–1945) (Warsaw, 1955).

[35] Joseph Tenenbaum, *Race and Reich: The Story of an Epoch* (New York, 1956). Tenenbaum published his first book on the destruction of the Jews in 1948, and a book detailing the Warsaw Ghetto Uprising in 1952. See *idem, In Search of a Lost People: The Old and New Poland* (New York, 1948), and *idem, Underground: The Story of a People* (New York, 1952).

[36] Raul Hilberg, *The Destruction of the European Jews*, 3 vols. (Chicago, 1961).

[37] See the letter of rejection quoted by Hilberg in *The Politics of Memory: The Journey of a Holocaust Historian* (Chicago, 1996). Cf. Roni Stauber, 'Confronting the Jewish Response during the Holocaust: Yad Vashem—A Commemorative and a Research Institute in the 1950s', *Modern Judaism*, 20 (2000), 283–93. For an excellent critique of the early historiography of the Holocaust, see Dan Stone, *Constructing the Holocaust: A Study in Historiography* (London, 2003), 106–15.

[38] Denise Dufurnier, *La Maison des mortes, Ravensbrück* (Paris, 1945); published in English as *Ravensbrück, the Women's Camp of Death* (London, 1948).

[39] e.g. Leo Baeck, 'Life in a Concentration Camp', *Jewish Spectator*, 11 (July 1946), 12–13, and Mark Dworetzki, 'A Day in the Ghetto', trans. Jacob Sloan, *Jewish Spectator*, 11 (Oct. 1946), 16–20.

[40] See e.g. Philip Friedman, 'Some Aspects of Concentration Camp Psychology', *American Journal of Psychiatry*, 105 (1949), 601–5, and *idem*, 'The Road Back for the DP's: Healing the Psychological Scars of Nazism', *Commentary*, 6 (1948), 502–10.

experience in suspicious terms, emphasizing a ruthless commitment to survival at any cost.[41]

Survivors wanted not only to testify to the atrocities they had witnessed, but to commemorate their lost homelands. To meet this task, immigrant associations—*Landsmanshaftn*—in countries such as the United States, Australia, Israel, and Argentina (and a few in the Displaced Persons' camps), prepared *Yizkor Bikher* (memorial books) as representations of their respective communities.[42] Written in Hebrew, Yiddish, or a mixture of the two languages, they are dedicated to the memory of Jewish life that was destroyed. Unlike the majority of survivor memoirs, they were intended primarily for fellow émigrés and their descendants, and were mostly printed only in small numbers. Many of the *Yizkor Bikher* memorialize very small communities, and often were read only by those who knew the editors of the volumes personally. The books (more than 1,000 have been written, and more continue to be published) contain excerpts from diaries, or in rare instances complete diaries (which have often not been published elsewhere), and other literary items dating from the Holocaust, and include articles by historians and survivors on the histories of the vanished communities; details of pre-war Jewish life, including maps and photographs; life in the ghettos, the uprisings, and resistance; concentration camps, labour camps, and death camps; the attitudes of the local populations; the plight of the survivors; and details regarding emigration to Israel.[43]

---

[41] See Ralph Segalman, 'The Psychology of Jewish Displaced Persons', *Jewish Social Service Quarterly*, 23/4 (1947), 363–5, and Bruno Bettelheim, 'Individual and Mass Behaviour in Extreme Situations', *Journal of Abnormal Psychology*, 38 (1943), 417–52.

[42] The pogroms following World War I also resulted in the publication of *Yizkor Bikher*. The first *Yizkor* book to respond to the Nazi genocide was *Lodzer Yiskor Bukh*, published in New York in 1943.

[43] For a discussion of the *Yizkor Bikher*, see Rosemary Horowitz, 'Reading and Writing during the Holocaust as Described in *Yisker* Books', in Jonathan Rose (ed.), *The Holocaust and the Book: Destruction and Preservation* (Amherst, Mass., 2001), 128–42. Cf. Judith Tydor Baumel, ' "In Everlasting Memory": Individual and Communal Holocaust Commemoration in Israel', in Robert Wistrich and David Ohana (eds.), *The Shaping of Israeli Identity: Myth, Memory and Trauma* (London, 1995), 146–70. For a discussion of the use of *Yizkor* books in historical research, see Abraham Wein, ' "Memorial Books" as a Source for Research into the History of Jewish Communities in Europe', *Yad Vashem Studies*, 9 (1973), 255–72.

EARLY MEMOIRS

For many survivors, before they could begin to commemorate their lost community, they had to inform the world of the suffering they had witnessed. Between 1945 and 1949, seventy-five memoirs were published in a variety of European languages:[44] fifteen in Yiddish, thirteen in Hebrew, and twelve in Polish. Additionally, seven testimonies were published in French, six in Hungarian, and several in English, including Mary Berg's *Warsaw Ghetto: A Diary* (1945);[45] Albert Menasche's *Birkenau (Auschwitz II): (Memoirs of an Eye-witness). How 72,000 Greek Jews Perished* (1947);[46] *Smoke over Birkenau* by Seweryna Szmaglewska (1947); *Prisoners of Fear* by Ella Lingens-Reiner, a non-Jewish Austrian doctor incarcerated in Ravensbrück and Auschwitz-Birkenau (1948); and Gisella Perl's *I Was a Doctor in Auschwitz* (1948).[47] The publication of these memoirs—and their translation into English—demonstrates that there was a market for this type of literature, although it was of course very different from the huge market that exists today.

The fact that many of the accounts written immediately after the war are in Yiddish is especially significant. Not only was the Yiddish-speaking world of East European Jewry destroyed by the Holocaust, but because the vast majority of English-speaking historians have little knowledge of Yiddish, these testimonies (like the *Yizkor Bikher*) have been largely overlooked until fairly recently, contributing to the idea of an all-pervasive post-war silence. Yiddish testimonies, like those written in Hebrew, were mostly restricted to a

---

[44] This is the figure provided by Yad Vashem, which holds fifty-four memoirs published between 1945 and 1947.

[45] Prior to its publication as a book in February 1945, Berg's diary was published in serial form in Yiddish in the *Jewish Morning Journal* in the autumn of 1944. Extracts also appeared in *Contemporary Jewish Record*, 7/5–6 (1944).

[46] Albert Menasche, *Birkenau (Auschwitz II): (Memoirs of an Eye-witness). How 72,000 Greek Jews Perished*, trans. Isaac Saltiel (New York, 1947).

[47] Gisella Perl, *I Was a Doctor in Auschwitz* (New York, 1948).

Jewish readership.[48] They speak of the Holocaust—or the *hurbn* (destruction—*hurban* is the traditional Hebrew term) as it is known in Yiddish—as the absolute obliteration not only of a people, but also of a culture.[49] The decision to write in Yiddish by those fluent in Hebrew, Russian, Polish, Lithuanian, or other European languages reflects an attempt to express the magnitude of the catastrophe that befell East European Jewry. Yiddish was the language which Jews spoke amongst themselves. Yiddish testimonies can also be seen as part of a longer tradition of rebellion against the dissolution of the Yiddish language. Yiddish was the language of the unassimilated Ashkenazi Jews, and since the first part of the nineteenth century, the use of Yiddish had been increasingly regarded as an obstacle to the emergence of a Jewish middle class. More importantly, assimilation-ists had believed that the adoption of the Polish language by Polish Jewry would not only provide the basis for assimilation, but would also resolve the 'Jewish question' in Poland.[50] While Yiddish was effectively abandoned in most of the German-speaking countries, in Eastern Europe it remained to a great extent intact. However, despite the expansion of the Yiddish-speaking community as a result of the great migration of the late nineteenth and early twentieth centuries, and the existence of a Yiddish press, theatre, and education, many Jews and Christians alike continued to regard Yiddish as a crude and faulty German and appealed to Eastern European Jewry to abandon their attachment to the language.[51] For many, the Holocaust turned the continued use of the Yiddish language and the preservation of Yiddish culture into an act of cultural, if not political, resistance. The

[48] It must further be noted that speaking Yiddish does not necessarily equate with reading Yiddish, as it is written in Hebrew characters. This was true for many Jews edu-cated in Polish schools.

[49] See Vladka Meed, *Fun beyde zaytn geto-moyer* (New York, 1948); published in English as *On Both Sides of the Wall*, trans. Benjamin Meed (Tel Aviv, 1973).

[50] Stephen D. Corrsin, 'Aspects of Population Change and of Acculturation in Jewish Warsaw at the end of the Nineteenth Century: The Census of 1882 and 1897', in Antony Polonsky (ed.), *Polin. Studies in Polish Jewry*, iii: *The Jews of Warsaw* (Oxford, 1988), 131.

[51] Lucy Dawidowicz, *The Jewish Presence: Essays on Identity and History* (New York, 1977), 137–8.

use of Yiddish can be regarded as an attempt to retain something of the pre-war world and not let it be erased from history.

While Yiddish was the *mame-loshen* (mother tongue) of East European Jewry, Hebrew was the language of the book. However, by the beginning of the twentieth century, when Yiddish was gaining strength in both the cultural and political spheres, advocates of Zionism were promoting Hebrew as the language of the Jewish future.[52] After World War II there was a renewed commitment to the Hebrew language and culture, and a rejection of Yiddish as the language of the Diaspora. Early post-war emigration to Israel had involved a number of former ghetto fighters, including Zivia Lubetkin, who arrived in 1946, and (Antek) Yitzhak Zuckerman who arrived in 1947.[53] For them, as for many of the 22,000 survivors who took part in Israel's War of Independence, it was important to stress the link between the historical fact of Jewish resistance during the Holocaust and the desire to fight to establish a Jewish state.[54] While a lot of the survivors had had little formal education and scant knowledge of Hebrew, former members of the East European Zionist movements were among those likely to have studied Hebrew, and saw it as vitally important that their memoirs be recorded in the language of the Jewish future.[55] In 1949, after the State of Israel was established, a group of former fighters and partisans—including Lubetkin and Zuckerman—founded Kibbutz Lohamei Hagheta'ot. As well as preserving the historical archives described in Chapter 1, they began publishing—and continue to publish—books and leaflets dealing with the resistance movements in occupied Europe, including memoirs by former fighters.

Writing about the Holocaust in both Hebrew and Yiddish can be understood not only as an attempt to focus on the Jewish significance

---

[52] Corrsin, 'Aspects of Population Change' 131.
[53] See Yablonka, 'Formation of Holocaust Consciousness', 120.
[54] Tom Segev, *The Seventh Million: The Israelis and the Holocaust*, trans. Haim Watzman (New York, 1993), 177.
[55] See e.g. Ruzhka Korchzak, *Lehavot Ba-efer* (Flames in the Ashes) (Tel Aviv, 1946).

of the catastrophe and to uncover its meaning for Jewish history, but also to distinguish Jewish from European Holocaust literature, and it thus continues the work of figures such as Emmanuel Ringelblum, who wrote in Yiddish, and Chaim Kaplan, who recorded his diary in Hebrew. Also, in Auschwitz members of the *Sonderkommando*, such as Zalman Gradowski, wrote in Yiddish. After the war, writing in Yiddish was an integral part of the attempt to resurrect a sense of the communal spirit which had stimulated many of the archival projects of the ghettos. For example, in May 1946 the Association of Polish Jews in Buenos Aires began *Dos Poylishe Yidntum* (Polish Jewry) series, which resulted in the publication of around 200 diaries, memoirs, and historical essays detailing the history of Polish Jewry prior to its destruction. Like Ringelblum and his colleagues in the Warsaw ghetto, the editors were committed to documenting as extensively as possible the suffering and destruction of Polish Jewry.

Writing in the Jewish languages of Yiddish and Hebrew emphasizes the specifically Jewish nature of the Nazi genocide and reaches out to an identifiable—but ultimately limited—body of readers. While writing in these languages became a means whereby survivors could mourn the loss of their communities through connections with fellow émigrés, it often meant exclusion from a wider readership, and also from their new countries. Hence, many testimonies originally written in Yiddish by Polish Jews who emigrated to the United States were translated into English soon afterwards.[56] It soon became apparent that in order to reach many Jewish readers in both the USA and Britain, it was necessary to publish in English.

Testimonies written in European languages such as French and German, which focused on the national rather than ethnic identities

---

[56] See e.g. Tuvia Borzykowski, *Tsvishn falndike vent* (Between Tumbling Walls) (Warsaw, 1949); Bernard Goldstein, *Finf yor in Varshever geto* (Five Years in the Warsaw Ghetto) (New York, 1947), published in English as *The Stars Bear Witness*, trans. Leonard Shatzkin (New York, 1949); Jacob Pat, *Ash un fayer* (New York, 1946), published in English as *Ashes and Fire: Through the Ruins of Poland*, trans. Leo Steinberg (New York, 1947); Jonas Turkow, *Azoy iz es geven: khurbn Varshe* (That is the Way It Was: The Destruction of Warsaw) (Buenos Aires, 1948); and Wiernik, *A yor in Treblinke*, trans. into English as *A Year in Treblinka*.

of the victims, immediately attracted more attention.[57] In particular, in France testimonies such as David Rousset's *L'Univers concentrationnaire* (The Universe of the Concentration Camp) (1946), written from the perspective of a non-Jewish political prisoner,[58] and Robert Antelme's *L'Espèce humaine* (The Human Species) (1947),[59] also a political prisoner, were widely reviewed.[60] The driving force behind these testimonies was the desire to let the world know of the brutality of the Nazis. Olga Lengyel, whose testimony *Souvenirs de l'au-delà* was published in France in 1947, writes: 'I want the world to read and to resolve that this must never, never, be permitted to happen again. That after perusing this account any will still doubt, I cannot believe.'[61] In Germany, Eugen Kogon's *Der SS-Staat: Das System der Deutschen Konzentrationslager* (The SS State: The System of the German Concentration Camps),[62] attempted an analysis of Nazism from the perspective of German history,[63] and Viktor Frankl's *Ein Psychologe erlebt das Konzentrationslager* (A Psychologist Experiences the Concentration Camps)[64] was a psychological study.

[57] Early reports written in German include Erich Altmann, *Im Angesicht des Todes: Drei Jahre in Deutschen Konzentrationslagern. Auschwitz, Buchenwald, Oranienburg* (In the Face of Death: Three Years in German Concentration Camps. Auschwitz, Buchenwald, Oranienburg) (Luxemburg, 1947), and Samuel Graumann, *Deportiert! Ein Wiener Jude Berichtet* (Deported! A Viennese Jew Reports) (Vienna, 1947).

[58] David Rousset, *L'Univers concentrationnaire* (Paris, 1946); published in English as *The Other Kingdom*, trans. Ramon Gutherie (New York, 1947).

[59] Robert Antelme, *L'Espèce humaine* (Paris, 1947); published in English as *The Human Race*, trans. Jeffrey Haight and Annie Mahler (Marlboro, Vt., 1992).

[60] Other early testimonies published in France include André Abraham David Lettich, *Trente-quatre mois dans les camp concentration* (Thirty-four Months in the Concentration Camps) (Tours, 1946), and Georges Wellers, *De Drancy à Auschwitz* (From Drancy to Auschwitz) (Paris, 1946).   [61] Lengyel, *Five Chimneys* (1995), 225.

[62] Eugen Kogon, *Der SS-Staat: Das System der Deutschen Konzentrationslager* (Munich, 1946); published in English as *The Theory and Practice of Hell: The German Concentration Camps and the System Behind Them*, trans. Heinz Norden (New York, 1949).

[63] See also Benedikt Kautsky, *Teufel und Verdammte: Erfahrungen und Erkenntnisse aus Sieben Jahren in Deutschen Konzentrationslagern* (Devils and the Damned: Experiences and Realizations from Seven Years in German Concentration Camps) (Zurich, 1946); published in English as *Devils and the Damned: The Story of Nazi Concentration and Extermination Camps* (London, 1960).

[64] Viktor E. Frankl, *Ein Psychologe erlebt das Konzentrationslager* (Vienna, 1946); published in English as *Man's Search for Meaning: An Introduction to Logotherapy*, trans. Ilse Lasch (Boston, 1959).

The majority of the early witnesses had either held important positions in the Jewish resistance movements or positions of some degree of privilege in the concentration camps.[65] For example, both Lingens-Reiner and Perl had worked as doctors. Lingens-Reiner explains: 'My personal position was peculiar, because I was an "Aryan", a "German", and a doctor who could work professionally all the time. This made my survival possible.'[66] She continues: 'It gave me an opportunity to see the various facets of the camp life, which others may not have known at all.'[67] Committed Communists Hermann Langbein and Bruno Baum also published testimonies early on, detailing the resistance movement in Auschwitz.[68]

Not only was a sizeable amount of survivor testimony published in Western Europe, but between 1945 and 1949 a fair amount was also published in Eastern Europe. Although the dissemination of these sources was limited, political interference into their publication, for the most part, was minimal. However, the onset of the Cold War, and the curtailment of religious freedom in Eastern Europe, meant that Jews who became trapped behind the Iron Curtain were soon prevented from telling the world of their experiences. The Jewish Anti-Fascist Committee, established in the Soviet Union in April 1942, had collected and printed a huge number of written and oral testimonies and other documents detailing the persecution and murder of Jews in the occupied territories of the Soviet Union.[69] The novelist

[65] See e.g. Marek Edelman, *Getto Walczy* (Warsaw, 1945); published in English as *The Ghetto Fights*, trans. Zofia Nalkowsak (New York, 1946).

[66] Lingens-Reiner, *Prisoners of Fear*, p. x. Cf. the account of the physician Désiré Haffner, a prisoner who worked in the men's camp at Auschwitz-Birkenau: Haffner, *Aspects pathologiques du camp de concentration d'Auschwitz-Birkenau* (Pathological Aspects of the Concentration Camp of Auschwitz-Birkenau) (Tours, 1946).

[67] Lingens-Reiner, *Prisoners of Fear*, p. x.

[68] See Bruno Baum, *Widerstand in Auschwitz* (Resistance in Auschwitz) (Berlin, 1949), and Hermann Langbein, *Die Stärkeren: Ein Bericht aus Auschwitz und anderen Konzentrationslagern* (The Stronger: A Report from Auschwitz and the other Concentration Camps) (Vienna, 1949).

[69] Mordechai Altshuler states that 'estimates of the number of Jewish Holocaust victims in the Soviet Union fluctuate between 2.5 million and 3.3 million' (Altshuler, *Soviet Jewry since the Second World War: Population and Social Structure* (New York, 1987), 4). Cf. Yitzhak Arad, 'The Holocaust of Soviet Jewry in the Occupied Territories of the Soviet Union', *Yad Vashem Studies*, 21 (1991), 47. For details of the Yiddish publications, see

Ilya Ehrenburg and the journalist Vasily Grossman intended these documents to form a *Black Book* to be published in Russian and Yiddish in the USSR, in Hebrew in Palestine, and in English in the United States. But, while a small amount of the material appeared in Yiddish in the Soviet Union between 1944 and 1945,[70] and the English edition of the *Black Book* was published in New York in 1946,[71] Stalin banned the distribution of the finalized version of the book, and in 1952 the Committee was dissolved, and its leaders imprisoned and executed.[72] Although the death of Stalin in March 1953 prevented the escalation of an anti-Jewish campaign, the devastation of the Jews remained a silent topic, and the *Black Book* never appeared in the Soviet Union.[73] The enormous suffering and destruction of World War II for a long time dwarfed the Jewish catastrophe and, significantly, the word 'Holocaust' was not used in Russia until the 1990s.[74] Soviet Jews, such as Hersh Smolar from Minsk, had his memoir, which had initially been published in both Russian and Yiddish shortly after liberation, subsequently censored and then banned; he was unable to revive it until 1989.[75]

Avraham Ben-Yoseph, 'Bibliography of Yiddish Publications in the USSR during 1941–1948', *Yad Vashem Studies*, 4 (1960), 135–66.

[70] Ilya Ehrenburg, *Merder fun felker: Materialn vegn di retsikhes fun di daytche farkhaper in di tsaytvaylik okupirte sovetishe rayonen* (Murder of Peoples: Materials on the Outrages of the German Conqueror in the Provisionally Occupied Soviet Areas) (Moscow, 1944).

[71] Jewish Black Book Committee, *The Black Book: The Nazi Crime against the Jewish People* (New York, 1946).

[72] See Joseph Kermish, 'The History of the Manuscript', in Ilya Ehrenburg and Vasily Grossman (eds.), *The Black Book: The Ruthless Murder of Jews by German-Fascist Invaders throughout the Temporarily-Occupied Regions of the Soviet Union and in the Death Camps of Poland during the War of 1941–1945*, trans. John Glad and James S. Levene (New York, 1981), pp. xix–xxvi. Cf. Lucy S. Dawidowicz, *The Holocaust and the Historians* (Cambridge, Mass., 1981), 81–2. On the suppression of the Holocaust in the Soviet Union and its reassertion post-Stalin, see John Klier, 'The Holocaust and the Soviet Union', in Dan Stone (ed.), *The Historiography of the Holocaust* (New York, 2004), 276–95.

[73] Zvi Gitelman, 'History, Memory, and Politics: The Holocaust in the Soviet Union', *Holocaust and Genocide Studies*, 5 (1990), 23–37.

[74] Thomas C. Fox, 'The Holocaust under Communism', in Stone (ed.), *Historiography of the Holocaust*, 423.

[75] Hirsh Smolar, *The Minsk Ghetto: Soviet-Jewish Partisans against the Nazis*, trans. Max Rosenfeld (New York, 1989); for the original memoir see *Fun Minsker geto* (From the Minsk Ghetto) (Moscow, 1946).

In Czechoslovakia, Richard Glazar wrote about his experiences of Treblinka immediately after liberation, but his testimony, originally written in Czech, was published for the first time in German only in 1992.[76] In Hungary, Béla Zsolt founded the *Haladás* magazine and published an account of his wartime experiences in serial format between 30 May 1946 and 27 February 1947. However, he died in 1949 without seeing his memoir published as a book; the subject of Communist prohibition, it appeared in print in his native country only in 1980.[77] The memoir, which describes the author's experiences in the Nagyvárad ghetto and as a forced labourer in the Ukraine, details both Hungarian fascism and the selfishness and cowardice of its victims. In Poland, in the immediate aftermath of the war, the short stories of the Polish poet Tadeusz Borowski received widespread attention, and testimonies such as Władysław Szpilman's *Śmierć Miasta* (Death of a City) (1946) were published.[78] The suppression of political and artistic freedom under communism, though, spelt the end of further testimonies, and also meant that Szpilman's testimony was published only in small numbers. In Poland, in particular, discussion of the specifically Jewish nature of the atrocities perpetrated by the Nazis was quickly suppressed. Other testimonies, such as that of Olga Lengyel, a Jewish doctor who survived Auschwitz and fled to Paris after liberation, but wrote her testimony in her native Hungarian, have never been published in Hungary.[79]

---

[76] See Glazar, *Die Falle mit dem Grünen Zaun*.

[77] Béla Zsolt, *Kilenc Koffer* (Budapest, 1980); published in English as *Nine Suitcases*, trans. Ladislaus Löb (London, 2004).

[78] See Tadeusz Borowski, *Pożegnanie z Maria* (Farewell to Maria) (Warsaw, 1948), and *idem*, *Kamienny Świat* (World of Stone) (Warsaw, 1948). For the combined publication in English, see *idem*, *This Way for the Gas, Ladies and Gentlemen*, trans. Barbara Vedder (Harmondsworth, 1967), and Władysław Szpilman, *Śmierć Miasta* (Warsaw, 1946); later published in English as *The Pianist: The Extraordinary Story of One Man's Survival in Warsaw, 1939–45*, trans. Anthea Bell (London, 1999).

[79] Susan Rubin Suleiman, 'Monuments in a Foreign Tongue: On Reading Holocaust Memoirs by Emigrants', *Poetics Today*, 17/4 (Winter 1996), 642. Suleiman provides a fascinating discussion of memoirs by mostly Hungarian survivors who, for a variety of reasons, are not writing in their native tongue (ibid. 639–57).

Early testimonies refer to revenge more explicitly than later memoirs.[80] The aftermath of the war was marked by the search not just for former SS concentration camp guards, but also for Jewish *Kapos* accused of brutal behaviour. Although many of the former *Kapos* attempted to conceal their pasts, they were often identified in the DP camps, and on occasion were beaten to death. After the establishment of the State of Israel, people often reported suspected collaborators to the Israeli police. But, until the Ministry of Justice introduced the Act against Jewish War Criminals in August 1949, and the Israeli parliament—the Knesset—passed the Nazi and Nazi Collaborators (Punishment) Law in 1950, they could not be prosecuted. Even with the law, the majority of investigations did not lead to indictments, and those accused were able to appeal against the stipulated death penalty and instead received prison sentences ranging from a few months to three years.[81]

For many survivors, this was particularly wounding. It was not until after liberation that they were able to express, or even feel, anger towards those who had maltreated them. Shamai Davidson, a psychiatrist who spent more than two decades interviewing survivors, explains: 'even the inner experience of rage or anger endangered the fragile psychological balance of the physically starved, abused and overworked captives during the Holocaust.'[82] Memoirs therefore offered a vehicle for the expression of these long suppressed feelings. A good example is Elie Wiesel's first autobiographical account, *Un di velt hot geshvign* (And the World Stayed Silent), written in Yiddish in 1955 (ten years after he was liberated from Buchenwald) and published in 1956 as volume 117 of *Dos Poylishe Yidntum* series.[83]

---

[80] On the neglected topic of revenge, see Berel Lang, 'Holocaust Memory and Revenge: The Presence of the Past', *Jewish Social Studies: History, Culture, and Society*, 2/2 (Winter 1996), 1–20.

[81] See Segev, *Seventh Million*, 259–61. On this subject, see Hanna Yablonka, 'The Nazis and Nazi Collaborators (Punishment) Law: An Additional Aspect of the Question of Israelis, Survivors and the Holocaust', *Katedra*, 82 (1996), 135–52 [Hebrew].

[82] Shamai Davidson, 'Human Reciprocity among the Jewish Prisoners in the Nazi Concentration Camps', in Gutman and Saf (eds.), *Nazi Concentration Camps*, 555–72.

[83] See Elie Wiesel, *Un di velt hot geshvign* (Buenos Aires, 1956).

The book is much more concerned with revenge than are his later works.[84] Naomi Seidman points out that while *Un di velt* is generally considered to be an earlier version of Wiesel's much acclaimed memoir *La Nuit*, published in France in 1958, there are some notable differences. First, while *La Nuit* is dedicated 'in memory of my parents and of my little sister, Tsipora', the dedication of *Un di velt* is angrier: 'This book is dedicated to the eternal memory of my mother Sarah, my father Shlomo, and my little sister Tsipora—who were killed by the German murderers.'[85] The Yiddish title also serves as an accusation of a world that stayed silent in the face of the Holocaust.[86]

A major theme in testimonies is the feeling of abandonment. It is not only the perpetrators who play a large part in survivors' memories, but also the notion of a world that stayed silent. For example, when Livia Bitton-Jackson heard the town crier announce that Jews and Gentiles were forbidden to speak to, or even acknowledge, one another, she did not believe it would be possible for either side to heed the order. However, she soon found: 'It was possible. It happened. . . . As non-existent shadows we moved on the streets, unrecognized, unacknowledged, unseen. . . . A sense of isolation pervaded our every waking moment. Alienation was becoming more tangible with every passing day.'[87] Olga Lengyel has written: 'I know that the world must share the guilt collectively. The Germans sinned grievously, but so did the rest of the nations, if only through refusing to believe and to toil every day and night to save the wretched and dispossessed by every possible means.'[88] And Elie Wiesel has stated: 'What hurts the victim most is not the cruelty of the oppressor but the silence of the bystander.'[89] Wiesel believes that it was the silence of the bystander that allowed the Holocaust to happen, that the Jew was seen as 'a kind of subhuman species, an unnecessary being, not like others; his disappearance did not count, did not weigh on the

---

[84] See Naomi Seidman, 'Elie Wiesel and the Scandal of Jewish Rage', *Jewish Social Studies: History, Culture, and Society*, 3/1 (Fall 1996), 1–19.   [85] Ibid. 5.

[86] Ibid.   [87] Bitton-Jackson, *Eli*, 29.

[88] Lengyel, *Five Chimneys* (1995), 218.

[89] Harry James Cargas, 'An Interview with Elie Wiesel', *Holocaust and Genocide Studies*, 1 (1986), 19.

conscience. He was a being to whom the concept of human brother-
hood did not apply, a being whose death did not diminish us, a being
with whom one did not identify.'[90]

That the motivation for revenge is suppressed in *Night* illustrates
an important development in Wiesel's understanding of the position
of the survivor-witness. While Wiesel's concern with the role of the
survivor began immediately upon liberation, he waited ten years
before writing his first book, because he felt he had to learn the role
before being able to express it. He explains:

I knew the role of the survivor was to testify. Only I did not know how. I
lacked experience. I lacked a framework. I mistrusted the tools, the proced-
ures. Should one say it all or hold it all back? Should one shout or whisper?
Place the emphasis on those who were gone or on their heirs? How does one
describe the indescribable? How does one use restraint in re-creating the fall
of mankind and the eclipse of the Gods? And then, how can one be sure that
the words, once uttered, will not betray, distort the message they bear? So
heavy was my anguish that I made a vow: not to speak, not to touch upon
the essential for at least ten years. Long enough to see clearly. Long enough
to learn to listen to the voices crying inside my own. Long enough to unite
the language of man with the silence of the dead.[91]

In a similar vein Charlotte Delbo, although having written of her
experiences of Auschwitz in 1946, waited almost twenty years before
having her work published.[92] She explains: 'I wanted to make sure it
would stand the test of time, since it had to travel far into the
future.'[93] For Wiesel, who since *Un di velt* has published in French
rather than in the language in which he experienced the events and
feelings he describes, there has also been an increasing sense of dislo-
cation—characterized by his move from the type of detailed historical
memoir encouraged by *Dos Poylishe Yidntum* to novelistic form—that

[90] Elie Wiesel, 'A Plea for the Dead', in *Legends of Our Time* (New York, 1982), 188.
[91] Elie Wiesel, 'An Interview Unlike Any Other', in *A Jew Today*, trans. Marion Wiesel
(New York, 1978), 15.
[92] See Charlotte Delbo, *Aucun de nous ne reviendra* (Geneva, 1965); published in
English as *None of Us Will Return*, trans. John Githens (Boston, 1965).
[93] Delbo, *Days and Memory*, p. x.

mirrors the other-worldly nature of the experiences being described. In the final chapter, it will be seen that for Wiesel the Holocaust constitutes an alternative reality that creates a new language.

Testimonies published in the immediate post-war period were not necessarily received in the manner their authors intended. Primo Levi's first book *Se questo è un uomo*, written just a few months after his return to Italy (following a number of repatriation camps in the Soviet Union), found a publisher in 1947, but did not attract much interest until later. He reflects:

> The manuscript was turned down by a number of important publishers; it was accepted in 1947 by a small publisher [De Silva in Turin] who printed only 2,500 copies and then folded. So this first book of mine fell into oblivion for many years: perhaps also because in all of Europe those were difficult times of mourning and reconstruction and the public did not want to return in memory to the painful years after the war that had just ended.[94]

Survivors had also not realized that their very survival made them objects of suspicion and unease. Primo Levi was soon to discover that people would 'judge with facile hindsight, or . . . perhaps feel cruelly repelled'[95] by survivor accounts. Nevertheless, a small number of testimonies continued to be published during the 1950s. Three in particular stand out: *Se questo è un uomo* was republished by the Turin-based publisher Einaudi in 1958, and Wiesel's *Un di velt* and *La Nuit* were first published in 1956 and 1958.

It was not only public attitudes that prevented many survivors from writing their testimonies. For at least a quarter of a century after the war, survivors needed to concentrate on rebuilding their lives. Anita Lasker-Wallfisch, a cellist in the orchestra of Birkenau, waited

---

[94] Levi, *Survival in Auschwitz*, 375. This is the American title used in the later reprinting of *If This is a Man*. For the history of the writing of *Survival in Auschwitz*, see Levi's own remarks in *The Reawakening*, trans. Stuart Woolf (New York, 1965), 195; published in the UK as *The Truce*, trans. Stuart Woolf (London, 1965); originally published in Italian as *La tregua* (Turin, 1963). Another early testimony published in Italy, is Giuliana Tedeschi, *Questo povero corpo* (This Poor Body) (Milan, 1946); published in English as *There is a Place on Earth: A Woman in Birkenau*, trans. Tim Parks (London, 1993).

[95] Levi, *The Drowned and the Saved*, 58.

forty years before writing about her experiences. First, she needed to concentrate on building a new life—on bringing up her children. She says that it is primarily for them that she decided to write her book, 'so that they could "inherit the truth" and keep alive the memory of those terrible days'.[96] Survivors such as Lasker-Wallfisch had to build new careers in new countries; those who had professional qualifications before the war were often prevented from practising their profession because of their new country's licensing requirements, and frequently had to accept more mundane employment.[97] In addition, they often had to learn a new language. A lot of survivors were children when the war broke out, with no secondary school education, and therefore they lacked the linguistic and conceptual tools necessary to theorize their experiences. For many, it was not until their children had grown up and left home that they felt able to speak of their experiences.

THE ESTABLISHMENT OF THE STATE OF ISRAEL AND THE TRIAL OF ADOLF EICHMANN

The establishment of the State of Israel diversified the type of survivors emigrating there. The state's principle of free immigration of Jews meant that during the first two years of Israel's existence 2,000 Jews were accepted. These survivors were older, and few had belonged to the pioneering youth movements.[98] Whereas early memorialization had focused on resistance, and in April 1951 the Knesset made 27 Nissan (30 April) in the Hebrew calendar (the middle of the period of the uprising in the Warsaw ghetto) the official date for the observance of *Yom Hashoah VeHamered* (Holocaust and Ghetto Rebellion Day), the subsequent change to *Yom Hashoah VeHagevurah* (Holocaust and Heroism Memorial Day) acknowledged this

[96] Anita Lasker-Wallfisch, *Inherit the Truth 1939–1945: The Documented Experiences of a Survivor of Auschwitz and Belsen* (London, 1996), 13–14.
[97] See Davidson, 'Human Reciprocity'.
[98] Yablonka, 'Formation of Holocaust Consciousness', 120.

diversification.[99] As Dalia Ofer points out, the concept of heroism 'leaves room for the admission of additional concepts, to be phrased in the Yad Vashem Law, such as spiritual valour, the struggle to retain one's humanness, and martyrdom'.[100] In 1953, the establishment of Yad Vashem, The Holocaust Martyrs' and Heroes' Remembrance Authority—the main institution in Israel dealing with the Nazi persecution and murder of the Jews—also attempted to acknowledge the different experiences. From the beginning, Yad Vashem, which in its infancy was staffed exclusively by survivors, was dedicated to the collection of testimonies.[101] It is significant that all these things happened before the trial of Adolf Eichmann in Jerusalem in 1961 (and his execution in 1962), for the trial is commonly regarded as the watershed for acknowledging the suffering of Israel's Holocaust survivors. The formal nature of the trial, which lasted from April to December, meant that Israel as a collective entity began to think more deeply about the Holocaust. It was reported on the radio and relayed in homes, buses, work places, and schools throughout the country. The Israeli writer Shulamith Hareven remembers: 'An entire nation went to work with the radio on. A bank clerk counted money and brushed back tears. A housewife stirred dinner and sobbed. A bus followed its route, its passengers sitting in hushed silence, hanging on every word without a moment's letup. . . . Whole classrooms sat at attention and listened.'[102]

The trial helped ordinary Israelis realize the full horror of the catastrophe and the helplessness of the victims.[103] The documents

[99] The more moderate name was later adopted. See James E. Young, 'When a Day Remembers: A Performative History of "Yom ha-Shoah"', *History and Memory*, 2/2 (Winter 1990), 54–75.

[100] Dalia Ofer, 'Israel and the Holocaust: The Shaping of Remembrance in the First Decade', *Legacy*, 1/2 (Summer 1997), 7.

[101] See Benzion Dinur, 'Problems Confronting "Yad [V]ashem" in its Work of Research', *Yad [V]ashem Studies*, 1 (1957), 7–30.

[102] Shulamith Hareven, 'The Man Who Descended into Inferno', in *The Vocabulary of Peace: Life, Culture, and Politics in the Middle East* (San Francisco, 1995), 144.

[103] For a discussion of the evolution of Holocaust memory in Israeli society, see Don-Yehiya Eliezer, 'Memory and Political Culture: Israeli Society and the Holocaust', *Studies in Contemporary Jewry*, 4 (1993), 139–62.

collected for the Nuremberg trials (1945–9) would have been enough to convict Eichmann,[104] but Gideon Hausner, the attorney-general in charge of prosecuting him, wanted 'people in Israel and the world to come close, through the trial, to this great catastrophe'.[105] This was to be achieved through the use of living witnesses. They were mostly provided by Rachel Auerbach (she herself testified at the trial), a former member of *Oneg Shabbat*, and head of the Department for Collecting Witness Accounts at Yad Vashem (most of the witnesses chosen had already published their testimonies), which was established in 1954.[106] Still, at the beginning of the trial, Hausner was met by the refusal of survivors to testify for fear of being publicly accused of 'going like sheep to the slaughter'. Indeed, on the eve of the trial, Meier Grossman, a long-time member of the Jewish Agency Executive, remarked that he found distasteful the idea of 'Jews stripping and showing their scars to the world like old beggars years after the scars have healed. The State of Israel has created an image of the courageous and self-reliant Jew standing up for his rights and fighting irrespective of odds which will be replaced by the old image of the sufferer crying his wrongs.'[107]

However, soon into the trial, survivors were queuing up to bring their experiences into the public domain (more than 100 testified at the trial). Many Israelis, who were themselves children of survivors, remember it as a time when their parents started to talk to them about their experiences. Likewise, in the United States and Britain, people generally became more interested in the experiences of survivors as a result of the reporting of the trial, although some believed the kidnapping and hanging of Eichmann to be a demonstration of Jewish vengeance. Peter Novick claims that while American Jews received reports of some of the worst atrocities carried out against the Jews

[104] See Donald Bloxham, *Genocide on Trial: War Crimes Trials and the Formation of Holocaust History and Memory* (Oxford, 2001), chs. 1–3. Cf. Michael Marrus, 'The Holocaust at Nuremberg', *Yad Vashem Studies*, 26 (1998), 5–41.

[105] Cited in Segev, *Seventh Million*, 338.

[106] Ibid. Cf. K. Y. Ball-Kaduri, 'Evidence of Witnesses, its Value and Limitations', *Yad [V]ashem Studies*, 2 (1958), 79–90.

[107] Grossman's remarks paraphrased in *The Jerusalem Post*, 31 March 1961, 5.

during the war itself, it was not until the trial of Eichmann in 1961 that they really began to view the destruction of European Jewry as a singular event—as the Holocaust. Twenty-eight memoirs were published in that year, compared with eleven in the previous year.[108]

Nevertheless, it is important not to overstate the significance of the trial in the developing position of the Holocaust witness.[109] Unlike the Nuremberg trials, which were predominantly concerned with establishing the fact and extent of the crimes of Nazism, the trial of Eichmann in Jerusalem was specifically concerned with what happened to the Jews; however, the vulnerability of survivors was still not fully appreciated. This is exemplified in Hannah Arendt's report of the Eichmann trial, which, on account of her claim that the *Judenräte* (Jewish Councils) allowed the Holocaust to take place through their compliance with the German authorities, is commonly interpreted as suggesting that the Jews allowed themselves to be 'led like sheep to the slaughter'.[110] While Arendt, herself a refugee from Nazi Germany, claimed that this was never her intention, and that her book was merely a report on the trial and nothing more, it does suggest that she failed to take into account the effect of her writing on survivors and their families.[111] In the final chapter it will be seen that the charge of being 'led like sheep to the slaughter' was so wounding that even survivors writing many years after the events of the Holocaust have felt

[108] This figure is provided by Yad Vashem.

[109] See Novick, *Holocaust and Collective Memory*, 133–45.

[110] See Hannah Arendt, *Eichmann in Jerusalem: A Report on the Banality of Evil* (New York, 1962). The report was originally published by *The New Yorker Magazine* in five instalments in early 1962. For responses to the controversy generated by Arendt, see Jacob Robinson, *And the Crooked Shall Be Made Straight: The Eichmann Trial, the Jewish Catastrophe, and Hannah Arendt's Narrative* (New York, 1965). Gershom Scholem's exchange with Arendt is reprinted in Gershom Scholem, *On Jews and Judaism in Crisis: Selected Essays*, ed. Werner J. Dannhauser (New York, 1976). For an overview of the controversy, see Richard I. Cohen, 'Breaking the Code: Hannah Arendt's *Eichmann in Jerusalem* and the Public Polemic: Myth, Memory and Historical Imagination', *Michael*, 13 (1993), 29–85.

[111] It is interesting to note that Arendt's report was not translated into Hebrew until 2000. Her critique of the trial as a 'show trial' likewise added to her lack of popularity. In the book she quotes David Ben-Gurion's statement that he agreed to the kidnapping of Eichmann, because 'it is necessary that our youth remember what happened to the Jewish people' (Arendt, *Eichmann in Jerusalem*, 10).

the need to explicitly discredit it in their testimonies.[112] Likewise, in the aftermath of the trial, many Jewish historians, such as Nora Levin,[113] took pains to stress the role of resistance in their work. Similarly, Hebrew anthologies such as *Sefer Hapartizanim Hayehudim* (The Book of Jewish Partisans) (1958) and *Lexicon Hagvurah* (Lexicon of Heroism), published by Yad Vashem between 1965 and 1968, took up the theme of armed resistance.[114]

THE SECOND WAVE OF MEMOIRS

Although the trial of Eichmann, like the Auschwitz trial in Frankfurt between 1963 and 1965,[115] resulted in an increase in the number of Holocaust testimonies published (particularly in Hebrew), it was not until the late 1960s and early 1970s that the number of memoirs published started to increase significantly. While the majority are in Hebrew, German, or English, the collapse of communism has brought with it memoirs in Hungarian, Russian, and Polish. It is only since the end of Communist rule (1989–91) that many survivors from the former Communist bloc have been able to talk about the specifically Jewish nature of their suffering.[116] However, the

[112] Elie Wiesel's 'A Plea for the Dead' was written in response to the uproar that Arendt's comments generated in the USA. Referring to the murdered Jews, Wiesel pleads: 'Let us leave them alone. We will not dig up those corpses without coffins. Leave them where they must forever be and such as they must be: wounds, immeasurable pain at the very depth of our being. Be content they do not wake up, that they do not come back to earth to judge the living. The day that they would begin to tell what they had seen and heard, and what they have taken so to heart, we will not know where to run, we will stop our ears, so great will be our fear, so sharp our shame' (*Legends of Our Time*, 179).

[113] See N. Levin, *The Holocaust*.

[114] Cited in Robert Rozett, 'Jewish Resistance', in Stone (ed.), *Historiography of the Holocaust*, 343.

[115] Twenty-two initial defendants (two were later dropped for health reasons) were charged with either perpetrating the murders committed at Auschwitz or acting as accomplices. See Adalbert Rückerl, *Die Strafverfolgung von NS-Verbrechen 1945–1978* (The Punishment Pursuit of Nazi Crimes) (Heidelberg, 1979).

[116] On this subject, see Zvi Gitelman (ed.), *Bitter Legacy: Confronting the Holocaust in the Soviet Union* (Bloomington, Ind., 1997). Cf. Gitelman, 'History, Memory, and Politics'.

emergence of long-suppressed memories also brings feelings of resentment and raises difficult questions regarding the complicity and comparative suffering of local populations. Similarly, the release of archival material from the former Soviet Union has also highlighted the role of local support in the process of destruction.[117]

In the West, and particularly in the United States, the Six-Day War in 1967 and the Yom Kippur War in 1973 stimulated increased interest in the Holocaust through renewed fears about the future of Jewish existence. Then in 1978 the American television docu-drama *Holocaust* definitively made the experiences of survivors a matter of public interest rather than a predominantly scholarly one. The nine and a half hour mini-series, which portrayed in soap-opera format the fate of German and Jewish neighbours, was presented by NBC-TV to an audience of 120 million. Since then, representations of the Holocaust have been slowly making their way into the mainstream media. While initially Hollywood filmmakers were reluctant to tackle the Holocaust in commercial cinema, since Steven Spielberg's *Schindler's List* in 1994, it has become an increasingly popular subject. In January 1995, the fiftieth commemoration of the liberation of Auschwitz brought survivors further into the public eye. In Britain, survivors such as Anita Lasker-Wallfisch were inundated with calls from the media. Although many survivors, including Lasker-Wallfisch, speak of badly conducted interviews with insensitive questions, the event marked an important development for the exposure of Holocaust testimonies. Finally survivors felt that they were being asked to speak about their experiences.

THE FAILURE OF LIBERATION

As the previous chapter illustrated, one of the greatest losses imposed by the concentration and death camps was the destruction of the matrix of meanings usually employed to understand the world. This

---

[117] Kushner, *The Holocaust and the Liberal Imagination*, 7.

resulted in what David Patterson calls 'The Failure of Liberation'.[118] Citing a statement by Primo Levi,[119] Patterson explains: 'The distance from home is not so much geographical as it is metaphysical. It lies not in the miles that separate Levi from Italy, but in the void that isolates him from the human beings around him, both living and dead.'[120] Although Primo Levi returned to his native Italy, and found his home and family intact, he could not leave the past behind. This is expressed in a dream described in *The Reawakening*, where he writes: 'I am in the Lager once more, and nothing is true outside the Lager.'[121] Tadeusz Borowski, a poet before the war, who started writing immediately after liberation, echoes this by writing all his stories about Auschwitz in the present tense, thereby 'ruling out any return to the world of the past or hope for the future'.[122] Whereas early memoirs were mostly concerned with documenting wartime experiences, later survivors had time to reflect on the enormity of their losses. Levi discovered that as a consequence of surviving extreme trauma, ordinary life loses its meaning; after living in extremity, it is difficult to take part in the mundanities of everyday life. The belief of Dawid Sierakowiak and his friends in the Łódź ghetto that 'if we survive the ghetto, we'll certainly experience a richness of life that we wouldn't have appreciated otherwise',[123] was, for many survivors, not true. Suffering is rarely a life-enhancing experience. This was particularly so for Borowski who committed suicide in 1951, and Levi, who is thought to have killed himself in 1987.[124] In *The Drowned and the*

---

[118] Patterson, *Sun Turned to Darkness*, 189.

[119] 'In the very hour in which a hope of a return to life ceased to be crazy, I was overcome by . . . the pain of exile, of my distant home, of loneliness' (Primo Levi, cited in Patterson, *Sun Turned to Darkness*, 189).

[120] Ibid.   [121] Levi, *Reawakening*, 67.

[122] Sidra Dekoven Ezrahi, 'Boundaries of the Present: Two Literary Approaches to the Concentration Camps', in Gutman and Saf (eds.), *Nazi Concentration Camps*, 657. Cf. Borowski, *This Way for the Gas, Ladies and Gentlemen*.

[123] Dawid Sierakowiak, *The Diary of Dawid Sierakowiak: Five Notebooks from the Łódź Ghetto*, trans. Kamil Turowski, ed. Alan Adelson (London, 1997), 209; originally published in Polish as *Dziennik Dawida Sierakowiaka* (Warsaw, 1960).

[124] See Myriam Anissimov, *Primo Levi: Tragedy of an Optimist*, trans. Steve Cox (London, 1998), 1–4.

Saved, published a year before his death, Levi writes: 'Just as they felt they were again becoming men, that is, responsible, the sorrows of men returned: the sorrow of the dispersed or lost family; the universal suffering all around; their own exhaustion, which seemed definitive, past cure; the problems of life to begin all over again amid the rubble, often alone.'[125]

Although many survivors did go on to have families, build careers, and experience happiness and success, most had to endure painful memories and nightmares, daily associations, the fear that history might be repeated, and, for many, the loss of loved ones. It is these types of experiences that indicate the limits of the concept of the Holocaust in signifying a beginning and end to a set of events. The nature of trauma means that the experiences of survivors are resistant ultimately to any final narrativization. The concept of the Holocaust also conceals the fact that behind the events is a lost past or heritage. Survivors not only have to deal with the nature and trauma of their wartime experiences, but also have to negotiate the rupture of not being able to live the life that was mapped out for them in childhood. Very few deportees realized when they left that they would never return. Patterson identifies the premature ageing of many survivors as a manifestation of this loss. He cites the example of Livia Bitton-Jackson, who was mistaken for a woman of 62 when she was only 14.[126] Although in time she regained the look of a young girl, she was unable to regain the life she expected to lead as that young girl. Survivors of the Holocaust, such as Bitton-Jackson, must learn to incorporate memories of a much-loved lost world into the context of the rest of their life. Increasingly, later memoirs include a section on pre-war life, providing detailed memories of former homes, including memories quite specific to the region of their origin—geography, food, education, and so on. They often present almost idealized images of childhood and family life. It seems likely that pre-war familial conflicts were superseded by the emergence of an increasingly

[125] Levi, *The Drowned and the Saved*, 70–1.
[126] See Patterson, *Sun Turned to Darkness*, 170.

hostile external environment.[127] This can also be seen as an attempt to emphasize how much was destroyed by the Nazis, and to show that the Holocaust constitutes more than just the suffering endured in the ghettos or concentration camps, or in hiding; it means the obliteration of individual histories.

The prohibition on talking about their experiences, which survivors felt soon after liberation, meant that it became difficult for many to see their survival as a victory over the Nazis. Moshe Sandberg explains: 'You spoke, but it was if you were talking to yourself, and you lived through it all again . . . so that even after his defeat the enemy continued doing his evil. Thus not a few of us were prevented from becoming adjusted to a new life, from returning to normal existence.'[128]

The challenge that survivors such as Sandberg faced was not to forget their wartime experiences, but to find some means of using their memories to overcome the pain of exile described by Primo Levi. One way was to attempt to draw out the wider significance of the memories. Tony Kushner, referring to survivors living in Britain, believes that this has been encouraged by the increasing interest in the Holocaust, fuelled by the 'growing commitment to multi-cultural and anti-racist strategies'.[129] Educating future generations has given survivors the means to incorporate their traumatic experiences into life after the events. However, the process of bearing witness, or the role of the survivor, demands a comprehensive, objective account of the Holocaust that may be beyond the subjective experiences of each individual. Not only this, but as the following chapters will illustrate, the writing of testimony is often a way to organize the experiences of a life in order to make sense of them and be able to function in the

[127] See Hillel Klein, 'The Survivors Search for Meaning and Identity', in Gutman and Saf (eds.), *Nazi Concentration Camps*, 547.

[128] Moshe Sandberg, *My Long Year in the Hungarian Labor Service and in the Nazi Camps*, trans. S. C. Hyman (Jerusalem, 1968), 2; originally published in Hebrew as *Shanah l'ayn kayts* (The Year Beyond Summer) (Jerusalem, 1967).

[129] Kushner, *The Holocaust and the Liberal Imagination*, 261. For a parallel discussion of the American experience, see Novick, *Holocaust and Collective Memory*.

present; also, memories are mediated not only by both the present and future concerns of each survivor, but by the dictates of collective memory.

The next chapter focuses on women's Holocaust testimonies to show how the hegemony of collective memory: testimonies' simultaneous universalization—its appeal to as wide an audience as possible, in order to show its universal relevance, and its role as an arbiter of moral judgement—but, therefore, homogenized outlook, determines the parameters of Holocaust representation, fostering an environment which necessarily excludes experiences that do not concur with accepted, easily comprehensible narratives.

4

Writing Ignored: Reading Women's Holocaust Testimonies

> The historian of the future will have to devote a fitting chapter to the role of the Jewish woman during the war. It is thanks to the courage and endurance of our women that thousands of families have been able to endure these bitter times.
>
> Ringelblum, *Notes from the Warsaw Ghetto*

When Emmanuel Ringelblum wrote these words in June 1942, he foresaw that the experiences of Jewish women under Nazism would become an important area of historical interest. Together with his assistant Cecilya Ślepak and the staff of *Oneg Shabbat*, Ringelblum studied the lives of Jewish women and children in the Warsaw ghetto between the winter of 1941 and the spring of 1942, prior to their deportation to Treblinka. Ślepak provided questionnaires asking the women about their lives, particularly their lives as wives and mothers. Some of the questionnaires and notes were discovered with Ringelblum's diary after the war in the ruins of the ghetto. It is significant that Ringelblum's words are cited in the introductions to two books on women and the Holocaust: Judith Tydor Baumel's *Double Jeopardy: Gender and the Holocaust* and *Women in the Holocaust* edited by Dalia Ofer and Lenore Weitzman. His findings have also inspired other books on the same theme. Such studies respond to Ringelblum's challenge by focusing on women's testimonies to highlight their moral, heroic, or noble behaviour, both in the ghetto and following deportation to the camps. Baumel, for example, believes that:

Any study of gender and the Holocaust is at the same time both tragic and uplifting. Tragic, as one cannot escape the awareness of how the gender factor supplied an added variable to the calculus of cruelty during a period when human beings were put to a daily moral, and mortal, test. Uplifting, in view of the women, both Jews and non-Jews, who did not succumb to the natural tendency to live for themselves alone and stretched out a helping hand to each other, transcending differences of race, religion and ideology to form a bond of sisterhood. These women, and their acts of kindness, have served as a beacon of light and humanity in an era of darkness.[1]

Although these 'women-centred' readings provide valuable insights into the specificity of women's Holocaust experiences and open up important areas of research—for example, there is some evidence to suggest that more women than men were deported from the ghettos to the concentration camps[2]—their focus is almost exclusively on women's roles as 'mothers' and 'caregivers'.[3] For example, an edited collection of oral testimonies given by women who survived the Holocaust is entitled *Mothers, Sisters, Resisters*—the editor, Brana Gurewitsch, states that 'all of the women here resisted their fates. They supported each other like sisters and nurtured each other like mothers'[4]—and on the front cover has a photograph taken in 1945 of

[1] Baumel, *Double Jeopardy*, 260.

[2] See Joan Ringelheim, 'Thoughts about Women and the Holocaust', in Roger S. Gottlieb (ed.), *Thinking the Unthinkable: Meanings of the Holocaust* (New York, 1990), 141–9. For an insightful comparison of the different experiences of Jewish women and men during the Holocaust, see Nechama Tec, *Resilience and Courage: Women, Men, and the Holocaust* (New Haven, 2003). Cf. *idem*, 'Sex Distinctions and Passing as Christians during the Holocaust', *East European Quarterly*, 18/1 (March 1984), 113–23.

[3] While the editorial component of Ofer and Weitzman (eds.), *Women in the Holocaust*, is problematic, and the general emphasis of the volume restrictive, it contains important original research concerning women's Holocaust experiences in Eastern and Western Europe. Of particular note are the essays by Paula Hyman and Joan Ringelheim, which will be discussed later in this chapter. It is also to the editors' credit that the volume includes essays written by those who are clearly in disagreement with their own perspective (see Lawrence Langer, 'Gendered Suffering? Women in Holocaust Testimonies', pp. 351–63).

[4] Brana Gurewitsch (ed.), *Mothers, Sisters, Resisters: Oral Histories of Women who Survived the Holocaust* (Tuscaloosa, Ala., 1998), p. xii.

five of the women holding their babies. Furthermore, research on women's experiences is generally presented as an addendum, or corrective, to existing androcentric work on the Holocaust.[5] *Different Voices: Women and the Holocaust*, edited by Carol Rittner and John Roth,[6] is explicitly intended as a response to the questions 'Where were the women during the Holocaust?' and 'How do the particularities of women's experiences in that event compare and contrast with those of men?'[7] Such approaches avoid questioning the categories of meaning they have applied to understanding women, and which women have applied to understanding themselves.[8] Closer attention could be paid to how women's experiences are particularly structured by preconceived gender roles, and how their identities have been shaped around gendered beliefs.[9] It will be seen that studies of women in the Holocaust favour stories that are seen as suitable or palatable for their readers, often avoiding those that do not accord with expected women's behaviour or pre-existing narratives of survival. This is exacerbated by the fact that testimony in general is often used to project easy comprehension of the Holocaust—it is employed to make sense of a difficult subject in an easy manner. Using a familiar, gendered conceptual framework, women's testimonies are often used to show us what we already want to see. But, assumptions about appropriate gender behaviour obscure the diversity of women's Holocaust experiences.

[5] Research into the specificity of women's Holocaust experiences has increased greatly since the first conference on 'Women Surviving the Holocaust' in March 1983. The conference was organized by Joan Ringelheim and sponsored by The Institute for Research in History in New York City. See Esther Katz and Joan Miriam Ringelheim (eds.), *Proceedings of the Conference on Women Surviving the Holocaust* (New York, 1983).

[6] Carol Rittner and John K. Roth (eds.), *Different Voices: Women and the Holocaust* (New York, 1993).   [7] Ibid., p. xi.

[8] See P. Cotteril and G. Letherby, 'Weaving Stories: Personal Autobiographies in Feminist Research', *Sociology*, 27/1 (1993), 67–80.

[9] Anna Hardman also argues that there is a tendency to read women's testimonies selectively to reinforce existing expectations. See her study, *Women and the Holocaust*, Holocaust Educational Trust Research Papers, 1/3 (2000). Cf. Zoë Waxman, 'Unheard Stories: Reading Women's Holocaust Testimonies', *Jewish Quarterly: A Magazine of Contemporary Writing and Culture*, 177 (Spring 2000), 53–8, and *idem*, 'Unheard Testimony, Untold Stories: The Representation of Women's Holocaust Experiences', *Women's History Review*, 12/4 (2003), 661–77.

This chapter focuses on the testimonies of women, not because it is they who are normally excluded from history, but because it is the representation of women's experiences that best illustrates how collective memory obscures the diversity of Holocaust testimonies. Studies of women in the Holocaust often project their own concerns, which set the agenda for future testimony. They tend to emerge from preconceived ideas regarding women's abilities to act in moral, heroic, or noble ways. However, the Holocaust was not discriminatory towards its victims. No moral test was required for the gas chamber, only a test of race. Of course, there were people who performed 'heroic' acts, but there were also many who merely did what they had to do in order to survive. To show that people are fallible and act just as human beings is not to demonize them, but to attempt to present a more rounded picture of responses to extreme suffering.

SECONDARY LITERATURE

Studies of women and the Holocaust tend to portray female witnesses in much the same way as child witnesses, as unproblematic victims. Little reference is made to the Jewish women who, as a result of intoler-able circumstances, acted contrary to traditional expectations of female behaviour, such as the women who placed their own survival above that of their children, and the few female Jewish *Kapos* who came to mimic the behaviour of the SS captors. Fania Fénelon, a member of the women's orchestra at Auschwitz-Birkenau, deported in January 1944 for her participation in the French Resistance Movement, describes what happened when her former friend, half-Jewish Clara, was appointed *Kapo*: 'Clara rose up before us, arm band in place, club in hand. . . . Everything that was left of the timid, bashful young girl had just disappeared, destroyed once and for all by the environment of the camp.' Fénelon tried to reason with Clara by pointing out that her actions would make her life difficult after Auschwitz:

'Clara, look at yourself! You've become a monster. If you lash out at your friends, you'll never dare to go back home. Remember your childhood, your girlhood, your parents. . . . Clara, look at yourself!'

Her eyes shone with a positively mineral brightness. . . . 'Be quiet and listen to me . . . it's me who's the stronger, it's me who's in charge. I've heard enough, now get away!'[10]

Responses such as Clara's might well have been the exception rather than the norm; it is hard to give figures, since women like her are precisely the ones who are least likely to record their testimonies. They are the ones who most want to forget the past, either because the pain of remembering is too great, or because of fears of retribution or condemnation. While Fénelon's memoir has been the subject of much controversy, her description of Clara should provoke further research into the complexities of women's responses to the Holocaust.[11] The heated nature of the debate surrounding Fénelon is illustrative of the problematic relationship between testimony, memory, and representation, and how women's responses in particular resist easy categorization and attempts to 'preempt' them. Here I used the term introduced by Lawrence Langer in *Preempting the Holocaust*, in the following words: 'When I speak of preempting the Holocaust, I mean using—and perhaps abusing—its grim details to fortify a prior commitment to an ideal of moral reality, community responsibility, or religious belief that leaves us with space to retain faith in their pristine value in a post-Holocaust world.'[12] This does not necessarily stem from cynical misappropriation. There is always a danger of imposing our concerns and beliefs on the events of the Holocaust because we lack the imagination to see that the issues we consider important might not be applicable. Langer cites Tzvetan Todorov's *Facing the Extreme: Moral Life in the Concentration Camps* as an example of the attempt to use the Holocaust to promote images of 'human dignity'.[13] Todorov does this through the use of survivor testimony, for he clearly views such testimony as carrying important lessons for the advancement of humanity. However, the point is that Todorov's reading of Holocaust testimonies did not lead him to an

[10] Fania Fénelon (with Marcelle Routier), *Playing for Time*, trans. Judith Landry (New York, 1977), 235–6; published in the UK as *The Musicians of Auschwitz*, trans. Judith Landry (London, 1977); originally published in French as Fania Fénelon, *Sursis pour l'orchestre* (Respite for the Orchestra) (Paris, 1976).

[11] For details of the controversy, see Hardman, 'Women and the Holocaust', 20–7.

[12] Langer, *Preempting the Holocaust*, 1.   [13] Ibid., p. xvi.

unanticipated discovery of 'moral life in the concentration camps'; rather, he believes that:

There are various perspectives from which the accounts of life in the camps can be read. One can ponder the precise chain of events that led to the creation of the camps and then to their extinction; one can debate the political significance of the camps; one can extract sociological or psychological lessons from them. Yet even though I cannot ignore those perspectives altogether, I would like to take a different approach. I want to look at the camps from the perspective of moral life.[14]

Todorov did not see the need to suppress his personal views of the world when reading the accounts of prisoners of concentration camps, and thus allowed his readings to reinforce his own deeply held convictions about the state of humanity. For Langer, the criticism of Todorov is also applicable to studies concerned with gender and the Holocaust. Langer uses the example of Judy Chicago's *Holocaust Project: From Darkness into Light*[15] to demonstrate how an interest in gender, or a commitment to feminist beliefs, often prefigures an interest in the Holocaust. For Chicago, patriarchy itself is indicted as part of what made the Holocaust possible—she cites as evidence the fact that the architects of the Third Reich were exclusively male.[16] Furthermore, Chicago does not just wish to offer a gendered reading of the Holocaust; she wants to use her beliefs about women to rescue the study of the Holocaust from a site of unremitting despair, as Todorov also attempted to do. As Langer has pointed out, the very title of Chicago's book is illustrative of this; she clearly could not envisage a project subtitled 'From Light into Darkness'.[17]

However, Langer goes too far when he claims that, due to the 'severely diminished role that gendered behaviour played during those cruel years',[18] studies of gender in the Holocaust are merely 'preempting the Holocaust'. While gendered roles and behaviour, in the same way as many pre-war roles and modes of interaction, were severely

---

[14] Todorov, *Facing the Extreme*, 31.
[15] Judy Chicago, *Holocaust Project: From Darkness into Light* (New York, 1993).
[16] Cited in Langer, *Preempting the Holocaust*, 13.   [17] Ibid. 10.
[18] Ibid. 43.

challenged by the Holocaust, an understanding of the intricacies of gender is important when looking at the testimonies of Holocaust witnesses. Societal constructions of gender must have continued to inform women's (and men's) actions, even if their behaviour did not conform to gendered expectations. As Chapter 2 has shown, concentration camp inmates' behaviour was still mediated by their pre-war lives, and many wanted to carry on with their familiar roles. The very fact that during the Holocaust women were often unable to meet these expectations has important and often ongoing traumatic repercussions for female survivors trying not only to represent their wartime experiences but also to connect them to their pre- and post-war lives.

In her book *Reading Auschwitz*, Mary Lagerwey writes that she

easily found evidence ... of women's unique experiences, of sexuality, friendship and parenting, their mutual concern for and assistance of each other, their emotional capacity, their unselfish and sacrificial sharing, and great flexibility—in sum, a moral superiority that even the horrors of Auschwitz could not obliterate. And, true to my expectations, I found that the stories written by men told of personal isolation, personal survival at any cost, ruthless competition, and pragmatic allegiances.[19]

Although she goes on to problematize this, and to state that 'Male survivors framed their narratives in order and coherence, and often de-emphasised emotions',[20] she does not explore the implications of such an observation: namely, that although there may not be inherent gender differences in the expression of emotions, social norms and expectations regarding masculinity and femininity may result in different emotional expressions.[21] The coping strategies of men and women might not be as different as the narrative structures that represent them suggest. What is often overlooked is the importance of gender differences in the *narration* of experience. Testimonies are not spontaneous outbursts of information, but come from the careful representation of experience, or the perceived 'appropriateness' of experiences for publication. For example, the development of Women's Studies has meant that women's Holocaust memoirs

---

[19] Mary D. Lagerwey, *Reading Auschwitz* (London, 1998), 75.   [20] Ibid.
[21] See Deborah Lupton, *The Emotional Self* (London, 1998), 55–61.

appearing from the mid-1970s onwards emphasize gender-related experiences—such as the loss of femininity, pregnancy, and fear of rape—to a much greater extent than is the case in earlier women's memoirs. It is interesting to note that the 1947 edition of Olga Lengyel's testimony is entitled *Five Chimneys: The Story of Auschwitz*, whereas the title of the 1995 edition has been changed to *Five Chimneys: A Woman Survivor's True Story of Auschwitz*.

WOMEN AS ACCESSIBLE WITNESSES

Publishers' comments on the dust jackets of testimonies of both men and women tend to promote them as cathartic acts of memory, and suggest that by reading them the reader is performing an act of psychological or even political solidarity. Holocaust testimonies, in other words, can ennoble both writer and reader. In the case of women's testimonies, and particularly those of young girls, this often expresses itself in a sentimentality that has nothing to do with the original concerns of the writer. For example, *Stolen Years*, Sara Zyskind's account of her teenage years spent in the Łódź ghetto, Auschwitz, and then the Mittelstein slave labour camp is described as 'an odyssey of agony that should never be forgotten . . . an epic of love and courage that the reader will want to remember forever'. Nowhere in her testimony does Zyskind state or imply that she views it as an 'epic of love and courage', and she, unlike her readers, lacks the luxury of deciding whether or not she wants to remember it forever. It is the suggestion of emotion, albeit not of traumatic emotion, that holds the possibility of providing a bond between witness and reader. Women, and in particular young women, are often seen as fulfilling this role.

Anne Frank is the most obvious example of this. Her diary, originally written in Dutch and published in 1947 as *Het Achterhuis* (The Room Behind the House),[22] sold only 1,500 copies at the time, but now sells millions of copies a year under the new title *The Diary of*

---

[22] Anne Frank, *Het Achterhuis* (Amsterdam, 1947).

a Young Girl.[23] In it, we hear the voice of an intelligent young girl whose life was cut tragically short—she was 13 when she started to write her diary, and 15 when she died—and the virtue of hope, which many seem reluctant to lose even in the context of the Holocaust, is read into her widely circulated photographic image.[24] The prevalence of this image and the 'personal' connotations of diary writing make many people feel that they actually knew Frank: she is an accessible Holocaust witness. However, she herself wrote: 'Although I tell you a lot, you only know very little of our lives. . . . It is almost indescribable.'[25]

Frank's diary is in many ways ideal for teaching or reading about the Holocaust while not actually dealing with its horrors. It shows an innocent young girl who, although hungry and suffering the misery of hiding in cramped conditions, still manages (until deportation) to write of more universally recognized teenage troubles, such as adolescent infatuations and disagreements with parents. It does not touch on her experiences of deportation and life at Westerbork, Auschwitz-Birkenau, and Bergen-Belsen. The 1999 film documentary *The Last Seven Months of Anne Frank*, by contrast, uses interviews with six women who knew Frank in the period after her arrest.[26] A childhood friend, Hannah Elisabeth Pick-Goslar, says of their meeting in Bergen-Belsen: 'It wasn't the same Anne. She was a broken girl.'[27] Rachel van Amerongen-Frankfoorder, who first met the Frank family in Westerbork, and Anne and her sister Margot again in Bergen-Belsen, remembers: 'The Frank girls were almost unrecognizable since their hair had been cut off. . . . And they were cold, just like the

[23] Anne Frank, *The Diary of a Young Girl*, trans. B. M. Mooyaart-Doubleday (London, 1952).
[24] All the photographs that exist of Anne Frank were taken before the war. No photographs were taken during the years the Frank family spent in hiding.
[25] Anne Frank, *The Diary of Anne Frank: The Critical Edition*, trans. Arnold J. Pomerans and B. M. Mooyaart-Doubleday, ed. David Barnouw and Gerrold van der Stroom (New York, 1989), 578–9.
[26] Filmmaker Willy Lindwer's book of the same name contains the complete transcript. See his *The Last Seven Months of Anne Frank*, trans. Alison Meersschaert (New York, 1991).   [27] Ibid. 27.

rest of us.'[28] Their memories of Anne are intermingled with memories of the concentration camp; for them, the fate of Anne Frank represents not a heroic tale of good over evil, but rather the terrible fate of so many concentration camp inmates (both Anne and her sister Margot died of typhus). As those who saw her shortly before she died testify, she looked very different from the photograph which manages to make so many feel as if they knew her. While this hardly undermines the power and value of the diary itself, it does call into question attempts to treat Frank as a 'symbol of the six million'. In the words of the journalist Anne Karpf: 'Anne Frank . . . has been hijacked by those who want their Holocaust stories to be about the triumph of the human spirit over evil and adversity.'[29] Hence, the most frequently cited of Frank's statements is: 'I still believe, in spite of everything, that people are truly good at heart.' This seems to have become her epitaph, rather than her last diary entry on Tuesday, 1 August 1944, which states: 'A voice within me is sobbing. . . . I get cross, then sad . . . and keep trying to find a way to become what I'd like to be and what I could be if . . . if only there were no other people in the world.'[30]

WOMEN AS SELFLESS CARERS?

To avoid 'preempting' the Holocaust, testimonies must not be taken as exhaustive of all Holocaust experiences. Not only are experiences of hiding different from those of living in the concentration camps, but also from those of life within the confines of the ghettos. Dalia Ofer and Lenore Weitzman highlight Emmanuel Ringelblum's observation that women's coping strategies and nurturing roles continued under wartime conditions, although they acknowledge that this might derive in part from the middle-class bias of Ringelblum's

---

[28] Ibid. 103.
[29] Anne Karpf, 'Let's Pretend Life is Beautiful', *The Guardian, Saturday Review*, 3 April 1999, 10.   [30] Frank, *Diary of a Young Girl*, 336.

subjects, whom they still present as typical 'women . . . fac[ing] overwhelming forces with incredible resourcefulness, courage, and persistence'.[31] In particular, they highlight Ringelblum's praise of the Jewish woman for her valiant attempts to care for her family. Indeed, this image is clearly evident in many testimonies. For example, Sara Zyskind writes of the Łódź ghetto:

Hunger was now stalking the ghetto. . . . Mother and I didn't feel the shortage of food so much, for even in good times we had eaten sparingly, but Father, with his healthy appetite, suffered badly from hunger pangs. Mother tried hard to supplement his diet, salvaging every grain of barley or crumb of bread to make an additional meal. To disguise the terrible taste of the rotten potatoes we were now receiving, she grated them finely and made fritters out of them. When Father discovered her hidden culinary talents, he responded with good-humoured praise.[32]

No doubt Sara and her mother did sometimes go hungry to spare their father and husband additional hunger. For Dalia Ofer and Lenore Weitzman, it is 'the portrait of a woman who saved her single ration of bread for her children, or that of a man who volunteered for forced labour because his wages were promised to his family—that restores individuality and humanity to the victims'.[33] But what about the unfortunate women who could not resist eating their paltry bread ration or the men too exhausted to even consider volunteering for such hard work? Their responses are just as human. The shame at not being able to control one's hunger can produce a terrible self-hatred. It is possible too that some did not even attempt to control their hunger. The phenomena of starvation and frustration in the ghettos were not just the preserve of the good. Furthermore, the valorizing of sacrifice often means that the struggles surrounding temptation are glossed over, although they could traumatize both those who gave in to temptation and those who fought desperately to overcome it. Sara Selver-Urbach writes of the terrible dilemmas of hunger she witnessed in the Łódź

[31] Ofer and Weitzman (eds.), *Women in the Holocaust*, 10.
[32] Zyskind, *Stolen Years*, 26.
[33] Ofer and Weitzman (eds.), *Women in the Holocaust*, 14.

ghetto. When food provisions became very low, people started to weigh whatever food they brought home. She writes:

Only people who participated in the weighing out of provisions in the presence of their whole family know what took place at those times: sharp, suspicious glances directed at the scales, mingled with shame and anger at having reached such a horrible degradation.

I relate these events with a heavy heart because we too, we too, started weighing our food. At first, we tried to justify this new step by claiming that the weighing would ensure an accurate and fair apportioning of our rations, so that no one could be wronged. Still, in our family, we never fought over our food, neither during the weighing of rations nor prior to it. . . .

But I could not be blind to the naked truth, at least where I was concerned. For I coveted greatly my own portion, and the weighing secured every gramme that was justly mine. A burning shame sweeps over me when I think back to those weighings, and I am consumed with remorse lest I was partial, here and there, to myself and added an extra crumb of my bread to my portion when it was my turn to weigh the food, though I know I would restore such a crumb on the very next occasion. And yet, this blot, this disgrace, will always remain with me, this shame at having had to lead such an inner struggle.

Until those days, I had never understood the full meaning of the Hebrew expression *Herpat Ra'av*, the literal translation of which is 'the disgrace of hunger'.

In later years, I tried to atone in various ways for that indelible stain on my soul, but no atonement is possible any more, there is no way to blot out these painful memories buried forever in my heart. All that remains for me to do is to look into the abyss of shame and regret and repeat again and again: How hast thou fallen, oh man![34]

WOMEN'S EXPERIENCES OF HIDING

In pointing out that women's particular skills and knowledge provided them with tools for survival, Lenore Weitzman rightly draws attention

---

[34] Selver-Urbach, *Through the Windows of My Home*, 77–8.

to women's ability to hide by disguising their Jewishness.[35] Her research, which is concerned with a largely neglected area in Holocaust studies, shows, *contra* Langer, that there are important differences in the wartime experiences of men and women. This is not surprising considering that women's lives in Eastern and Western Europe, during the 1920s and 1930s, revolved around specific gender roles. Paula Hyman explains that while Jewish women in more affluent Western Europe tended not to participate in business, higher education, and politics, and were therefore denied access to knowledge of the Gentile world and the possibility of assimilation, in Poland and other countries in Eastern Europe, where the majority of Jews were far less affluent and women needed to help out financially, women were likely to have a considerable knowledge of local languages and customs.[36]

When it came to passing as Aryan, women had certain advantages over men, in particular a physical one: in Eastern Europe it was very rare for any man not Jewish to be circumcised. If a man was suspected of being Jewish, he was ordered to undress. Piotr Rawicz, describes his constant fear that his circumcision would betray his Jewishness.[37] Women at least knew they could not be discovered by physical examination, although having stereotypically Jewish features such as dark hair and eyes, the markings of emotional and physical suffering, as well as a lack of financial resources, similarly prohibited the ability to pass.[38] They hid either with forged documents, moving from place to place in both cities and small villages, in convents, in factories, and sometimes in forced-labour camps, or without documents by physically concealing themselves in fields, forests, attics, and stables. In Warsaw it is estimated that about two-thirds of Jews in hiding on the Aryan side were women.[39] In towns and cities, women had to learn to

[35] See Weitzman, 'Living on the Aryan Side in Poland'.
[36] See Paula E. Hyman, 'Gender in the Jewish Family in Modern Europe', in Ofer and Weitzman (eds.), *Women in the Holocaust*, 25–34.
[37] Piotr Rawicz, *Blood from the Sky*, trans. Peter Wiles (New York, 1964).
[38] See Weitzman, 'Living on the Aryan Side in Poland', 201–5.
[39] See Paulsson, *Secret City*. Cf. *idem*, 'The Demography of Jews in Hiding in Warsaw, 1943–1945', in Polonsky (ed.), *Polin. Studies in Polish Jewry*, xiii: *Focusing on the Holocaust and its Aftermath*, 78–103.

enter any place with the placard 'No Jews Allowed' without showing any signs of fear. In rural areas things were not necessarily any easier. Alicia Appelman-Jurman, who, while a young girl, hid in Podole—a part of the Ukraine annexed by Poland after World War I—with her mother, remembers:

My mother and I decided on a plan that called for her to remain hidden in the ravine while I worked on building up a rapport with the local farmers. It wasn't enough just to work for them in the summer; I also had to earn their fondness and sympathy for the wintertime, when there would be no work and I would have to go begging. It was out of the question for my mother to try to work; she would be too easily recognised as a Jewess. The sadness and pain that had settled permanently in her eyes would betray her.

We agreed that she would hide in the wheat fields or in the ravine during the day, and I would bring food for her after my work was through. When I thought of my mother hiding day in day out in the wheat—trembling at every sound, wondering if I would come back or if I had been found out and caught, and waiting, waiting all day with nothing to do, totally dependent on her child for survival—my heart ached for her. But that was how it had to be if we were to survive.[40]

Women who survived the war in hiding did not necessarily suffer less, but were left with a legacy of trauma different from that of those who survived the camps.[41] The experience of Anne Frank and her family was rare, for it was hardly ever the case that families hid together. Like those deported to the concentration camps, most of those in hiding had already experienced many losses. For Alicia Appelman-Jurman it was the loss of her father and brothers that prompted her and her mother's attempt to escape the Gestapo. Testimonies of the appalling horrors of the concentration camps illustrate that at least one thing was not missing in the camps—human company. While they describe the unbearable overcrowding in the barracks, the sharing of sleeping quarters and eating vessels, there is

[40] Alicia Appelman-Jurman, *Alicia: My Story* (New York, 1990), 134.
[41] See Maria Einhorn-Susułowska, 'Psychological Problems of Polish Jews who Used Aryan Documents', in Polonsky (ed.), *Polin. Studies in Polish Jewry*, xiii: *Focusing on the Holocaust and its Aftermath*, 104–11.

very little talk of feelings of isolation. Indeed, as was shown in the previous chapter, for many concentration camp survivors it was liberation that introduced feelings of loneliness into their lives.

For those who survived the war by passing as Aryan, feelings of isolation, of being able to trust no one—not even other Jews in hiding—greatly defined their experiences. For them, it was the fear of discovery rather than the fear of the gas chamber that was always present. Ida Fink's semi-autobiographical novel *The Journey*[42] describes such feelings. Fink's father, a doctor, was wealthy enough to purchase Aryan birth certificates for his daughters. The two sisters, assuming their false identities, stayed for a while in a German work camp. Fink describes her meeting with a fellow Jewess:

Nothing about the way she looked would arouse the slightest suspicion. She was absolutely perfect, and in the best sense of the word, completely natural, not at all flashy. She had delicate features, thick, lustrous, chestnut-coloured hair; her eyes were chestnut-coloured, too. What was striking was the winsome, simple beauty of her round, slightly childish face. But I recognized her immediately, and she recognized me too. She tossed her head and turned away. I could tell she was angry. I watched her sulking; I looked at her delicate profile, her ski boots, her elegant, bell-shaped, light blue coat . . . and I thought: That's the fifth one [Jew], and who knows if she's the last.[43]

Part of the context of publication for any testimony is the existence of other testimonies. This creates not only a sense of 'witness' as a shared identity, but also a feeling of what is and what is not appropriate to talk about. The fact that Anne Frank's story has become the paradigm of hiding has meant that it is widely assumed that the only danger people in hiding faced was being caught by the Nazis.[44] However, there were other problems for women in hiding. Although the Nazi policy of *Rassenschande* (race defilement) firmly prohibited sexual relations between Aryan men and Jewish women, and the

---

[42] Ida Fink, *The Journey*, trans. Joanna Weschler and Francine Prose (London, 1992).
[43] Ibid. 77.
[44] Joan Ringelheim, 'The Split between Gender and the Holocaust', in Ofer and Weitzman (eds.), *Women in the Holocaust*, 345.

incidence of rape and sexual assault seems to have been relatively rare in the concentration camps—although, as will be seen shortly, there are reported cases of rapes perpetrated by other prisoners, in particular by low-level functionaries—numerous acts of sexual violence were committed against 'non-Aryan' women throughout Eastern Europe.[45] Women were particularly sexually vulnerable when in hiding. Fanya Gottesfeld Heller tells the story of a Gestapo raid which resulted in the rape of her aunt:

> Unable to find me, Gottschalk and his henchman left and went looking for me at the home of one of my aunts. When they didn't find me there, they raped her and forced her husband to watch. The rape had to be kept secret because if the Gestapo [presumably she is referring to the higher ranks of the Gestapo] found out about it they would have killed her immediately, since Germans were forbidden to 'fraternise' with 'subhuman' Jews. My aunt told a few members of the family but they didn't believe her—they didn't want to hear or know about it. She never told her children, and for that reason, I have not disclosed her name.[46]

Gottesfeld Heller herself waited fifty years before telling the story. She also describes what she terms as a consensual sexual relationship between herself as a teenager and the Ukranian militia man who rescued and protected her family. Clearly, whether or not a sexual relationship based on such an extreme power imbalance can be understood as consensual makes for a contentious discussion. The feminist researcher Joan Ringelheim gives a further example of a Jewish survivor called 'Pauline' who was molested by male relatives of the people hiding her. Pauline was told that if she complained they would denounce her.[47] The effects of this on her life are enduring. In

[45] See Birgit Beck, 'Vergewaltigung von Frauen als Kriegsstrategie im Zweiten Weltkrieg?' (The Rape of Women as a War Strategy in World War Two?), in Andreas Gestrich (ed.), *Gewalt im Krieg: Ausübung, Erfahrung und Verweigerung von Gewalt in Kriegen des 20. Jahrhunderts. Jahrbuch für Historische Friedensforschung* (Violence in War: Practice, Experience and Refusal of Violence in Wars of the 20th Century. Yearbook for Historical Peace Research), 4 vols. (Munich, 1996), 34–50.

[46] Fanya Gottesfeld Heller, *Strange and Unexpected Love: A Teenage Girl's Holocaust Memoirs* (Hoboken, NJ, 1993), 81.

[47] Ringelheim, 'Split between Gender and the Holocaust', 343.

Writing Ignored

an interview she told Ringelheim: 'I can still feel the fear. . . .
Sometimes I think it was equally as frightening as the Germans. It
became within me a tremendous . . . I (didn't) know how (to deal
with it) . . . what to do with it. I had nobody to talk (to) about it.
Nobody to turn to.'[48] It is an experience which, as Pauline herself
realizes, is not easily reconciled with traditional Holocaust narratives.
She states: 'In respect of what happened, (what we) suffered and
saw—the humiliation in the ghetto, seeing people jumping out and
burned—is this (molestation) important?'[49] In the words of
Ringelheim: 'Her memory was split between traditional versions of
Holocaust history and her own experience.'[50] In other words, traditional Holocaust narratives can make it difficult to discuss anything
considered to be outside the range of accepted Holocaust experiences
as outlined by existing testimony. Witnesses may feel obliged to stay
silent about certain aspects of their experiences for fear that they do
not belong to the history of the Holocaust, or that the experiences
will not be easily understood.[51] This can prevent us from challenging
traditional narratives, or adding to them by acquiring further
information about the diversity of experiences during the Holocaust.

RAPE AND SEXUAL ABUSE

While the observation that rape and sexual assault were relatively rare
in the concentration camps is based upon the absence of descriptions
of sexual abuse in testimonies, it is possible that such an absence
inhibits other witnesses who did experience abuse from including
descriptions of it in their testimonies. Ringelheim presents the case of

---

[48] Ringelheim, 'Split between Gender and the Holocaust', 343.   [49] Ibid.
[50] Ibid.
[51] See Annie G. Rogers *et al.*, 'An Interpretative Poetics of Languages of the Unsayable',
in Ruthellen Josselson and Amia Lieblich (eds.), *Making Meaning of Narratives* (London,
1999), 77–106, for a discussion of the importance of being aware of the possibility of 'the
unspeakable' in making sense of narratives of lived experience. For Rogers *et al.* 'what is
unspeakable exists as a deep and haunting sense of something that begs for words but is
also absolutely forbidden to be spoken', 86.

'Susan', who was deported to Auschwitz when she was 21 years old and quickly became a 'privileged prisoner'. A male Polish prisoner came to Susan one day and offered her some sardines. He told her when and where to meet him, and not realizing his motives, she did. Then, as Susan confessed to Ringelheim, 'he grabbed and raped me'.[52] While it is significant that Susan is careful to point out that it was not a Jewish prisoner, but a Polish prisoner who raped her—thereby connecting herself to classic narratives by talking of Polish anti-Semitism—Ringelheim is correct to observe: 'I believe that we avoid listening to stories we do not want to hear. Sometimes we avoid listening because we don't understand the importance of what is being said. Without a place for a particular memory, without a conceptual framework, a possibly significant piece of information will not be pursued.'[53]

As the examples of both Pauline and Susan indicate, Holocaust survivors may feel that traditional versions of Holocaust history prohibit them from telling their stories. Perhaps it is only because Susan's assailant was Polish rather than Jewish that she is able to speak of the assault at all. But, although Ringelheim is right to suggest that women were vulnerable to rape or sexual abuse, she fails to acknowledge that men were also at risk from such attacks. Although they occurred, these incidents have almost never been published. One of the very few testimonies to testify to the experience of rape comes from a male survivor. Roman Frister's testimony *The Cap or the Price of a Life*, which, like Gottesfeld Heller's memoir, was written a long time after the events it describes, tells the story of a young Jewish boy born in Poland and his rape in Auschwitz at the age of 15 by a fellow inmate who then stole his uniform cap. Inmates who appeared at morning roll-call without it would be shot on the spot. Presumably this was the rapist's intention. In order to survive, Frister promptly stole another cap from a sleeping prisoner. Three hours later, at roll-call, the prisoner was shot dead. In contrast to many survivors who tend to supply their experiences with a positive moral or emotional

[52] Ringelheim, 'Split between Gender and the Holocaust', 341.
[53] Ibid. 342. Ringelheim also makes the important point that, unlike in Bosnia (or Kosovo), rape was not part of the genocidal strategy.

subtext, Frister states quite bluntly that at the time he had no qualms. Today, however, he does feel guilt, but suggests that it is probably irrational; believing morality to be a relative rather than a universal concept, he asks: 'Does anyone have the right to judge me against the standards of our civilised society for acts I committed in the darkness of the human jungle? Survival is the law of the jungle, and yes, I willingly submitted to that law.'[54] It is noticeable that Frister focuses on the morality, or lack of morality, of stealing the cap, rather than on the trauma of the rape, thereby turning the story into a further opportunity to explore the more familiar territory of the nature of morality in the concentration camps. It will not be until comprehension of the Holocaust is broadened to acknowledge types of experience that stand outside traditional narratives that stories such as Frister's will be understood and explored.

MOTHERHOOD

Research on the particularity of women's Holocaust experiences is right to draw attention to the role of mother, but this must be put in the context of the difficulty in fulfilling that role under a Nazi regime ruthlessly committed to destroying the Jewish family. In November 1941, Ringelblum recorded: 'Jews have been prohibited from marrying and having children. Women pregnant up to three months have to have an abortion.'[55] While Avraham Tory wrote in his diary in the Kovno ghetto, 'From September on, giving birth is strictly forbidden. Pregnant women will be put to death', he went on to write on 4 February 1943: 'It was terrible to watch the women getting on the truck; they held in their arms their babies of different ages and wrapped in more and more sweaters so that they would not catch cold on the way (to their death).'[56] Also in the Theresienstadt ghetto a

[54] Roman Frister, *The Cap or the Price of a Life*, trans. Hillel Halkin (New York, 1999), introduction.   [55] Ringelblum, *Notes from the Warsaw Ghetto*, 230.
[56] Avraham Tory, *Surviving the Holocaust: The Kovno Ghetto Diary*, trans. Jerzy Michalowicz (Cambridge, Mass., 1990), 114, 195.

decree for compulsory abortion was issued in July 1943, and afterwards any woman who refused to comply with this order, or who gave birth, was placed on the next transport to the concentration camps in the East.[57] Women's responses to this climate of anti-mothering are complex and varied.

In March 1943, when the Germans began liquidating the Polish city of Lwów, forcing the Jews from the ghetto and murdering thousands, a small group, including several small children, managed to escape into the sewers. They lived in a confined space among the city's waste for 14 months. One of the members of the group, Genia Weinberg, gave birth to a baby boy, assisted only by her comrades with a pair of rusty scissors and a towel. Needless to say, it would be almost impossible to care for a baby under such conditions. The dilemma was whether to attempt to raise the child at all costs, or to sacrifice its life for the sake of the group, since its cries could attract attention. Due to the appalling nature of such a choice, it is not surprising that there are differing versions of what happened. The mother herself provides the following version of events: 'The group quickly realized the hopelessness of trying to care for a baby. . . . The baby's cries would alert people in the street of their presence and so it was agreed, unanimously, that the baby be terminated. It was taken away, killed, and disposed of.'[58] In this account Mrs Weinberg seems to be trying to distance herself both from her baby and from a personal decision to end its life. However, an alternative version of events is provided by a family called Chiger and confirmed by a woman named Klara Margulies. They recall: 'Mrs Weinberg showed no sign of wanting to suckle the baby, so, in order to quieten the little boy's cries, Paulina tried to feed him some sweet water. She dipped a piece of clean material in the water and placed it against the baby's mouth. Instinctively, he began to suck. . . . The baby had been given to Genia to hold but she appeared uninterested in it.' The Chigers' daughter

[57] Ofer and Weitzman (eds.), *Women in the Holocaust*, 7.
[58] Cited in Robert Marshall, *In the Sewers of Lvov: The Last Sanctuary from the Holocaust* (London, 1991), 125.

Kristina, who was 7 years old at the time, recalled: 'I remember seeing my mother crawling towards the baby and trying to give it a little water, and Mrs Weinberg was taking the baby away from my mother. I saw my mother fighting with her, my mother was trying to give some water and Mrs Weinberg was pulling the baby away. And Ignacy Chiger records:

She [Mrs Weinberg] began to hug the baby closer and closer to herself, covering its face with a towel or rag, supposedly to quiet the sound of his whimpering. But my wife realized that she was in fact trying to suffocate the baby and she tried to pull the cloth away.

The struggle continued for some time until the two women were just too exhausted to continue. . . . In the morning, the little corpse was lying beside his mother, who had fallen into a sullen trance.[59]

Leopold Socha, another member of the group, was horrified by what had happened, but, rather than condemning the mother, he developed great affection for her, perhaps realizing the trauma that she had been through. As Primo Levi has observed, 'a person who has been wounded tends to block out the memory so as not to renew the pain; the person who has inflicted the wound pushes the memory deep down, to be rid of it, to alleviate the feeling of guilt.'[60] If Mrs Weinberg did suffocate her own baby, her testimony of events can be read either as a coping strategy to avoid facing the full horror of what had happened, or as a partial suppression of a painful truth. She can be understood not just as a mother (and possibly as a bad mother for failing to live up to the ideals celebrated by Ofer and Weitzman), but as a woman who had perhaps not yet relinquished her hope for a future.

On arrival at the concentration camps, men and women were separated before being murdered in the gas chambers or sent to separate camps or barracks. At Auschwitz-Birkenau, women who refused to be separated from children under the age of 14 were sent to the gas chambers with them. Mothers were faced with what Lawrence Langer

---

[59] Marshall, *In the Sewers of Lvov*, 126.   [60] Levi, *The Drowned and the Saved*, 23.

calls 'a choiceless choice':[61] they could attempt to dissociate them-selves from their children in the uncertain hope of survival or accom-pany them to a certain death. Some women did not realize that they were going with their children to their deaths, as the Nazis took pains to conceal the reality of the gas chambers until it was too late. Experienced prisoners, who did know the truth, sometimes tried to tell the mothers to hand the children over to the elderly, for the eld-erly were already condemned to death on account of their age. However, studies of women and the Holocaust continue the theme of the dutiful mother by suggesting, for example, that on arrival at Auschwitz 'most women clung to their children (and many young girls to their mothers) and were sent to the gas chambers with them'.[62] This statement, taken from Ofer and Weitzman's *Women in the Holocaust*, may indeed be true of most women, but there are exceptions.

In his semi-autobiographical work *This Way for the Gas, Ladies and Gentlemen*, which recalls events he is known to have experienced but are filtered through the voice of 'Tadek', Tadeusz Borowski tells the story of a young woman's attempt to distance herself from her crying child by pretending no knowledge of it, although she in fact fails and is forced to share the child's fate:

Here is a woman—she walks quickly, but tries to appear calm. A small child with a pink cherub's face runs after her and, unable to keep up, stretches out his little arms and cries: Mama! Mama!

'Pick up your child, woman!'

'It's not mine, sir, not mine!', she shouts hysterically and runs on, covering her face with her hands. She wants to hide, she wants to reach those who will not ride the trucks, those who will go on foot, those who will stay alive. She is young, healthy, good-looking, she wants to live.

---

[61] In *Versions of Survival*, Langer describes a 'choiceless choice' as occurring when 'cru-cial decisions did not reflect options between life and death, but between one form of abnormal response and another, both imposed by a situation that was in no way of the victims' own choosing' 72.

[62] Ofer and Weitzman (eds.), *Women in the Holocaust*, 11.

But the child runs after her, wailing loudly: 'Mama, mama, don't leave me!'

'It's not mine, not mine, no!'

Andrei, a sailor from Sevastopol, grabs hold of her. His eyes are glassy from vodka and the heat. With one powerful blow he knocks her off her feet, then, as she falls, takes her by the hair and pulls her up again. His face twitches with rage.

'Ah, you bloody Jewess! So you're running from your own child! I'll show you, you whore!' His huge hand chokes her, he lifts her in the air and heaves her on the truck like a heavy sack of grain.

'Here! And take this with you, bitch!' and he throws the child at her feet.

'*Gut gemacht*, good work. That's the way to deal with degenerate mothers,' says the S.S. man standing at the foot of the truck. '*Gut, gut, Russki.*'[63]

It is not easy to make sense of this young mother's response within frameworks of interpretation based on the notion of the dutiful mother. If this mother had lived, and had possibly become a mother to other children, she would need to find some way of binding her memories. She would have to assign a boundary to her suffering if she were to be able to function in a new life. If she did give voice to her story, the woman might find a less self-incriminating framework in which to tell of the loss of her child. However, this does not mean that she would not continue to suffer silently the trauma and guilt of what she had done.

Pregnant woman were occasionally admitted to the camps, either because they were married to Gentile husbands, or because their pregnancy was not yet noticeable. Some would undergo induced miscarriages, often as late as the fourth or fifth month.[64] The 'choiceless choice' finds particular expression when women gave birth in the camps. Ilona Karmel explores pregnancy in the slave labour camps, to understand the moral dilemmas of survival. Karmel, who survived such camps herself, points out that there were many responses to

---

[63] Borowski, *This Way for the Gas, Ladies and Gentlemen*, 43.

[64] See Lucie Adelsberger, *Auschwitz: A Doctor's Story*, trans. Susan Ray (London, 1996), 100–2; originally published in German as *Auschwitz: Ein Tatsachenbericht. Das Vermächtnis der Opfer für uns Juden und für alle Menschen* (Auschwitz: A Factual Report. The Legacy of the Victims for us Jews and for all People) (Berlin, 1956).

motherhood. For example, she contrasts one woman's 'longing for a child' with another's sense of her unborn baby as 'a tormentor who sucked her strength, snatched every crumb away'.[65] Significantly, newborn children were not allowed to survive: if discovered, it meant certain death for both mother and child. Therefore, many of the inmate doctors decided that such children must die so that the mother might live. They saved poison for this purpose, but in its absence were forced to smother the babies. Sometimes they managed to kill the baby without the mother's knowledge, in the expectation that this would spare her some measure of pain; but on other occasions she was aware of the situation. Lucie Adelsberger, a Jewish doctor, who worked in the make-shift hospital barracks at Birkenau remembers: 'One time there was no poison available, and so the mother strangled the child she had just delivered. . . . She was a Pole, a good mother who loved her children more than anything else. But she had hidden three small children back home and wanted to live for them.'[66] Judith Sternberg Newman, a nurse at Auschwitz, describes the drowning of a newborn baby:

Two days after Christmas, a Jewish child was born on our block. How happy I was when I saw this tiny baby. . . . Three hours later, I saw a small package wrapped in cheese cloth lying on a wooden bench. Suddenly it moved. A Jewish girl employed as a clerk came over, carrying a pan of cold water. . . . She picked up the little package—it was the baby, of course—and it started to cry with a thin little voice. She took the infant and submerged its little body in the cold water. . . . After about eight minutes the breathing stopped.[67]

Ilona Karmel tells us what happened when women did try to save a newborn baby, when Nazi doctors had ordered that the child be placed in cotton wool but not fed anything, including water. The women involved risked their own lives to feed the baby sugar water, but the baby died anyway, its suffering prolonged.[68]

---

[65] Ilona Karmel, *An Estate of Memory* (New York, 1986), 242. Karmel, who survived the Buchenwald concentration camp, chooses to narrate her experiences through the medium of documentary fiction.   [66] Adelsberger, *Auschwitz*, 101.

[67] Judith Sternberg Newman, *In the Hell of Auschwitz: The Wartime Memoirs of J. S. Newman* (New York, 1963), 42–3.   [68] Karmel, *An Estate of Memory*, 255.

CARING FOR OTHERS

Studies of women in the concentration camps pay a great deal of attention to stories of mutual support, primarily women who survived with close relatives—daughters, mothers, sisters, cousins. Some realized that they could only survive the camps by being caring to one another. In her memoir *Rena's Promise: A Story of Sisters in Auschwitz*, Rena Kornreich Gelissen recalls the words she spoke to her sister while at Auschwitz: '[T]his is my dream, Danka—I am going to bring you home [to Tylicz in Poland]. We're going to walk through our farmhouse door and Mama and Papa will be there waiting for us. Mama will hug and kiss us, and I'm going to say, "Mama, I got your baby back."' [69] Rena makes it clear that the presence of her sister in Auschwitz allowed her to maintain a connection with the past and hope for the future. Her need to be a good sister and daughter is illustrative not only of a desire to help another, but also of a very important survival strategy that provides Rena with a sense of purpose and a means to survival.

While the ability to maintain familial or emotional bonds was for many an important contributory factor to survival, not least psychologically, the representation of these close relationships often loses the context in which they occur. For example, Aranka Siegal, in describing Mrs Hollander—a fellow prisoner who had cared for her— repeats the words spoken by Mrs Hollander throughout their march from Christianstadt to Bergen-Belsen: 'I want to live long enough to feed my daughters just once more and then I will die happy.' [70] When placed within the context of the rest of Siegal's memoir, this tableau of Mrs Hollander is illustrative of Siegal's sanctification of motherhood, resulting from the loss of her own mother on arrival at Auschwitz.

Accounts of mutual care and concern become problematic when used to obscure the horrors of the concentration camps by introducing a redemptive message into the Holocaust. Testimonies document

---

[69] Rena Kornreich Gelissen (with Heather Dune Macadam), *Rena's Promise: A Story of Sisters in Auschwitz* (London, 1996), 73.   [70] Siegal, *Grace in the Wilderness*, 8.

the sharp and often violent divisions among prisoners within the concentration camps based on factors like position in the camp hierarchy, political affiliation, religious observance, or geographical origin. Helen Lewis describes the deep sense of division in Auschwitz between the Yiddish-speaking *Ostjuden* (Eastern European Jews) and the more assimilated Western European Jews:

There were three hundred of us newcomers who had previously been in Terezin and in the family camp at Birkenau. We came from Czechoslovakia, Germany and Austria and we shared a fairly similar background and outlook. . . . The five hundred prisoners who had arrived some weeks earlier came from Poland and the Baltics, as well as Hungary and Romania. Most of them had had a strict religious upbringing, which gave them a strong sense of identity, but sadly manifested itself in their hostility towards us and their rejection of our group. They could speak the languages of their home countries, but preferred to talk to each other in Yiddish, a language which I and the rest of my group didn't understand. They bitterly resented our lack of religious ardour; we thought them uneducated, uncivilised even.[71]

The brutality and deprivation of the concentration camps dictated that both on a group and an individual level any sense of solidarity, friendship, or familial feeling would have its dark side. The scope for action was so constrained that caring for someone invariably meant doing so at somebody else's expense. When Rena manages to get her sister a place on her bunk, she acknowledges: 'I do not ask what will happen to the girl who was sleeping next to me. . . . This is a selfish act, perhaps, but I have a sister who I have to keep alive and she is all that matters.'[72]

Ultimately, too, prisoners could share their bread, but in most cases could not protect those they loved from starvation, from disease, from brutality, or ultimately from death. They continually had to endure situations that in their pre-war lives they could have acted upon. Those unaware of the limits to the possibility of noble action were soon disillusioned. Sara Selver-Urbach tells the following story

---

[71] Helen Lewis, *A Time to Speak* (Belfast, 1992), 75.
[72] Gelissen, *Rena's Promise*, 72.

concerning a fellow inmate who had previously been a highly respected physician in the Łódź ghetto:

She broke down completely from the start, lost control over her bodily functions. . . . Her daughter, who was another of our inmates, did her utmost to conceal her mother's state to protect her. A Kapo who'd noticed the daughter's efforts beat her so cruelly that she fainted. The rest of us, inmates, watched the brutal punishment mutely, stonily, acknowledging in our despair the omnipotence of the laws that governed Auschwitz.

All of us, that is, except Salusha, who had not yet grasped sufficiently the supremacy of those laws (the incident occurred on one of our first days in that camp). To our horrified stupefaction, Salusha's childish voice spoke suddenly, in the deadly silence: 'Why are you beating her? It's so unfair!'

Salusha had barely finished her remark when the fat Kapo burst into a wild fit of laughter, her colleagues—who ruled over our blockhouse with her—joining in the sickening merriment.

'Fairness! She's looking for fairness! Did you hear that?' They screeched raucously, holding their bellies, their faces contorted. One of them imitated in a strident, almost bestial voice, Salusha's outburst, stressing exaggeratedly every syllable: 'Whey-are-you-bea-ting-her-it's-so-un-fair-hi-hi-hi . . . !'

But the incident did not end there. Far from it!

The Kapo punished Salusha. She dragged her out of the line-up and made her climb on top of the stove which ran the length of the blockhouse. There, she forced Salusha onto her knees, placed heavy bricks in her hands and ordered her to raise hands and bricks above her head, a position which poor Salusha was compelled to stay in for some hours. Never again did Salusha ask for fairness and justice.[73]

The inability to intervene results in the corrosion of a sense of self, which is a common theme of many Holocaust memoirs. In an essay entitled 'Shame', Primo Levi writes:

Few survivors feel guilty about having deliberately damaged, robbed or beaten a companion. Those who did so (the kapos, but not only them) block out the memory. By contrast, however, almost everybody feels guilty of having omitted to offer to help. The presence at your side of a weaker—or less

[73] Selver-Urbach, *Through the Window of My Home*, 130–1.

cunning, or older, or too young—companion, hounding you with his demands for help or with his simple presence, in itself an entreaty, is a constant in the life of the lager.[74]

Women's testimonies in particular also highlight the trauma of losing a sense of one's physical self. For example, for many women, and particularly religious women, it was the first experience of the showers that eroded their sense of self and will to live. A comparative study of women's and men's testimonies suggests that more women describe the trauma of their initiation into the concentration camp world. Women write of the agony of having to stand naked in front of men, of being searched for hidden valuables, of being subjected to obscene remarks, of being shorn of all their hair, and of being tattooed.[75] Rena Kornreich Gelissen remembers: 'I try to prevent tears from falling down my disinfected cheeks. Only married women shave their heads [orthodox Jewish women shave their heads after marriage]. Our traditions, our beliefs, are scorned and ridiculed by the acts they commit.'[76]

Many women found the experience so traumatic that they went to their deaths soon after. A further step in the erosion of the self was the stopping of menstruation shortly after arrival at the concentration camps. (While this might have been the result of shock or starvation, it was also rumoured that the food the women ate was laced with bromide as part of an experiment in mass sterilization.) This made some women fearful that they would be infertile forever.[77] Livia Bitton-Jackson writes: 'Married women keep wondering about the bromide in their food again and again. Will they bear children again? What will their husbands say when they find out?'[78] Some even tried to eat less food in the hope that it would cause less damage.[79] However, hunger generally made this a short-lived strategy.

---

[74] Levi, *The Drowned and the Saved*, 78.
[75] The internal examinations were conducted mostly by SS men, and the shaving and tattooing by both male and female prisoners.   [76] Gelisssen, *Rena's Promise*, 63.
[77] It was also rumoured that male prisoners were subjected to emasculating potions.
[78] Bitton-Jackson, *Eli*, 103–4.   [79] Ibid.

MOTHERS OR MURDERERS?

Assumptions about women's behaviour obscure the diversity of their Holocaust experiences. The Holocaust was indiscriminate in its targeting of the Jews—every Jew, male and female, was condemned to death. The religious, the secular, the educated, the ignorant, the good, and the corrupt were all sentenced to the same fate. For those who survived, feelings of guilt can exist regardless of whether or not they are justified. The identities of women are constructed on the basis of roles such as 'mother', 'caregiver', 'daughter', and testimonies are often selected to reinforce these pre-existing ideals. Many testimonies do focus on the desire to fulfil traditional gendered expectations. While in Auschwitz, Rena was determined to prove herself a caring sister. Since she and her sister both survived, she was able to maintain this self-image. Other testimonies describe the split between the desire to meet particular expectations and the realization that they could not be attained. Ilona Karmel tells us that when women did try to save a baby by secretly feeding it, very often they were merely prolonging the child's suffering. Other women such as Clara abandoned all ideals of female (or human) decency and became vicious *Kapos*. They refused to acknowledge who they had been or might be expected to be. Women such as Clara show that under extreme circumstances people can act in unexpected ways. Before arriving at Auschwitz, the young mother described by Tadeusz Borowski might have fulfilled all the criteria demanded of 'mother', but realizing that her child was sentenced to die, tried to abandon him in order to live. She, like the majority of those who experienced the Holocaust, did not survive to write her testimony.

Survivors who write testimony can feel compelled to make their experiences compatible with pre-existing narratives of survival. Part of the process of writing a testimony may be to record a story of survival in a way that helps the survivor to carry on with his or her own life within a culture in which gender norms are strong. For example, Genia Weinberg might need to deny suffocating her child in order to go on living. For most survivors, Holocaust testimony is rooted in traumatic experiences, and the act of writing a testimony involves the rediscovering of an identity—be it witness, survivor, Jew, loving mother, or dutiful daughter, to name but a few. For many, the desire to be a witness was present at the time of the Holocaust. The post-war adoption of the role of the witness can provide survivors with a sense of purpose, or identity, but their testimony is mediated by the myriad of factors which play a part in a survivor's narrative, especially the accepted Holocaust narratives, studies, and testimonies. As will be noted in the next chapter, the function of collective memory is not to focus on the past in order to find out more about the Holocaust, but to use the past to inform and meet present concerns. In the case of women, the purpose is to say something universal about women, not about their particular Holocaust experiences. Unfortunately, the distressing stories of people who acted desperately, under appalling circumstances, in order to survive, are often overlooked. It is, of course, understandable that many people shy away from confronting the full horrors of the Holocaust, yet this will continue as long as testimonies are projected as 'epics of love and courage'.

5

Writing the Ineffable:
The Representation of Testimony

[B]y its uniqueness the holocaust defies literature.

Wiesel, cited by Berger

Auschwitz cannot be explained . . . the Holocaust transcends history.

Wiesel, 'Trivialising the Holocaust'

This chapter focuses on the mediation between the memory of witnessing the atrocities of the Holocaust and the role played by the subsequent comprehension and conception of the Holocaust as a historical event in constructing and reconstructing testimony. It looks at the way in which the concept of the Holocaust acts as an organizer of memory, not only for events contained within its own description—how it shapes, what it excludes, and the manner of its functioning—but also for memories of other events. The role of the witness has expanded to incorporate not only commentary on the human condition but also to offer warnings against future cases of ethnic cleansing and genocide. Although many survivors—for example, Anita Lasker-Wallfisch, Elie Wiesel, Primo Levi, and Henry Wermuth—have accepted this role, the merging of individual experiences of suffering into a collective historical memory both conceals the diversity of experiences it seeks to represent and mediates the writing of testimony.

Many Holocaust testimonies contain a section in which the author attempts to explain why he or she has decided to record his or her experiences. Apart from paying homage to the dead, or leaving a document for their children, the most prominent reason motivating survivors to write their testimonies is to ensure that *we never forget*; the view being that such a momentous crime against humanity must always be remembered. This involves the feeling that the magnitude of their terrible experiences should not be diminished by being compared to other genocides. Lasker-Wallfisch speaks for many survivors when she says that she is wary of historians who try to universalize the event. Showing how testimony does not operate in isolation from wider historiographical concerns, she believes that the only historian who can be trusted is the Israeli historian Yehuda Bauer, because he stresses the Holocaust's uniqueness;[1] something Lasker-Wallfisch believes to be its most important aspect.[2]

The perceived uniqueness of the Holocaust means that the act of recording one's memories is often one of duty rather than one of release. At a conference at the British Library in 1999, Lasker-Wallfisch stated that she and other survivors resent any suggestion that talking or writing about their experiences allows for resolution, feeling that this implies that readers or interviewers are 'doing them a favour'.[3] Henry Wermuth, writing in his introduction to *Breathe Deeply My Son*, states that he was persuaded by his cousin that it was 'my duty to overcome my doubts and reluctance and write my story'.[4] In his self-reflexive examination of his motivation for writing down his experiences, Wermuth explains: 'My main aim is to counter those people, who, incredible as it sounds, are hard at work in diminishing

[1] See Yehuda Bauer, *The Holocaust in Historical Perspective* (London, 1978). However, in a recent book entitled *Rethinking the Holocaust*, Bauer explains that 'to avoid misunderstandings, and contrary to my usage in previous publications, I am now using unprecedented instead of unique' (*idem, Rethinking the Holocaust* (New Haven, 2001), 278 n. 6).

[2] Anita Lasker-Wallfisch, 'A Survivor's Perspective', paper read at *Taking Testimonies Forward: Oral Histories of the Holocaust* (conference held at the British Library, 15 Nov. 1999). On the debate over 'uniqueness' see Stone, *Constructing the Holocaust*, ch. 5.

[3] Lasker-Wallfisch, 'A Survivor's Perspective'.

[4] Henry Wermuth, *Breathe Deeply My Son* (London, 1993), 1.

the dimension of the unspeakable crimes, to whittle down the figures of those killed—or to deny the *Shoah*, or *Hurban*, altogether.'[5]

THE POSITION OF THE WITNESS

Wermuth's very literal take on the role of the witness—to counteract false belief and prove something to be true—makes very particular demands of the survivor-writer: it demands objectivity. Understanding this, Primo Levi has written: 'I have deliberately assumed the calm sober language of the witness, neither the lamenting tones of the victim nor the irate voice of someone who seeks revenge.'[6] He explains that survivors testify because 'they know they are witnesses in a trial of planetary and epochal dimensions'.[7] The importance of using 'calm sober language' correlates with the view that the Holocaust holds messages for the advancement of humanity: the impassivity of the bystander, the dangers of racism, the importance of community, the triumph of the human spirit. However, there is a tension. Although Levi hopes that reading *If This is a Man* 'should be able to furnish documentation for a quiet study of certain aspects of the human mind',[8] he also explains that his impulse for writing the book 'had taken on . . . the character of an immediate and violent impulse'.[9] Expressions of revenge are suppressed in later testimonies; survivors, such as Levi, were to learn that any display of anger would detract from the sober position of the witness. This overlooks the fact that it was the very desire to testify *against the Nazis* that in part fuelled the will to survive.

Because the Holocaust is regarded as an event with pedagogic implications, survivors are seen as having a unique source of historical knowledge. This is made implicit in the very concept of 'witnessing', which is usually defined as 'first-hand seeing'. Though I have argued throughout this book that the subsequent giving of testimony, or the bearing of witness, is mediated by a multiplicity of factors—that it

---

[5] Wermuth, *Breathe Deeply My Son*, 3.   [6] Levi, 'Afterword', 382.
[7] Levi, *The Drowned and the Saved*, 121.   [8] Levi, *If This is a Man*, 15.
[9] Ibid.

holds no immediacy for itself—I reject the notion that the traumatic nature of the events themselves renders witnesses' testimony opaque. Influenced by the work of Freud, some writers, such as the survivor (and psychoanalyst) Dori Laub, believe that it was impossible to witness the Holocaust at the time because it involves the assumption that witnesses are capable of transcending their traumatic experiences. Freud's early writings on trauma, developed in conjunction with his hermeneutical understanding of memory, concentrate on how traumatic memory can be dealt with successfully by its integration into other non-traumatic memories. Such a perspective is very much one of 'management' rather than 'confrontation' of painful past memories.[10] The actual traumatic memory can never be represented, for 'the cause of trauma is precisely the impossibility of experiencing, and subsequently memorizing, an event. From this perspective it is contradictory to speak of traumatic experience or memory.'[11] It is, then, only the repression of the trauma, or the retrospective meaning attributed to the trauma, that can be read in narrative accounts of the Holocaust. As Laub states: 'The degree to which bearing witness was required, entailed such an outstanding measure of awareness and of comprehension of the event—of its radical *otherness* to all human frames of reference—that it was beyond the limits of human ability (and willingness) to grasp, to transmit, or to imagine.'[12]

Judith Herman agrees, stating that 'traumatic memories lack verbal narrative and context',[13] and are in essence 'fragmentary sensation . . . image without context . . . a series of still snapshots'.[14] However,

[10] Michael Roth, 'Trauma, Representation, and Historical Consciousness', *Common Knowledge*, 7/2 (Fall 1998), 100.

[11] Ernst Van Alpen, 'Symptoms of Discursivity: Experience, Memory, and Trauma', in Mieke Bal, Jonathan Crewe, and Leo Spitzer (eds.), *Acts of Memory: Cultural Recall in the Present* (Hanover, NH, 1999), 26.

[12] Dori Laub, 'An Event without a Witness: Truth, Testimony and Survival', in Shoshana Felman and Dori Laub, *Testimony: Crises of Witnessing in Literature, Psychoanalysis, and History* (New York, 1992), 84.

[13] Judith Lewis Herman, *Trauma and Recovery* (New York, 1992), 38.

[14] Ibid. 175. The image of 'still snapshots' is attributed to F. Snider of the Boston Area Traumatic Study Group. Cited in Henry Greenspan, *On Listening to Holocaust Survivors: Recounting and Life History* (Westport, Conn., 1998), 176–7.

Laub and Herman make two important errors. Not only do they judge the events of the Holocaust from the viewpoint of the *concept* of the Holocaust, from the post-war comprehension of the events—for example, the knowledge of the magnitude of the killing—but they underestimate survivors' (including Laub's) abilities to negotiate traumatic experiences. As shown in Chapter 2, survivors were able to manage their trauma by embarking on survival strategies; for example, Livia Bitton-Jackson writes: 'The fear is gone. Amazing how fast one learns. . . . Even swallowing the daily mush became easier. Lying on the hard floor is much easier now, and the *Zählappell* quite bearable.'[15]

A considerable amount of bearing witness did take place during the events of the Holocaust, thereby arguing against Dori Laub's and Judith Herman's conception of trauma, which claims that witnessing the Holocaust could take place only after the event, that meaning is garnered only retrospectively. In the face of certain death, the men of the *Sonderkommando* not only wrote about the terrible crimes they had been forced to witness, but buried their writings, clearly explaining that they wanted the world to know the suffering inflicted upon the Jews. In a similar manner, many Jews in the ghettos wrote of their suffering. Primo Levi's concern for 'the calm sober language of the witness' is an echo of Emmanuel Ringelblum's implicit conception of testimony as articulated in the Warsaw ghetto. Both presuppose that the traumatic events and the bearing of witness are not incompatible. In the ghetto, Ringelblum explained on behalf of the staff of *Oneg Shabbat* that 'We deliberately refrained from drawing professional journalists into our work, because we did not want it to be sensationalized. Our aim was that the sequence of events in each town . . . should be conveyed as simply and faithfully as possible.'[16]

Even Anne Frank, as a child in hiding, intended her diary to be more than just a personal life narrative. She came to see it as a testimony to the ordeal of hiding. Initially, she saw her writing as a

---

[15] Bitton-Jackson, *Eli*, 95.
[16] Cited in Roskies, *Jewish Search for a Usable Past*, 22.

creative and emotional outlet for herself, but when in 1944 an exiled member of the Dutch government, Gerrit Bolkestein, stated in a radio broadcast from London that after the war he wished to collect eyewitness accounts of the experiences of the Dutch people under the German occupation, she started to see its wider significance. She dedicated herself to rewriting and editing her diary, making improvements, omitting what she did not think would be of interest, and so on. She did this at the same time as keeping her original, more private diary.[17] For Frank, the idea that her experiences would be historically interesting allowed her to see herself as more than a suffering child. *Contra* Frank *et al.*, Laub's and Herman's viewpoints are tantamount to asserting that the testimony of these witnesses is not only unreliable, but impossible. Witnessing and the bearing of witness are both, of course, mediated by the trauma of the events, but not necessarily eclipsed by them.[18]

While the difficulties of writing during the Holocaust are readily accepted, what is somewhat less evident and accepted is that the bearing of witness after the events has its own set of problems. Survivors such as Primo Levi, Elie Wiesel, Anita Lasker-Wallfisch, and Henry Wermuth have all clearly accepted the role of the survivor-witness over that of the victim. This is expressed through the desire to educate future generations about the Holocaust, and is a way of incorporating their traumatic experiences into life after the events. While Chapter 1 has shown that Ringelblum's aim 'to convey the whole truth'[19] could not be achieved, either because witnesses did not have access to information about all the events that were going on, or because of fears that the archives would be discovered prematurely, it is also true that the survivor can offer only a singular account. In the process of bearing witness, the role of the survivor demands a comprehensive and objective account of the Holocaust that may be beyond the subjective

[17] Otto H. Frank and Mirjam Pressler, 'Foreword', in Anne Frank, *The Diary of a Young Girl: The Definitive Edition*, trans. Susan Massotty, ed. Otto H. Frank and Mirjam Pressler (London, 1997).

[18] Cf. the discussion of trauma in Stargardt, *Witnesses of War*, 9–10.

[19] Ringelblum, 'O.S.', 9.

experience of any one individual. Not only this, but memories are also mediated by both the present and future concerns of each survivor, and the writing of testimony is often a way to organize the experiences of a life in order to make sense of them and function in the present. It is not always the case that the identity, concerns, or experiences of a survivor tally with the concerns of collective memory. Survivors' experiences are multifaceted and heterogeneous. As was seen in the previous chapter, there are many Holocaust stories that do not easily accord with accepted Holocaust narratives: for example, the brutal behaviour of some Jewish *Kapos*, instances of rape in the camps and in hiding, the killing of others in order to survive, and the contradictory behaviour of certain 'perpetrators'. As Kitty Hart explains:

we heard that Hössler [*Lagerführer* (Camp Leader) at Auschwitz I] had been arrested and was coming up for trial. . . . It was he who had responded to my mother's plea and had freed me from *Kanada* to travel with her. I would not have been alive today but for him. We knew he had committed many brutalities in Auschwitz but we owed him a lot and felt someone ought to speak up for him. . . . We explained that we'd been in the camp and knew of Hössler's crimes, but also knew of some good he had done. We wanted only to give simple, straightforward evidence in his defence. It was not allowed.[20]

The accepted concept of the Holocaust and the role of collective memory place two demands on the survivor. First, they seek to homogenize survivors' experiences, and secondly, they assume that, in adopting the role of the witness, survivors will adopt a universal identity. But, in negotiating the hegemony of accepted Holocaust narratives, some survivors' experiences are either pushed towards the margins or neglected altogether. Survivors not only need to find an identity that enables them to cope with their experiences and find meaning in their lives, they also have to worry about how the representation of their experiences relates to the *modus operandi* of collective memory, the concept of the Holocaust, and the accepted role of the witness. Focusing on women's Holocaust testimonies has shown that there are many events that are still largely unspoken about

[20] Hart, *Return to Auschwitz*, 205.

because they are deemed incompatible with the above. Therefore, testimony is mediated by both the concerns of collective memory and the concerns of the individual survivor, the latter often writing as an act of atonement or even exorcism in an attempt to assimilate overwhelming memories.

However, as Lawrence Langer points out, the clinical formula for treating trauma is not applicable to Holocaust survivors; their narratives can rarely be liberating, for 'forgetting would be the ultimate desecration'.[21] This returns us to the point made by Anita Lasker-Wallfisch and Henry Wermuth, that the writing of testimony is a matter of duty rather than release, the primary duty being to carry on the memory of family and friends who did not survive. Some did not realize, or did not allow themselves to accept, that when they said goodbye, they would never see their families again. Wermuth writes that when he and his father said goodbye to his mother and sister, 'We did not kiss or hug unduly as we would not allow ourselves to feel this was a final goodbye.'[22] The loss of his 13-year-old sister, whom Wermuth anticipated would be the only member of the family to survive—'her young features could blend easily with any European race and her Polish was excellent'[23]—was particularly painful. His testimony is dedicated to his parents, to the 6 million Jews 'who were murdered in the cruellest manner during the greatest crime in human history . . . and especially . . . to Hanna—my beloved little sister who so wanted to live'.[24] Olga Lengyel, who believed initially that she had sent her 11-year-old son to join his brother in the children's camp, cannot forgive herself for not realizing that no such camp existed. She declares at the start of her testimony: '*Mea culpa*, my fault, *mea maxima culpa!* The world understands that I could not have known, but in my heart the terrible feeling persists that I could have, I might have, saved them.'[25] For Lengyel in particular, because her testimony is compounded by both loss and guilt, there can be neither forgetting nor a sense of liberation through the written record.

[21] Langer, *Preempting the Holocaust*, 68.
[22] Wermuth, *Breathe Deeply My Son*, 58.   [23] Ibid. 59.
[24] Ibid., dedication.   [25] Lengyel, *Five Chimneys* (1995), 11.

Some survivors include in their memoirs an acknowledgement that their survival was gained at the cost of another's life.[26] This can dramatically affect the narrative structure of testimonies. Michael Berg, aware that he was saved when a man named Alexander Donat accidentally took his place in a death brigade, wrote his memoir, *The Holocaust Kingdom*, in Donat's name, thus acknowledging both the interchangeability of fate and his debt to the dead. Primo Levi has gone further, suggesting that fate, rather than being random, was a 'process of negative selection' whereby 'The worst survived, that is, the fittest; the best all died.'[27] Levi is not suggesting that those who survived did so, like Berg, at the cost of another's life, or that survivors committed immoral acts in order to live—he himself has experienced the pain of being 'judge[d] with facile hindsight'[28]—rather, it is simply the fact that he survived while millions did not that haunts him.

'PREEMPTING THE HOLOCAUST'

While Levi was aware that his training as a chemist helped to save him by providing him with useful skills, other witnesses have tried to explain their survival by focusing on other seemingly innocuous factors. However, the fear of being 'judge[d] with facile hindsight' is so strong that many survivors feel they have to focus on the morality of their behaviour, believing that any suggestion of impropriety in order to survive detracts attention away from the real perpetrators of the Holocaust. This tendency is fuelled by the secondary literature, which attempts to analyse the experiences of survivors, and has particular potency for survivors wanting to find an explanation for their survival other than 'luck'. This provides a further example of Lawrence Langer's 'preempting the Holocaust', as outlined in the previous chapter. Terrence Des Pres, who in 1976 produced the first major study of the psychology of Holocaust survivors, like Tzvetan

---

[26] See the discussion of Frister's *The Cap or the Price of a Life* in the previous chapter.
[27] Levi, *The Drowned and the Saved*, 82.   [28] Ibid. 78.

Todorov, also writes that testimonies teach us something positive about the human spirit: 'for survivors the struggle to live—merely surviving—is rooted in, and a manifestation of, the form-conferring potency of life itself.'[29] Likewise, Martin Gilbert, who has worked with testimony extensively to produce his monumental work *The Holocaust*, finishes with the words: 'Simply to survive was a victory of the human spirit.'[30] It is perhaps not surprising, therefore, that many later testimonies are written in a similar tone. For example, Livia Bitton-Jackson writes in the Foreword to the revised edition of her memoir of Auschwitz: 'My stories are of gas chambers, shootings, electrified fences, tortures, scorching sun, mental abuse, and constant threat of death. . . . But they are also stories of faith, hope, triumph and love. They are stories of perseverance, loyalty, courage in the face of overwhelming odds and of never giving up. . . . My story is my message: Never give up.'[31]

Halina Birenbaum goes even further, suggesting that being a witness to the Holocaust—in particular to Auschwitz—has given her a certain moral authority:

The number tattooed on my left arm—personal evidence from Auschwitz—. . . for me it is a kind of certificate of maturity, from a period in which I experienced life and the world in their naked forms, a desperate struggle for a piece of bread, a breath of air and a little space, from a period in which I learned to distinguish between truth and falsehood . . . between goodness, nobility and evil baseness.[32]

Similarly, while imprisoned in Bergen-Belsen, Hanna Lévy-Hass decided: 'I shall keep firmly in my mind everything that I have seen, everything that I have experienced and learnt, everything that human nature has revealed to me. . . . I shall judge each man according to the way he has behaved, or could have behaved, in these conditions that surround us.'[33] This is difficult to square with Jean Améry's

[29] Terrence Des Pres, *The Survivor: An Anatomy of Life in the Death Camps* (Oxford, 1976), 177.   [30] M. Gilbert, *The Holocaust*, 828.
[31] Livia E. Bitton-Jackson, *I Have Lived A Thousand Years: Growing Up in the Holocaust* (London, 1999), 9.   [32] Birenbaum, *Hope is the Last to Die*, 245.
[33] Hanna Lévy-Hass, *Inside Belsen*, trans. Ronald Taylor (Brighton, 1982), 41.

declaration: 'We did not become wiser in Auschwitz, if by wisdom one understands positive knowledge of the world. We perceived nothing that we would not already have been able to perceive on the outside; not a bit of it brought us practical knowledge or guidance.'[34] It is not her tattoo that allows Birenbaum to distinguish between good and evil, but the identity of Holocaust witness and the homogenizing concerns of collective memory that instruct her to seek positive moral insights retrospectively. As Langer would point out, the moral universe in which Birenbaum struggled for life is different from that in which she is writing now. This does not mean that there was no morality in the camps, but rather that it lacked the neat separations described above.[35]

Kitty Hart does, however, provide a useful insight into how morality could be negotiated in the camps:

Very early on, Mother and I had agreed that no matter what happened, we would not play the Nazi game. Life in Auschwitz was a matter of organizing, of grabbing the bare necessities wherever you could find them. But we would never let ourselves be demoralized into cheating the living. If we took anything it must be from the dead. People today may flinch from such an idea. But what use had the dead for their clothes or pitiful rations? . . . To rob the living, or the half-living, was to speed them on the way to their death. To organize the relics of the dead was to acquire material which helped keep the living alive, and keep the half-living breathing, with just enough strength maybe to survive until the gates opened on to a freer, sweeter world outside.[36]

Hart's acknowledgement that 'people today' might find her actions difficult to understand may be traced back to her treatment immediately after liberation, when she and other survivors were suspected of surviving by ruthless means, or of doing nothing to resist their fate. Just as Hart has emphasized, 'I'm not ashamed of anything I did there and not ashamed to be alive today',[37] so other survivors have

[34] Améry, *At the Mind's Limits*, 19–20.
[35] See Levi, 'The Grey Zone', in *The Drowned and the Saved*, 22–51.
[36] Hart, *Return to Auschwitz*, 94.   [37] Ibid. 227.

responded to the accusation of passivity. For example, Trudi Levi, as well as outlining her role in sabotaging the German war effort—by leaving the caps loose on the grenades she was preparing while working as a slave-labourer in a munitions factory—adds: 'Because of these activities, I resent the allegations that we Jews went like lambs to the slaughter.'[38] Even those who lacked such an opportunity for sabotage have tried to frame their narratives around the theme of resistance by emphasizing the role of spiritual resistance in their survival. This highlights how testimony is not written in a vacuum but is mediated by concerns such as the perceived passivity of the Jewish victims of the Holocaust. For Améry it is 'Thanks to the insurgent Jews in some of the camps, above all in the Warsaw ghetto, [that] today the Jew can look at his own human face, as a human being'.[39] And Elie Wiesel goes so far as to admit that in his memoirs 'certain events will be omitted, especially those episodes that might embarrass friends, and of course, those that might damage the Jewish people'.[40]

BEARING WITNESS TO 'THE HOLOCAUST'

It is not just for themselves that survivors want to dispute unjust accusations; they also want to protect the memory of the dead, and apart from remembering individual relatives, to honour the 6 million. The task is so great that certain figures have become emblematic. A particularly poignant image is that of the little boy photographed in the Warsaw ghetto with his hands in the air; for many, this photograph symbolizes the Jewish children murdered during the Holocaust. Yala Korwin sums up its legacy in the following poem:

> Your image will remain with us,
> and grow and grow
> to immense proportions,

[38] Trudi Levi, *A Cat Called Adolf* (London, 1995), 22.
[39] Jean Améry, *Radical Humanism: Selected Essays*, trans. Sidney Rosenfeld and Stella P. Rosenfeld (Bloomington, Ind., 1980).
[40] Elie Wiesel, *All Rivers Run to the Sea: Memoirs* (New York, 1995), 17.

to haunt the callous world,
to accuse it, with ever stronger voice
in the name of the million
youngsters who lie,
pitiful ragdolls their eyes forever closed.[41]

Gisella Perl could be talking about this image and other photographs of those we now know to be dead when she warns: 'The dead are speaking to you here. The dead who do not ask you to avenge them but only to remember them and to be watchful that no more innocent victims of German inhumanity ever swell their ranks.'[42] By holding his hands up, the little boy reminds people that the memory of the Holocaust is not just of the victims but also of the perpetrators. More importantly, the photographic image of the child becomes a way of (re)-humanizing the dead.

The story of Mala Zimetbaum and Edward Galiński's escape from Auschwitz also features prominently in many memoirs, as if to emphasize the dignity of the dead. On 24 June 1944, Mala Zimetbaum, a Jewish girl from Belgium, escaped from Birkenau with her Polish boyfriend Edward Galiński. Zimetbaum's position as *Lauferin* (runner)—she was fluent in Flemish, French, German, Polish, and Yiddish—gave her access to important information in the camp, and she was often able to remove names from selection lists. The pair managed to escape using stolen SS uniforms and identity documents. Although there is little conclusive information about their escape, prisoner rumours suggest that Zimetbaum managed to steal documents giving details about the gassings, which she intended to smuggle to the outside world. Accounts vary as to how they were captured, but it is thought that approximately two weeks after their

---

[41] Yala Korwin, 'The Little Boy with His Hands Up', in *To Tell the Story: Poems of the Holocaust* (New Haven, 1987), 75. Cf. the discussion of the photograph by Henry Rapport in *Is There Truth in Art?* (Ithaca, NY, 1997). For a discussion of photographs of the Holocaust as powerful instruments of 'postmemory', see Marianne Hirsch, 'Past Lives: Postmemories in Exile', *Poetics Today*, 17/4 (Winter 1996), 659–86; *idem*, 'Projected Memory: Holocaust Photographs in Personal and Public Fantasy', in Bal *et al.* (eds.), *Acts of Memory*, 3–23; and *idem*, *Family Frames: Photography, Narrative, and Postmemory* (Cambridge, Mass., 1997).   [42] Perl, *I Was a Doctor in Auschwitz*, 12.

escape, Zimetbaum and Galiński were arrested and returned to Auschwitz to be publicly executed.[43] The Yad Vashem archives contain numerous testimonies recording Zimetbaum slapping the face of the SS man about to hang her before slashing her wrists with a razor blade that she had concealed. Although there can be no exact account of her final moments, the significance of the story is clearly that Mala Zimetbaum, a young girl, in refusing to die the death the SS had planned for her, was able to achieve heroism.

The story of Galiński and Zimetbaum also allows witnesses to have some shared temporal point of contact. It helps to create a sense of 'witness' as a shared identity. A further example of this is the way in which many survivors write that they met the infamous Dr Mengele on the arrival ramp at Auschwitz, regardless of whether they knew his identity at the time. Judith Magyar Isaacson writes in reference to the SS officer who decided whether she was to live or die: 'I shall call him Dr. Mengele, because of what I've read of his role, and because several of my former comrades recognized him later from his photo. But personally, I did not think to study his features and I cannot be sure.'[44]

In a similar vein, the time spent in Auschwitz has now become the focal point of many survivor testimonies, regardless of whether they spent longer periods in less well-known concentration camps. This leaves the survivor who experienced the war away from the famous sites of Jewish suffering in a particular predicament. For those who survived the war by passing themselves off as Aryan, or who witnessed mass shootings, not only is their position as witness to the Holocaust less identifiable than that of those who survived the camps, but they also lack many of the shared experiences to which concentration camp survivors appeal.

Nevertheless, the post-war role of the survivor as witness demands that survivors bear witness to the magnitude of the suffering; but, as

[43] See M. Gilbert, *The Holocaust*, 695. Cf. Giza Weisblum, 'The Escape and Death of the "Runner" Mala Zimmetbaum', in Suhl (ed.), *They Fought Back*, 182–281.

[44] Isaacson, *Seed of Sarah*, 84.

Primo Levi wrote, 'we, the survivors, are not the true witnesses'.[45] Henry Wermuth adds:

How could I even attempt to describe all the wretched misery, the death-cries of millions of innocent people, the open and secret tortures, the agony of parents seeing their babies dragged away and thrown like discarded rubbish on to lorries, sometimes alive, sometimes killed, their limbs torn apart or their heads smashed in? How could I, or anyone put into words the last moments of even one family inside a gas chamber, stripped, degraded, humiliated, embracing and looking into each other's terrified eyes, the strongest of them forced to see their loved ones dying slowly and in agony.[46]

Wermuth cannot put into words the last moments of a family inside a gas chamber, because he has not been there; he is aware of this and reminds his readers: 'the closest witnesses to violent and forcible death are dead.'[47] This points to a very important historiographical issue: in wanting to bear witness to the Holocaust, survivors have to refer to matters outside their own experience. As seen in the previous chapter, the prisoners of the *Sonderkommando* were sentenced to death on account of their very specific knowledge of the undressing rooms, the gas chambers, and the crematoria. Filip Müller, who worked in crematorium I at Birkenau from May 1942 to July 1943, was one of the very few who survived.[48] He describes himself as 'the oldest member of the Auschwitz and Birkenau *Sonderkommando* and the only one to have lived through everything'.[49] Therefore, the vast majority of prisoners would find resonance with Wermuth's reminder to his readers that '[b]eing in these camps does not, contrary to the assumptions of many, imply that I knew all and everything there was

---

[45] Levi, *The Drowned and the Saved*, 63. Levi also notes that 'the history of the Lagers has been written almost exclusively by those who like myself, never fathomed them to the bottom' (ibid. 6).   [46] Wermuth, *Breathe Deeply My Son*, 1.
[47] Ibid. 3.
[48] The Jewish doctor Miklos Nyiszli, cited in Ch. 2, is another *Sonderkommando* prisoner who survived and produced a memoir (see Nyiszli, *Auschwitz*).
[49] Cited in Ota Kraus and Erich Kulka, *The Death Factory: Documents on Auschwitz*, trans. Stephen Jolly (Oxford, 1966), 156; originally published in Czech as *Továrna na smrt: document o Ozvetimi* (Prague, 1946). Kraus and Kulka worked as craftsmen and repairmen in Auschwitz, and assembled a collection of accounts of life in Auschwitz.

to know about them. . . . My overriding concern was to stay alive.'[50] Sara Selver-Urbach, who spent a week in Auschwitz, admits that she 'even lacked the time to become convinced that the crematoriums with their smoking chimneys were indeed consecrated to the burning of human beings'.[51] She explains that it was only after liberation that she and her friends learnt 'the total horror of such places as Auschwitz and Treblinka and Majdanek, both from survivors of those death camps who'd witnessed these horrors with their own eyes, and from written reports in newspapers and books as well as from various exhibitions'.[52]

Even when describing their own experiences, survivors often have to read testimonies and works of history to fill the gaps in their memories; otherwise they risk making factual mistakes. This is illustrated by an example supplied by Dori Laub, describing the testimony of a woman who witnessed the *Sonderkommando* uprising at Birkenau: 'All of a sudden . . . we saw four chimneys going up in flames, exploding. The flames shot into the sky, people were running. It was unbelievable.'[53] However, only one chimney was blown up, and later the woman's videotaped testimony was presented at a conference and provoked considerable debate among historians who claimed that this inaccuracy called into the question the veracity of the woman's testimony in general. But, as Laub pointed out: 'The woman was testifying . . . not to the number of chimneys blown up, but to something else, more radical, more crucial: the reality of an unimaginable occurrence. One chimney blown up in Auschwitz was as incredible as four. . . . She testified to the breakage of a framework. That was historical truth.'[54]

While the woman described by Laub might have been prevented from making this error had she read other testimonies, conversely, there is the possibility of receiving false information from them. Selver-Urbach, who admits that much of her understanding of the Holocaust was achieved after the war, writes that as well as learning

[50] Wermuth, *Breathe Deeply My Son*, 139.
[51] Selver-Urbach, *Through the Window of My Home*, 125. [52] Ibid. 188.
[53] Felman and Laub, *Testimony*, 59. [54] Ibid. 60.

about the gas chambers and crematoria at Auschwitz, '[a] grisly detail about life in the ghetto was revealed as well'.[55] She explains to her readers: 'The green soap that had been so plentiful and had smelled so unpleasantly—the soap imprinted with the initials R.J.F.—had been processed from the bodies of cremated Jews! The initials stood for *Reines Juden Fett* (pure Jew fat).'[56]

In fact, Yad Vashem officially states that the German concentration camp authorities at no time made soap from the dead bodies. During the war, when Germany suffered a shortage of fats, and the production of soap came under government supervision, bars of soap were imprinted with the initials R.I.F., a German acronym for 'pure industrial fat'. A few people mistakenly read the letters as R.J.F., and the rumour spread among the ghettos. Evidence suggests that Nazi officials, including the governor of Poland, Hans Frank, also believed the soap to be the product of human fats. Before the end of the war, a laboratory in Danzig had begun conducting experiments to find out whether human fats could be used in food production. Subsequently, Yad Vashem concluded that there was no such thing as Jewish soap.[57]

The problem of the factual accuracy of testimony was also considered in the ghettos, where witnesses were living through the events they were writing about. In the Warsaw ghetto, Chaim Kaplan wrote: 'I risk my life with my writing, but my abilities are limited; I don't know all the facts; those that I do know may not be sufficiently clear, and many of them I write on the basis of rumors whose accuracy I cannot guarantee.'[58] Kaplan decided that although it was ultimately impossible to meet Ringelblum's criterion of 'a photographically true and detailed picture of what the Jewish population had to experience, to think and to suffer',[59] he could be true to the essence of their suffering, thereby reaching a similar definition of historical truth to that of Laub: 'But for the sake of truthfulness, I do not require individual facts, but rather manifestations of the fruits of a great many facts that

---

[55] Selver-Urbach, *Through the Window of My Home*, 222.   [56] Ibid.

[57] The history of this myth can be found in Segev, *Seventh Million*, 184.

[58] Kaplan, *Scroll of Agony*, 30.   [59] Ringelblum, 'O.S.', 8.

leave their impression on the people's opinions, on their mood and morale. And I can guarantee the factualness of these manifestations because I dwell among my people and behold their misery and their soul's torments.'[60]

In a similar vein, Charlotte Delbo has written: 'Today, I am not sure that what I wrote is true. I am certain it is truthful.'[61] Sim Kessel echoes this, stating: 'On the ground of truth or sincerity I could not I think be reproached. But on many points I wanted to be more precise.'[62] Kaplan is writing from inside the event, and Delbo and Kessel after it. Delbo and Kessel, although privy to the information and sense of perspective which Kaplan never lived to experience, have to contend with the contingencies and inevitable limitations of memory. As Primo Levi writes: 'The memories which lie within us are not carved in stone; not only do they tend to become erased as the years go by, but often they change, or even increase by incorporating extraneous features.'[63]

A common preoccupation of Holocaust survivors is the fear that they will not be believed. In Chapter 2 Szymon Laks described how an SS guard told him that even in the unlikely event that he did survive, no one would believe his stories, and therefore the Germans would never be brought to justice. Countless testimonies tell cautionary tales of how during the Holocaust many refused to believe witness accounts. For example, Elie Wiesel's *Night* tells of the widespread disbelief with which Moché the Beadle was met when he attempted to warn the Jews of Sighet of their impending doom. Moché, who was expelled in 1942 as a foreign Jew, returned after several months to relate his escape from a Gestapo massacre of Jews in the Polish forests. He was not believed. While he pleaded 'Jews, listen to me. . . . Only listen to me,'[64] his words were dismissed as the ravings of a lunatic. The 15-year-old narrator of *Night* himself wondered: 'Why are you so anxious that people should believe what you say? In your place, I

---

[60] Kaplan, *Scroll of Agony*, 30.   [61] Delbo, *None of Us Will Return*, 1.

[62] Sim Kessel, *Hanged at Auschwitz*, trans. Melville and Delight Wallace (New York, 1972), 11; originally published in French as *Pendu à Auschwitz* (Paris, 1970).

[63] Levi, *The Drowned and the Saved*, 11.   [64] Wiesel, *Night*, 5.

shouldn't care whether they believed me or not.'[65] However, as Wiesel
and other survivors were later to learn, even after liberation, being
believed was extremely important.[66] The prevalent notion that
survivors were neglected in the immediate post-war period fuels the
general understanding that responding to the stories of survivors has
moral significance. For example, referring to their post-war treatment, Wiesel has stated that the suicides of Tadeusz Borowski, Joseph
Wulf, Paul Célan,[67] and Benno Werzberg condemn society, for it
carries out the task that the killers did not complete.[68] Wiesel de-
historicizes the category of perpetrator by suggesting that it is not a
historically contingent position limited to the events of the
Holocaust, but can be applied post-Holocaust, to those who do not
treat survivors in an ethical manner.

These sorts of concerns were evident in the case of the fraudulent
testimony *Fragments: Memories of a Childhood, 1939–1948*, written
by Binjamin Wilkomirski, which told of his recollections of being
separated from his family and friends and imprisoned in the
Majdanek death camp when just 3 or 4 years old.[69] Even those who
were suspicious of Wilkomirski's story—who believed that it was
unlikely that such a young child would have survived Majdanek—
were reluctant to publicly accuse a so-called Holocaust survivor of
lying and face the consequences. Additionally, while the book is
written from the standpoint of a child, supposedly to allow the
reader to view the experiences through a child's eyes, the voice of the
adult author, which cannot help but infiltrate the text, provides an

[65] Wiesel, *Night*, 5.

[66] For a discussion of the role of the listener in Holocaust survivor testimony, see Dori
Laub, 'Bearing Witness, or the Vicissitudes of Listening', in Felman and Laub (eds.),
Testimony, 57–74.

[67] Paul Célan famously wrote 'Niemand zeugt für den Zeugen' (No one bears witness
for the witness).

[68] Wiesel, *A Jew Today*, 219. Cf. Wiesel's thoughts on Primo Levi, Jerzy Kozinski, and
Piotr Rawicz in the chapter entitled 'Three Suicides', in Elie Wiesel, *And the Sea is Never
Full*, trans. Marion Wiesel (New York, 1999), 345–51.

[69] Binjamin Wilkomirski, *Fragments: Memories of a Childhood, 1939–1948*, trans.
Carol Brown Janeway (London, 1996); originally published in German as *Bruchstücke:
Aus einer Kindheit 1939–1948* (Frankfurt, 1995).

additional theme: the ongoing trauma of a survivor who has been forced to suppress his agonizing memories of the Holocaust—something to which the book constantly makes reference. At the end of the book Wilkomirski explains that writing it was an attempt to set himself 'free'.[70] He states a further reason for writing the book: 'the hope that perhaps other people in the same situation would find the necessary support and strength to cry out . . . so that they too could learn that there really are people today who will take them seriously, and who want to listen and understand'.[71] *Fragments* received a great deal of public commendation; as well as receiving endorsements by prominent survivors, it was translated very quickly into a dozen languages, and was awarded such honours as the Jewish Quarterly Prize in London, the Prix de Mémoire de la Shoah in Paris, and the National Jewish Book Award in New York, where finalists included Alfred Kazin and Elie Wiesel. As a child who survived the horrors of the Holocaust and committed himself to helping other child survivors of the camps, Wilkomirksi enjoyed a great deal of respect.[72]

However, Daniel Ganzfried, a Swiss writer and son of Holocaust survivors, researched Wilkomirski's past and wrote an article accusing him of having forged his identity. Ganzfried discovered a birth certificate and school documents which showed that the Latvian-born, Jewish Wilkomirski was in reality Bruno Grosjean (later Dösseker), an illegitimate Protestant child born in neutral Switzerland, whose Swiss mother had placed him in a children's home before giving him up for adoption in 1945.[73] Since Ganzfried's exposure of Wilkomirski, further attempts have been made to discover why

---

[70] Ibid. 155.   [71] Ibid.

[72] It was not until May 1991 and the 'First International Gathering of Children Hidden during World War Two' in New York City that such experiences were brought into the public eye. On the experiences of children who survived the Holocaust, see Jane Marks, *The Hidden Children: The Secret Survivors of the Holocaust* (London, 1993), and Paul Valent, *Child Survivors: Adults Living with Childhood Trauma* (Port Melbourne, Victoria, 1994).

[73] Daniel Ganzfried, 'Die Geliehene Holocaust-Biographie—The Purloined Holocaust Biography', trans. Katherine Quimby Johnson, *Die Weltwoche*, 27 Aug. 1998.

somebody who had not lived through the events of the Holocaust would wish to adopt the identity of a concentration camp survivor.[74] The studies are based on extensive interviews and involve meticulous research. While the authors clearly state that they are not psychologists, and that it is difficult to form any conclusive opinions as to why somebody would decide to take on such a role, they convincingly suggest that Wilkomirski decided consciously or subconsciously to translate traumatic childhood memories into a historical event with collective significance. This would explain the seeming sincerity of the emotions, which appear in a narrative we now know to be false. As the writer Elena Lappin, who was the editor of *The Jewish Quarterly* magazine when it awarded Wilkomirski the prize, notes: 'the similarities between *Fragments*, the early life of Benjamin Wilkomirski, and what we know of the childhood of the real Bruno Grosjean are too striking to resist.'[75] For Lappin, whose observations are extremely similar to those of the historian Stefan Maechler, Bruno Dösseker in wishing to 'remove himself as far as possible from his native environment . . . declared himself a Jew', and to him 'being a Jew was synonymous with the Holocaust'.[76] More than this, Dösseker was responding to a specific representation of the Holocaust: one in which victims are sharply differentiated from perpetrators, and where good and evil or innocence and guilt are easily distinguished. It could be suggested that the appeal of *Fragments* was in large measure due to the desire to view the Holocaust along such sharply dichotomized lines. Wilkomirski as a young, suffering child, like the little boy photographed in the Warsaw ghetto, could not fail to illicit the total, unquestioning moral support of his readers. Moreover, in reading of his continued suffering post-war, it appears that readers wished to believe that their belated response to a young child's suffering would

---

[74] See esp. Philip Gourevitch, 'The Memory Thief', *New Yorker*, 14 June 1999, 48–68; Elena Lappin, 'The Man with Two Heads', *Granta*, 66 (Summer 1999), 7–65; and Stefan Maechler, *The Wilkomirski Affair: A Study in Biographical Truth*, trans. John E. Woods (New York, 2001). A BBC1 television documentary entitled *Child of the Death Camps: Truth and Lies*, Wednesday, 3 Nov. 1999, also attempted to throw some light on the matter.
[75] Lappin, 'Man with Two Heads', 63.   [76] Ibid.

in some way protect him from further hurt.[77] It is significant that even after the book was declared fictional, withdrawn from book-shops, and dropped by publishers, it has continued to attract readers eager to believe its veracity. For them, responding to Wilkomirksi has become an act of faith. However, the incident raises serious questions regarding the use and accuracy of witness testimonies.

THE REPRESENTATION OF EXPERIENCE

It is not just individual facts that are hard to recall; emotions too can be difficult to retrieve. Charlotte Delbo, a non-Jew who was deported to Auschwitz as a member of the French Resistance, writes of the split between experience and representation:

[W]hen I talk to you about Auschwitz, it is not from deep memory that my words issue. They come from external memory . . . from intellectual memory, the memory connected with the thinking processes. Deep memory preserves sensations, physical imprints. It is the memory of the senses. For it isn't words that are swollen with emotional charge. Otherwise, someone who has been tortured by thirst for weeks on end could never again say, 'I'm thirsty. How about a cup of tea.' This word has also split in two. Thirst has turned back into a word for commonplace use. But if I dream of the thirst I suffered in Birkenau, I once again see the person I was, haggard, halfway crazed, near to collapse; I physically feel that real thirst and it is an atrocious nightmare.[78]

Although Delbo re-experiences the horror of Auschwitz in her dreams, when speaking, she finds language inadequate to commun-icate her experiences. As the scholar Cathy Caruth explains, the trans-lation of traumatic memory into narrative memory means that what is being remembered loses its 'essential incomprehensibility, the face of its *affront to understanding*'.[79] The very act of writing changes a witness's relationship to their experiences. It translates the extreme

---

[77] For a discussion of the contemporary urge to view experience in terms of trauma and the pitfalls of 'collective' and 'individual' trauma as a dominant frame of reference, see Stargardt, *Witnesses of War*, 9–10.   [78] Delbo, *Days and Memory*, 3–4.
[79] Cathy Caruth (ed.), *Trauma: Explorations in Memory* (Baltimore, 1995), 154.

into the familiar. Lasker-Wallfisch writes both of the difficulty of conveying the extremity of her suffering in a way that will make sense to her readers and also her unease in doing so: 'I don't know how to describe *hunger*, not the type everybody is familiar with when a meal has been skipped but hunger that causes actual *pain*; or what it is to be *cold* without any prospect of ever becoming warm again; or the sensation of *real fear* and total misery.'[80] In making her testimony transmittable, Lasker-Wallfisch has to use words which evoke shared human experience, such as 'pain' or 'cold', but, obviously uncomfortable about doing so, she feels the need to counteract their familiar usage through the use of italics.[81] She believes it is impossible to represent the events of the Holocaust, because their horror is beyond comprehension. This is what Primo Levi meant when he spoke of 'the ineffable universe of the camps'.[82] However, the role of the survivor also demands that the events be told. This aporia is illustrative of what philosopher Jean-François Lyotard has termed 'the différend', which is the 'unstable state and instant of language wherein something which must be put into phrases cannot yet be'.[83]

In order to stress the unique and ineffable nature of their Holocaust experiences, witnesses invariably end up drawing upon inherited categories of comprehension. Lasker-Wallfisch unconsciously validates James Young's assertion that '[n]arrative testimony documents *not* the experience it relates, but rather the conceptual presuppositions through which the narrator has apprehended experience'.[84] Young argues that, once written, the original authorial

[80] Lasker-Wallfisch, *Inherit the Truth*, 16.

[81] Primo Levi has stressed the need to represent the Holocaust in easily accessible writing: 'since we the living are not alone, we must not write as if we were alone. As long as we live we have a responsibility: we must answer for what we write, word by word, and make sure that every word reaches its target' (Primo Levi, 'On Obscure Writing', in *Other People's Trades*, trans. Raymond Rosenthal (London, 1995), 161–2; originally published in Italian as, *L'altrui mestiere* (Turin, 1985)).

[82] Primo Levi, 'Revisiting the Camps', in James E. Young (ed.), *The Art of Memory: Holocaust Memorials in History* (Munich, 1994), 185.

[83] Jean-François Lyotard, *The Différend: Phrases in Dispute*, trans. Georges van den Abbeele (Manchester, 1988), 13.

[84] James E. Young, 'Interpreting Literary Testimony: A Preface to Rereading Holocaust Diaries and Memoirs', *New Literary History*, 18/2 (Winter 1987), 420.

intention when writing a Holocaust testimony is quickly disseminated into all manner of other meanings. Meaning is not necessarily controlled by what the writer declares is his or her aim or objective, and the text increasingly becomes a substitute for the survivors as they leave us. The words they write will take the place of the past, and it is these words, rather than the events themselves, which will be remembered.[85] What Young is alluding to is the split between experience and its subsequent representation. Although, as critical theorist Theodor Adorno reminds us, the original experiences of survivors, like memories, 'cannot be preserved in drawers and pigeon-holes; in them the past is indissolubly woven into the present',[86] it is wrong to deny the essential dialectical relationship between the concepts 'through which the narrator has apprehended experience' and experiences *per se*. To split them apart suggests that the events have a life independent of their being experienced. Indeed, Young suggests a tenuous link between representation and the events themselves. While testimony is certainly mediated by the post-war comprehension and/or concept of the Holocaust, survivors' original understandings of the events were not wholly inadequate to comprehend or judge the horrors for themselves. That the Holocaust cannot be re-presented but must be represented is one of its many contradictions. To argue that the Holocaust defies representation is also to argue that it defies comprehension; contradictorily, two judgements have been made: the severity of the Holocaust's crimes, and that this severity cannot be uttered or comprehended.[87] Language may not be adequate to convey the horrors of the Holocaust, but this does not mean that nothing can be said, or that the events cannot be comprehended. It is certainly a difficulty faced by survivors who believe that it is the words they write which form a memorial not only for themselves but also for those who did not survive.

---

[85] See Hilberg, *Politics of Memory*.
[86] Theodor W. Adorno, *Minima Moralia: Reflections from Damaged Life*, trans. E. F. N. Jephcott (London, 1978), 166.
[87] Mark Greenaway, 'The Entelechy of Auschwitz' (unpublished MS, 1995).

THE LIMITS OF REPRESENTATION

At least two generations of postmodern philosophers have profoundly affected how the Holocaust has been considered: Maurice Blanchot's *The Writing of the Disaster*;[88] Jean-François Lyotard's *The Différend: Phrases in Dispute*; the writings of Jacques Derrida and Emmanuel Levinas;[89] and, more recently, Philippe Lacoue-Labarthe and Jean-Luc Nancy.[90] The most influential theme has been Lyotard's claim that the Holocaust defies representation: it is 'not sublatable into a concept',[91] and, 'with Auschwitz something new has happened in history . . . a différend is born from a wrong and is signalled by a silence'.[92] These writers have had a significant influence on survivors.[93] Elie Wiesel believes that the only way to preserve the inexplicability of the original event is through silence: 'by its uniqueness the holocaust defies literature',[94] and 'Auschwitz cannot be explained . . . the Holocaust transcends history'.[95] Arguably, he is also in danger of turning the extremity of the violence into mysticism when he states:

Even if you studied all the documentation, even if you listened to all the testimonies, visited all the camps and museums and read all the diaries, you would not be able to even approach the portal of that eternal night. That is the tragedy of the survivor's mission. He must tell a story that cannot be told.

[88] Maurice Blanchot, *The Writing of the Disaster*, trans. Ann Smock (Lincoln, Nebr., 1995).

[89] See e.g. Jacques Derrida, 'Force of Law: The Mystical Foundation of Authority', *The Cardozo Law Review, Destruction and the Possibility of Justice*, 11/5–6 (July–Aug. 1990), 973–1039, and Emmanuel Levinas, 'Ethics as First Philosophy', in Sean Hand (ed.), *The Levinas Reader* (Oxford, 1989), 75–87.

[90] See Philippe Lacoue-Labarthe, *Heidegger, Art and Politics: The Fiction of the Political*, trans. Chris Turner (Oxford, 1990), and Jean-Luc Nancy, 'Our History', *Diacritics*, 20/3 (Fall 1999), 97–115.   [91] Lyotard, *Différend*, 88.

[92] Ibid. 57.

[93] For a fascinating discussion of the relationship between postmodern approaches to the Holocaust and testimony, see Robert Eaglestone, *The Holocaust and the Postmodern* (Oxford, 2004).

[94] Cited in Alan L. Berger, 'Elie Wiesel', in Steven T. Katz (ed.), *Interpreters of Judaism in the Late Twentieth Century* (Washington, 1993), 377.

[95] Elie Wiesel, 'Trivialising the Holocaust: Semi-Fact and Semi-Fiction', *The New York Times*, 2/1 (16 April 1978), 29.

He must deliver a message that cannot be delivered. . . . In this sense the enemy, ironically, realized his goal. Since he extended the crime beyond all bounds, and since there is no way to cross those bounds except through language, it is impossible to tell the full story of the crime.[96]

While Wiesel as a witness believes that silence is the only true response to the Holocaust, his dual status as a victim means that he cannot abandon what he has described as 'the obsession to tell the tale'.[97] Moreover, Wiesel's memoir *Night* tells us that it was Wiesel's strength of will that allowed him to survive, and indicates that he already knew 'the role of the survivor was to testify'. However, he asks: 'how is one to say, how is one to communicate that which by its very nature defies language?'[98] Survivors such as Wiesel believe that it is impossible to represent the Holocaust, because to do so is sacrilegious. Wiesel maintains that the Holocaust is a sacred event, and that its significance is 'equal to the revelation at Sinai' in its religious importance.[99] He also believes that it is impossible to fathom God's presence at Auschwitz, because, as Lyotard has argued, the Holocaust represents an epistemological crisis.

Wiesel has afforded himself the ability to judge the severity of the Holocaust's crimes and at the same time judge that that severity cannot be uttered or comprehended. For Wiesel, testimony is the only way of reaching this unreachable event because it is given by survivors, who, as the living dead, possess an epistemological, if not ontological authority. In Wiesel's opinion, 'no one who has not experienced the event will ever be able to understand it.'[100] Wiesel exempts testimony from the contingencies of representation; rather than a witness writing testimony, he feels himself to *be* testimony. He further argues: 'what happened at Auschwitz should be conveyed in the same manner that the Talmud was taught, "transmitted from

---

[96] Elie Wiesel, 'Questions That Remain Unanswered', in *Papers for Research on the Holocaust*, 7 (Haifa University, 1989), 4. Cited in Segev, *Seventh Million*, 158.
[97] Harry James Cargas (ed.), *Harry James Cargas in Conversation with Elie Wiesel* (New York, 1976), 87.   [98] Wiesel, *A Jew Today*, 235.
[99] Elie Wiesel, 'Words from a Witness', *Comparative Judaism*, 21 (Spring 1967), 43.
[100] Elie Wiesel, 'Trivialising Memory', and 'Testimony at the Barbie Trial', in *From the Kingdom of Memory: Reminiscences*, trans. Marion Wiesel (New York, 1990), 166, 187.

mouth to ear, from eye to eye".'[101] The act of witnessing is part of the Jewish tradition, the tradition by which one reaffirms oneself as a Jew: the Ten Commandments are referred to as 'the two tables of the testimony',[102] and the observance of the Sabbath bears witness to the fact that it was God, rather than man, who created the world in six days.

In the Torah the command to bear witness is explicitly stated: 'And he is a witness whether he has seen or known of it; if he does not utter it, then he shall bear his iniquity' (Lev. 5: 1).[103] Not to bear witness would be an act of betrayal. Bruno Bettleheim, who survived Buchenwald and Dachau, and began writing soon after arriving in the USA in 1942, writes: 'If we remain silent, then we perform exactly as the Nazis wanted: behave as if it never did happen.'[104] This is supported by Anita Lasker-Wallfisch, who believes that it is 'almost a criminal offence not to speak for the dead who can never be heard'.[105] Other witnesses, such as Samuel Drix, write of bearing witness as a 'sacred duty I owe to the martyrs of Janowska camp and Ghetto Lwów so that they should not be forgotten'.[106]

If the argument that the Holocaust defies comprehension is accepted, and Wiesel is correct in his assertion that what happened at Auschwitz is 'a mystery begotten by the dead',[107] then it is not just his commitment to bear witness that is sacred, but testimonies themselves take on a sacred status.[108] While Wiesel's theological interpretations of

---

[101] Elie Wiesel, *One Generation After*, trans. Lily Edelman and Elie Wiesel (New York, 1970), 235.

[102] It is written: 'When He made an end of speaking with Moses upon Mount Sinai, He gave unto him the two tables of testimony, tables of stone, written with the finger of God' (Exod. 31: 18, RSV).

[103] Cited in Young, *Writing and Rewriting the Holocaust*, 18.

[104] Bruno Bettelheim, *Surviving and Other Essays* (New York, 1960), 97.

[105] Lasker-Wallfisch, 'Taking Testimonies Forward'.

[106] Samuel Drix, *Witness to Annihilation: Surviving the Holocaust* (London, 1964), p. xv.

[107] Wiesel, *One Generation After*, 43.

[108] For an essay specifically concerned with the theme of Holocaust testimony as sacred text, see Isabel Wollaston, ' "Memory and Monument": Holocaust Testimony as Sacred Text', in Jon Davies and Isabel Wollaston (eds.), *The Sociology of Sacred Texts* (Sheffield, 1993), 37–44. Cf. Wollaston's study of the various ways in which the Holocaust is understood and remembered: *idem*, *A War against Memory? The Future of Holocaust Remembrance* (London, 1996).

testimony are widely known, it should be noted that, despite his famous declaration ('There is Auschwitz, so there cannot be God'[109]), Primo Levi suggests that testimonies of witnesses can be understood as 'stories of a new Bible'. Writing of a fellow prisoner he states:

He told me his history, and today I have forgotten it, but it was certainly a sorrowful, cruel and moving story; because so are all our stories, hundreds of thousands of stories, all different and all full of tragic, disturbing necessity. We tell them to each other in the evening, and they take place in Norway, Italy, Algeria, the Ukraine and are simple and incomprehensible like the stories in the Bible. But are they not themselves stories of a new Bible?[110]

However, the 'new Bible' of which Levi speaks is very different from the traditional Hebrew Scriptures. In his poem 'Shemà', which prefaces *If This is a Man*, Levi shows how the traditional injunction to remember God is replaced by one to remember Auschwitz.[111] The last eight lines of the poem are as follows:

> I commend these words to you.
> Carve them in your hearts
> At home, in the street,
> Going to bed, rising;
> Repeat them to your children,
>   Or may your house fall apart,
>   May illness impede you,
>   May your children turn their faces from you.[112]

Levi believes that the language of Holocaust testimony, like that of the Bible, is 'simple and incomprehensible', and that it reveals

---

[109] Cited in Ferdinando Camon, *Conversations with Primo Levi*, trans. John Shepley (Marlboro, Vt., 1989), 68.

[110] Levi, *Survival in Auschwitz*, 59. Cf. *idem*, *If This is a Man*, 71–2.

[111] In the Shemà it is written: 'Hear, O Israel: the Lord is Our God, the Lord is alone. You shall love the Lord your God with all your heart, and with all your soul, and with all your might. Keep these words that I am commanding to you today in your heart. Recite them to your children and talk about them when you sit in your house, when you are away, when you lie down and when you rise. Bind them as a sign on your hand, fix them as an emblem on your forehead, and write them on the doorposts of your house and on your gates' (Deut. 6: 4–9; as trans. in *Daily Prayer Book: Ha-Siddur Ha-Shalem*, trans. Philip Birnbaum (New York, 1949)).   [112] Levi, *If This is a Man*, 17.

something completely new. Like Anita Lasker-Wallfisch, Levi believes that the concentration camps demand a new language:

Just as our hunger is not that feeling of missing a meal, so our way of being cold has need of a new word. We say 'hunger', we say 'tiredness,' 'fear,' 'pain,' we say 'winter' and they are different things. They are free words, created and used by free men who lived in comfort and suffering in their homes. If the Lagers had lasted longer a new, harsh language would have been born; and only this language could express what it means to toil the whole day in the wind, with the temperature below freezing, wearing only a shirt, under-pants, cloth jacket and trousers, and in one's body nothing but weakness, hunger and knowledge of the end drawing nearer.[113]

For Levi, there is an unbridgeable gap between the world of the concentration and death camps and the world of the interpreter. He even casts doubt on his own authority to speak for the dead and his ability to act as a 'true' witness. For Wiesel, the gap must be approached with 'fear and trembling'.[114] He explains:

Now, one generation after the event, one can still say—or one can already say—that what is called the literature of the Holocaust does not exist, cannot exist. It is a contradiction in terms, as is the philosophy, the theology, the psychology of the Holocaust. Auschwitz negates all systems, opposes all doctrines. . . . The past belongs to the dead, and the survivor does not recognize himself in the words linking him to them. A novel about Treblinka is either not a novel or not about Treblinka; for Treblinka means death—absolute death—death of language and of the imagination.[115]

This position is also adopted by the literary critic George Steiner:

These books and the documents that have survived are not for 'review'. Not unless 'review' signifies, as perhaps it should in these instances, a 'seeing-again', over and over. As in some Borges fable, the only completely decent 'review' of the Warsaw Diary or of Elie Wiesel's *Night* would be to re-copy the book, line by line, pausing at the names of the dead and the names of the children as the orthodox scribe pauses, when recopying the Bible, at the

[113] Levi, *Survival in Auschwitz*, 112–13.   [114] Wiesel, *A Jew Today*, 237.
[115] Elie Wiesel, 'Art and Culture after the Holocaust', in Eva Fleischner (ed.), *Auschwitz: Beginnings of a New Era?* (Hoboken, NJ, 1977), 405.

hallowed name of god. Until we know many of the words by *heart* (knowledge deeper than mind) and could repeat a few at the break of morning to remind ourselves that we live *after*, that the end of the day may bring 'inhuman trial or a remembrance stronger than death'.[116]

Why then, it might be asked, did Ringelblum and the staff of *Oneg Shabbat* take such pains to collect material for future historians, and why did prisoners in the concentration camps risk their lives to bear witness? Those writing in the Warsaw ghetto were also concerned with the inadequacy of words to express what they were witnessing. An anonymous contributor to *Oneg Shabbat* wrote: 'The desire to write is as strong as the repugnance of words. We hate them, because they too often served as a cover for emptiness and meanness.'[117] Steiner is not advocating that we do not respond to the catastrophe, but rather that we are careful in our response, avoid superfluous comment or empty words, and recognize the difficulty of representation. For Wiesel, this translates as meaning that only those who were there can write about the Holocaust: 'any survivor', he insists, 'has more to say than all the historians combined about what happened'.[118] He explains: 'facts, on which historians base their research, are only facts, whereas survivors reveal the truth.'[119]

This sentiment is repeated by many other survivors, including Livia Bitton-Jackson: 'Only one who was there can truly tell the tale. And I was there.'[120] Such claims to ownership of the truth are problematic, though, for survivors can ultimately know the truth only of their own experience. For example, knowledge of the concentration camps was dependent on a prisoner's position within a particular camp's structure, and was therefore limited to an individual's subjective experience. Wiesel himself must have realized this, for he stated

116 George Steiner, *Language and Silence: Essays 1958–1966* (London, 1967), 193.
117 Kermish (ed.), *To Live with Honor and Die with Honor!*, 704.
118 Cargas, 'Interview with Elie Wiesel', 5.
119 Elie Wiesel, 'Twentieth Anniversary Keynote', in F. H. Little, A. L. Berger, and H. G. Locke (eds.), *What Have We Learned? Telling the Story and Teaching the Lessons of the Holocaust: Papers of the Twentieth Anniversary Scholars' Conference* (Lewiston, Me., 1993), 7–8.   120 Bitton-Jackson, *I Have Lived a Thousand Years*, 9.

that in his quest to learn more about the Holocaust, he 'read every single book that appeared on the Holocaust'.[121] However, what is clear is that survivors such as Wiesel and Bitton-Jackson feel a proximity to the events of the Holocaust that clearly demarcates them from the historians who were not there. The observation of David Roskies might be added: 'For the historian, the Holocaust is a segregated past. For the survivor it is everything.'[122]

UNIQUENESS VERSUS UNIVERSALISM

Like Wiesel and Bitton-Jackson, Lasker-Wallfisch feels that it is very important to retain the distinction between 'those who "know" and those who "don't know"': '[If] you have been a witness to this twentieth-century outrage of sophisticated cruelty of man to man, you will inevitably live in some kind of double limbo, cut off from the rest of the world. I have accepted the reality that there are those who "know" and those who "don't know"; and there the story seems to end.'[123]

The conflict that is apparent in many Holocaust memoirs is the attempt to bear witness to the Holocaust—while insisting on the uniqueness of the severity of its horror—at the same time ensuring that posterity *never forgets*, and therefore *never lets it happen again* by universalizing its importance. However, as Peter Novick observes, 'the extremity of the Holocaust makes the applicability of lessons difficult.'[124] He asks: 'Above all, what is the relevance of these lessons on surviving in the Hell of Hitler's Europe for living our lives, safely and peacefully in the here and now?'[125]

One answer is to present the Holocaust as a warning from history. David Rousset, a non-Jew and professor of philosophy in Paris before the Nazi occupation, who was incarcerated in Buchenwald for

[121] Cargas (ed.), *Harry James Cargas in Conversation with Elie Wiesel*, 89.
[122] Roskies, *Jewish Search for a Usable Past*, 15.
[123] Lasker-Wallfisch, *Inherit the Truth*, 16.
[124] Novick, *Holocaust and Collective Memory*, 261.   [125] Ibid. 244.

disseminating information to Allied sources, wrote as early as 1945: 'The existence of the camps is a warning. . . . Under a new guise similar effects may appear tomorrow.'[126] However, while the word 'similar' might be taken to imply that the Holocaust is unique, it is unlikely that Rousset writing in 1945 was able to predict the concern with uniqueness that many survivors have today. An example is illustrated by Elie Wiesel in his foreword to Rezak Hukanović's *The Tenth Circle of Hell: A Memoir of Life in the Death Camps of Bosnia*[127]—the first such account to be published. Wiesel introduces the book, stating that 'Dante was wrong. Hell consists not of nine circles, but of ten. Rezak Hukanović takes you to the latest one, the most dreadful and the most heartbreaking';[128] but then Wiesel feels compelled to point out that the murder of European Jewry was more cataclysmic than any other genocidal mass slaughter: 'Omarska was not Auschwitz. Nothing, anywhere, can be compared to Auschwitz.'[129] Wiesel manages to connect and separate the two genocides. He is pointing out that the legacy of Auschwitz is not yet over, and at the same time clearly stating that 'Omarska was not Auschwitz', which can be decoded as meaning 'Omarska was not as bad as Auschwitz'. This allows him to maintain his monolithic view of the Holocaust, while also using his position as a survivor of the Holocaust to provide indispensable moral insights.

In contrast to the difficulties they have experienced in writing their testimonies, many survivors, such as Lasker-Wallfisch, Wermuth, and Wiesel, express in unequivocal terms their acceptance of the identity of Holocaust witness. Having waited a long time to be accepted as valued historical witnesses, they are reluctant to lose that position. Yet, the multiplicity of Holocaust experiences renders the unified concept of the Holocaust problematic. Apart from the actual physical differences in experience—for example, geographical location, age,

[126] Rousset, *Other Kingdom*, 112.
[127] Rezak Hukanović, *The Tenth Circle of Hell: A Memoir of Life in the Death Camps of Bosnia*, trans. Colleen London and Midhat Ridjanović (London, 1998).
[128] Elie Wiesel, Foreword to Hukanović, *Tenth Circle of Hell*, p. v.
[129] Ibid.

and gender—witnesses will inevitably focus on particular aspects of their experience. Particularly important in the context of Lasker-Wallfisch's distinction is whether the survivor actually witnessed mass destruction in the ghettos or concentration camps, or whether she or he acquired the information retrospectively. And, many survivors do feel the distinction between those who witnessed the Holocaust and those who did not to be very important. Without the concept of the Holocaust and its connotations of uniqueness, a part of their identity would disappear. However, while assuming the role of the survivor, or the identity of the witness, has given survivors of the Holocaust a sense of purpose, their activities are inextricably mediated by the post-war comprehension or concept of the Holocaust and by the effects of testimony becoming a part of collective memory.

Epilogue

> To argue for silence, prayer, the banishment equally of poetry
> and knowledge, in short, the witness of 'ineffability', that is non-
> representability, is to mystify something we dare not understand,
> because we fear that it may be all too understandable, all too
> continuous with what we are—human all too human.
>
> Rose, 'Beginnings of the Day'

Jews writing in the ghettos and concentration camps of Eastern
Europe consciously recorded their experiences of suffering and persecution, with the aim that they would not be forgotten by future historians. In the aftermath of liberation—at a time when many survivors
were experiencing not the joy of freedom but rather the pain of feeling lost in the world—survivors bore witness not only for themselves,
but for those they had lost. Today survivors are still coming forward
to tell their stories, leaving behind not only a record for their children
and grandchildren, but evidence for posterity. Without all these
documents, knowledge of what European Jewry was forced to endure
would be extremely limited. They are invaluable in allowing us to try
to understand what it meant to live under German occupation: its
effect on the individual, the family, community, education, religion,
and culture. In describing Jewish life before the war, they also help us
to appreciate the world that was destroyed. They urge us to ensure
that we never forget; that such a momentous crime against humanity
is always remembered. Perhaps most importantly of all, in documenting the vanished communities—details of pre-war Jewish life; life in
the ghettos, the uprisings, and resistance; concentration camps,
labour camps, and death camps; and the daunting task of rebuilding

shattered lives—they also remind us that the extremity and magnitude of the Holocaust makes it resistant to any final narrativization. Despite the plethora of testimonies that now exist, it is clear that we are still far from knowing all there is to know about the Holocaust.

However, the collectivization of Holocaust memory has led to a homogenization of Holocaust comprehension that eschews difficult testimony or stories that fall outside accepted narratives. Although we now know much more about the events of the Holocaust, the outcome has been a diluted comprehension that accords with 'official' forms of Holocaust representation. Yet, while survivors such as Elie Wiesel want to emphasize the dignity of the Jewish victims, they do not want their testimonies to be used to convey comforting notions about the triumph of hope or goodness, far removed from the terrible suffering of the Holocaust. In a similar manner, although witnesses writing in the ghettos and concentration camps emphasized the theme of Jewish resistance, to refute the possibility of unjust accusations of Jewish passivity, they wanted to stress Jewish suffering in at least equal measure. For Wiesel, the problem is that the Holocaust has become a 'desanctified theme, or if you prefer, a theme robbed of its passion, its mystery'.[1] The experience of Sally Grubman, a survivor of Auschwitz and Ravensbrück, illuminates the problems faced when using the Holocaust as a pedagogic model:

There is a tremendous interest in the Holocaust that we didn't see when we came [to the United States]. . . . I see an awakening of consciousness, but also some confusion about the reality. American Jewish teachers invite me into their classrooms to speak, but they do not want me to make the Holocaust a sad experience. They want me to turn us into heroes and create a heroic experience for the survivors. There is this book they use, *The Holocaust: A History of Courage and Resistance*, but the Holocaust never was a history of courage and resistance. It was a destruction by fire of innocent people, and it's not right to make it something it never was. We are not heroes. We survived by some fluke that we do not ourselves understand. And people have said, 'Sally, tell the children about the joy of survival.' And I can

[1] Wiesel, 'A Plea for Survivors', in *A Jew Today*, 237–8.

see that they don't understand it at all. If you're in a canoe and your life is in
danger for a few minutes and you survive, you can talk about the joy of survival. We went through fire and ashes and whole families were destroyed.
And we are left. How can we talk about the joy of survival?[2]

Grubman's unease is with the attempt to portray a uniformity of
experience, and one that conveys 'heroic' sentiments. Arguing against
attempts to extract universal meaning from the testimonies of survivors, Lawrence Langer believes that the study of survivors' stories
should be 'an experience of unlearning; [where] both parties are
forced into the Dantean gesture of abandoning all stage props as they
enter and, without benefit of Virgil, make their uneasy way through
its vague domain'.[3] For Langer, all attempts to focus on the meaning
of survivors' testimonies are bogus; he is also critical of readers who
concentrate on particular episodes or individual lines of testimony as
'keys to the mystery of why one Jew survived while another did not'.[4]
He believes that the recent explosion of interest in the Holocaust has
fostered an environment that imposes unnecessary structures upon
Holocaust representation; in particular, it has led to the elevation of
testimonies that exhibit morally correct behaviour. The banalization
of the Holocaust—whereby we no longer look at testimony to tell us
something about the past, but instead use it to tell us something
about the present or about ourselves—means that when we return to
the archives of, for example, *Oneg Shabbat*, it is to confirm our
current concerns.

If Lawrence Langer is right, if no meaning can be discerned from
the reading of Holocaust testimonies, then we return to Elie Wiesel's
understanding of the Holocaust as 'a mystery begotten by the dead'.[5]
But, at the same time, we are warned against forgetting. This is the
arena that the battle for Holocaust memory has to traverse: on the
one hand, the Holocaust is treated as unique, and, on the other, it is
the test of morality. Nevertheless, witnesses writing in the ghettos and

[2] Cited in Greenspan, *On Listening to Holocaust Survivors*, 44–5.
[3] Langer, *Art from the Ashes*, 6–7.   [4] Langer, *Preempting the Holocaust*, 27.
[5] Wiesel, *One Generation After*, 43.

concentration camps wanted future generations to do more than just remember them—they wanted to provide historical documentation of Jewish life during German occupation. Furthermore, Emmanuel Ringelblum and the other members of *Oneg Shabbat*, as a result of the constraints they were under, realized that their diaries were fallible documents which were themselves subject to distortions and would therefore need to be interpreted and validated in the future; they did not want their writings to be treated as untouchable, sacred relics.

As the events of the Holocaust recede further into the past, it becomes increasingly important to engage in the task of active remembering. James Young, speaking of Holocaust monuments, suggests that, 'once we assign monumental form to memory, we have to some degree divested ourselves of the obligation to remember. In shouldering the memory work, monuments may relieve viewers of their memory burden.'[6] While survivors such as Halina Birenbaum, and critics such as Tzvetan Todorov, can be accused of using the Holocaust reductively to mobilize a simplistic morality, unlike Langer, they eschew the ineffable and err on the side of comprehension. Equally, although Primo Levi and Elie Wiesel have written of the limitations of traditional categories of explanation in confronting the Holocaust—albeit in very different ways—they have dedicated their lives to trying to understand its events. Without an understanding of the complex nature of testimony and representation, and a willingness to document fully the lives of witnesses and the diversity of their experiences, it is likely that the Holocaust will remain a dark period of history that is constantly referred to but never fully comprehended or explored.

[6] James E. Young, *The Texture of Memory: Holocaust Memorials and Meanings* (New Haven, 1993), 5.

Bibliography

ADELSBERGER, LUCIE, *Auschwitz: Ein Tatsachenbericht. Das Vermächtnis der Opfer für uns Juden und für alle Menschen* (Berlin: Lettner, 1956); published in English as *Auschwitz: A Doctor's Story*, trans. Susan Ray (London: Robson Books, 1996).

ADLER, HANS GÜNTHER, *Theresienstadt 1941–1945: Das Antlitz einer Zwangsgemeinschaft—Geschichte, Soziologie, Psychologie* (Tübingen: Mohr, 1955).

ADORNO, THEODOR W., *Minima Moralia: Reflections from Damaged Life*, trans. E. F. N. Jephcott (London: Verso, 1978).

AGAMBEN, GIORGIO, *Remnants of Auschwitz: The Witness and the Archive*, trans. Daniel Heller-Roazen (New York: Zone, 1999).

AINSZTEIN, REUBEN, *The Warsaw Ghetto Revolt* (New York: Schocken, 1979).

ALTMANN, ERICH, *Im Angesicht des Todes: Drei Jahre in Deutschen Konzentrationslagern. Auschwitz, Buchenwald, Oranienburg* (Luxemburg: Luxemburgensia, 1947).

ALTSHULER, MORDECHAI, *Soviet Jewry since the Second World War: Population and Social Structure* (New York: Greenwood, 1987).

AMÉRY, JEAN, *Jenseits von Schuld und Sühne: Bewältigungsversuche eines Überwältigten* (Munich: Szczesny, 1966); published in English as *At the Mind's Limits: Contemplations by a Survivor on Auschwitz and its Realities*, trans. Sidney Rosenfeld and Stella P. Rosenfeld (Bloomington, Ind.: Indiana University Press, 1980).

—— *Radical Humanism: Selected Essays*, trans. Sidney Rosenfeld and Stella P. Rosenfeld (Bloomington, Ind.: Indiana University Press, 1980).

ANISSIMOV, MYRIAM, *Primo Levi: Tragedy of an Optimist*, trans. Steve Cox (London: Aurum Press, 1998).

ANTELME, ROBERT, *L'Espèce humaine* (Paris: Gallimard, 1947); published in English as *The Human Race*, trans. Jeffrey Haight and Annie Mahler (Marlboro, Vt.: Marlboro Press, 1992).

APENSZLAK, JACOB (ed.), *The Black Book of Polish Jewry: An Account of the Martyrdom of Polish Jewry under the Nazi Occupation* (New York: American Federation for Polish Jews, 1943).

APPELMAN-JURMAN, ALICIA, *Alicia: My Story* (New York: Bantam, 1990).

ARAD, YITZHAK, 'The Holocaust of Soviet Jewry in the Occupied Territories of the Soviet Union', *Yad Vashem Studies*, 21 (1991), 1–47.

—— GUTMAN, YISRAEL, and MARGALIOT, ABRAHAM (eds.), *Documents on the Holocaust: Selected Sources on the Destruction of the Jews of Germany and Austria, Poland, and the Soviet Union*, 4th edn. (Jerusalem: Yad Vashem, 1981).

ARENDT, HANNAH, *Eichmann in Jerusalem: A Report on the Banality of Evil* (New York: Viking, 1962).

AUERBACH, RACHEL, *Varshever tsavoes: bagegenishn, aktivitetn, goyroles 1933–1943* (Tel Aviv: Israel Book, 1974).

BAECK, LEO, 'Life in a Concentration Camp', *Jewish Spectator*, 11 (July 1946), 12–13.

BALL-KADURI, K. Y., 'Evidence of Witnesses, its Value and Limitations', *Yad [V]ashem Studies*, 2 (1958), 79–90.

BARKAI, MEYER (ed.), *The Fighting Ghettos* (Philadelphia: Jewish Publication Society, 1962).

BARKOW, BEN, *Alfred Wiener and the Making of the Holocaust Library* (London: Vallentine Mitchell, 1997).

BAU, JOSEPH, *Dear God, Have You Ever Gone Hungry?*, trans. Shlomo Yurman (New York: Arcade, 1990).

BAUER, YEHUDA, *The Holocaust in Historical Perspective* (London: Sheldon Press, 1978).

—— *Rethinking the Holocaust* (New Haven: Yale University Press, 2001).

BAUM, BRUNO, *Widerstand in Auschwitz* (Berlin: Kongress, 1949).

BAUMEL, JUDITH, TYDOR, ' "In Everlasting Memory": Individual and Communal Holocaust Commemoration in Israel', in Robert Wistrich and David Ohana (eds.), *The Shaping of Israeli Identity: Myth, Memory and Trauma* (London: Frank Cass, 1995), 146–70.

—— 'DP's, Mothers and Pioneers: Women in the *She'erit Hapletah*', *Jewish History*, 11/2 (1997), 99–110.

—— *Double Jeopardy: Gender and the Holocaust* (London: Vallentine Mitchell, 1998).

BECK, BIRGIT, 'Vergewaltigung von Frauen als Kriegsstrategie im Zweiten Weltkrieg?', in Andreas Gestrich (ed.), *Gewalt im Krieg: Ausübung, Erfahrung und Verweigerung von Gewalt in Kriegen des 20. Jahrhunderts. Jahrbuch für Historische Friedensforschung*, 4 vols. (Munich: LIT, 1996), 34–50.

BENTWICH, NORMAN, *They Found Refuge: An Account of British Jewry's Work for the Victims of Nazi Oppression* (London: The Cresset Press, 1956).

BEN-YOSEPH, AVRAHAM, 'Bibliography of Yiddish Publications in the USSR during 1941–1948', *Yad Vashem Studies*, 4 (1960), 135–66.

BERENBAUM, MICHAEL (ed.), *A Mosaic of Victims: Non-Jews Persecuted and Murdered by the Nazis* (London: Tauris, 1990).

BERG, MARY, *Dziennik z Getta Warszawkiego* (Warsaw: Czytelnik, 1945); published in English as *Warsaw Ghetto: A Diary*, trans. Norbert Guterman and Sylvia Glass, ed. S. L. Shneiderman (New York: Fischer, 1945).

BERGER, ALAN L., 'Elie Wiesel', in Steven T. Katz (ed.), *Interpreters of Judaism in the Late Twentieth Century* (Washington: B'nai B'rith, 1993), 369–91.

BETTELHEIM, BRUNO, 'Individual and Mass Behaviour in Extreme Situations', *Journal of Abnormal Social Psychology*, 38 (1943), 417–52.

—— *Surviving and Other Essays* (New York: Knopf, 1960).

BIRENBAUM, HALINA, *Nadzieja Umiera Ostatnia* (Warsaw: Czytelnik, 1967); published in English as *Hope is the Last to Die: A Personal Documentation of Nazi Terror*, trans. David Welsh (New York: Twayne, 1971).

BITTON-JACKSON, LIVIA E., *Eli: Coming of Age in the Holocaust* (London: Grafton, 1984).

—— *I Have Lived a Thousand Years: Growing Up in the Holocaust* (London: Simon & Schuster, 1999).

BLANCHOT, MAURICE, *The Writing of the Disaster*, trans. Ann Smock (Lincoln: University of Nebraska Press, 1995).

BLATT, THOMAS TOVI, *From the Ashes of Sobibor: A Story of Survival* (Evanston, Ill.: Northwestern University Press, 1997).

BLOXHAM, DONALD, *Genocide on Trial: War Crimes Trials and the Formation of Holocaust History and Memory* (Oxford: Oxford University Press, 2001).

—— and KUSHNER, TONY, *The Holocaust: Critical Historical Approaches* (Manchester: Manchester University Press, 2005).

BODER, DAVID, *I Did Not Interview the Dead*, 16 vols. (Urbana, Ill.: University of Illinois Press, 1949).

BOROWSKI, TADEUSZ, *Pożegnanie z Maria* (Warsaw: Pánstwowy Instytut Wydawniczy, 1948).

—— *Kamienny Swiat* (Warsaw: Pánstwowy Instytut Wydawniczy, 1948).

—— *This Way for the Gas, Ladies and Gentlemen*, trans. Barbara Vedder (Harmondsworth: Penguin, 1967).

BORZYKOWSKI, TUVIA, *Tsvishn falndike vent* (Warsaw: Merkaz Hehalutz, 1949).

BRONNER, ERIC STEPHEN, 'Making Sense of Hell: Three Meditations on the Holocaust', *Political Studies*, 47/2 (1999), 314–28.

BROWNING, CHRISTOPHER R., *Collected Memories: Holocaust History and Postwar Testimony* (Madison: University of Wisconsin Press, 2003).

BULLOCK, ALAN, *Hitler: A Study in Tyranny* (London: Odhams Press, 1952).

CAMHI FROMER, REBECCA, *The Holocaust Odyssey of Daniel Bennahmias, Sonderkommando* (Tuscaloosa, Ala.: University of Alabama Press, 1993).

CAMON, FERDINANDO, *Conversations with Primo Levi*, trans. John Shepley (Marlboro, Vt.: Marlboro Press, 1989).

CARGAS, HARRY JAMES, 'An Interview with Elie Wiesel', *Holocaust and Genocide Studies*, 1 (1986), 11–25.

—— (ed.), *Harry James Cargas in Conversation with Elie Wiesel* (New York: Paulist Press, 1976).

CARUTH, CATHY (ed.), *Trauma: Explorations in Memory* (Baltimore: Johns Hopkins University Press, 1995).

CESARANI, DAVID, *Justice Delayed: How Britain Became a Refuge for Nazi War Criminals* (London: Heinemann, 1992).

—— *Britain and the Holocaust* (London: Holocaust Educational Trust, 1998).

CHICAGO, JUDY, *Holocaust Project: From Darkness into Light* (New York: Viking, 1993).

COHEN, NATHAN, 'Diaries of the Sonderkommando in Auschwitz: Coping with Fate and Reality', *Yad Vashem Studies*, 20 (1990), 273–312.

—— 'Diaries of the Sonderkommando', in Yisrael Gutman and Michael Berenbaum (eds.), *Anatomy of the Auschwitz Death Camp* (Bloomington, Ind.: Indiana University Press, 1994), 522–34.

COHEN, RICHARD I., 'Breaking the Code: Hannah Arendt's *Eichmann in Jerusalem* and the Public Polemic: Myth, Memory and Historical Imagination', *Michael*, 13 (1993), 29–85.

CONWAY, JOHN S., 'The First Report about Auschwitz', *Simon Wiesenthal Center Annual*, 1 (1984), 133–51.

CORRSIN, STEPHEN D., 'Aspects of Population Change and of Acculturation in Jewish Warsaw at the End of the Nineteenth Century: The Census of 1882 and 1897', in Antony Polonsky (ed.), *Polin. Studies in Polish Jewry*, iii: *The Jews of Warsaw* (Oxford: Littman Library, 1988), 122–41.

COTTERIL, P., and LETHERBY, G., 'Weaving Stories: Personal Autobiographies in Feminist Research', *Sociology*, 27/1 (1993), 67–80.

CZECH, DANUTA, *Auschwitz Chronicle, 1939–1945: From the Archives of the Auschwitz Memorial and the German Federal Archives* (New York: Henry Holt, 1990).

CZERNIAKÓW, ADAM, *Adam Czerniaków, yoman geto Varsha: 6.9.1939–23.7.1942*, ed. Joseph Kermish (Jerusalem: Yad Vashem, 1968); published in English as *The Warsaw Diary of Adam Czerniakow: Prelude to Doom*, ed. Raul Hilberg, Stanislaw Staron, and Josef Kermisz (New York: Stein & Day, 1973).

Daily Prayer Book: Ha-Siddur Ha-Shalem, trans. Philip Birnbaum (New York: Hebrew Publishing, 1949).

DAVIDSON, SHAMAI, 'Human Reciprocity among the Jewish Prisoners in the Nazi Concentration Camps', in Yisrael Gutman and Avital Saf (eds.), *The Nazi Concentration Camps: Proceedings of the Fourth Yad Vashem International Conference, January 1980* (Jerusalem: Yad Vashem, 1984), 555–72.

DAWIDOWICZ, LUCY S., *The War against the Jews, 1933–1945* (New York: Holt, Rinehart & Winston, 1975).

—— *The Jewish Presence: Essays on Identity and History* (New York: Holt, Rinehart & Winston, 1977).

—— *The Holocaust and the Historians* (Cambridge, Mass.: Harvard University Press, 1981).

DELBO, CHARLOTTE, *Aucun de nous ne reviendra* (Geneva: Éditions de Minuit, 1965); published in English as *None of Us Will Return*, trans. John Githens (Boston: Beacon Press, 1965).

—— *Auschwitz et après* (Paris: Éditions de Minuit, 1970).

—— *La Mémoire et les jours* (Paris: Berg International, 1985); published in English as *Days and Memory*, trans. Rosette C. Lamont (Marlboro, Vt.: Marlboro Press, 1990).

DERRIDA, JACQUES, 'Force of Law: The Mystical Foundation of Authority', *The Cardozo Law Review, Destruction and the Possibility of Justice*, 11/5–6 (July–August 1990), 920–1045.

DES PRES, TERRENCE, *The Survivor: An Anatomy of Life in the Death Camps* (Oxford: Oxford University Press, 1976).

DINNERSTEIN, LEONARD, *America and the Survivors of the Holocaust* (New York: Columbia University Press, 1982).

DINUR, BENZION, 'Problems Confronting "Yad [V]ashem" in its Work of Research', *Yad [V]ashem Studies*, 1 (1957), 7–30.

DOBROSZYCKI, LUCJAN, 'Restoring Jewish Life in Post-war Poland', *Soviet Jewish Affairs*, 3/2 (1973), 58–72.

—— (ed.), *The Chronicle of the Łódź Ghetto, 1941–44*, trans. Richard Lourie, Joachim Neugroschel, *et al.* (New Haven: Yale University Press, 1984).

DONAT, ALEXANDER, *The Holocaust Kingdom: A Memoir* (London: Corgi, 1967).

DRIX, SAMUEL, *Witness to Annihilation: Surviving the Holocaust* (London: Fount, 1964).

DUFOURNIER, DENISE, *La Maison des mortes: Ravensbrück* (Paris: Hachette, 1945); published in English as *Ravensbrück: The Women's Camp of Death* (London: Allen & Unwin, 1948).

DWORETZKI, MARK, 'A Day in the Ghetto', trans. Jacob Sloan, *Jewish Spectator*, 11 (October 1946), 16–20.

DWÓRK, DEBORAH, and JAN VAN PELT, ROBERT, *Auschwitz: 1270 to the Present* (London: Norton, 1996).

EAGLESTONE, ROBERT, *The Holocaust and the Postmodern* (Oxford: Oxford University Press, 2004).

EDELHEIT, ABRAHAM J., and EDELHEIT, HERSHEL, *History of the Holocaust: A Handbook and Dictionary* (Boulder, Colo.: Westview, 1994).

EDELMAN, MAREK, *Getto Walczy* (Warsaw: CK Bundu, 1945); published in English as *The Ghetto Fights*, trans. Zofia Nalkowsak (New York: American Representation of the General Jewish Workers' Union of Poland, 1946).

EHRENBURG, ILYA, *Merder fun felker: Materialn vegn di retsikhes fun di daytche farkhaper in di tsaytvaylik okupirte sovetishe rayonen* (Moscow: Melukhe-farlag, 1944).

—— and GROSSMAN, VASILY (eds.), *The Black Book: The Ruthless Murder of Jews by German-Fascist Invaders throughout the Temporarily-Occupied Regions of the Soviet Union and in the Death Camps of Poland during the War of 1941–1945*, trans. John Glad and James S. Levene (New York: Holocaust Library, 1981).

EINHORN-SUSUŁOWSKA, MARIA, 'Psychological Problems of Polish Jews who Used Aryan Documents', in Antony Polonsky (ed.), *Polin. Studies in Polish Jewry*, xiii: *Focusing on the Holocaust and its Aftermath* (London: Littman Library, 2000), 104–11.

EISENBACH, ARTUR, *Hitlerowska Polityka Eksterminacji Żydów w Latach 1939–1945 Jako Jeden z Przejawów Imperializmu Niemieckiego* (Warsaw: Jewish Historical Institute, 1953); published in Yiddish as *Di Hitleristishe politik fun yidn-farnikhtung in di yorn 1939–1945* (Warsaw: Yiddish-Bukh, 1955).

ELIAS, RUTH, *Triumph of Hope: From Theresienstadt and Auschwitz to Israel*, trans. Margot Bettauer Dembo (New York: John Wiley, 1998).

ELIEZER, DON-YEHIYA, 'Memory and Political Culture: Israeli Society and the Holocaust', *Studies in Contemporary Jewry*, 4 (1993), 139–62.

ENGELKING, BARBARA, *Holocaust and Memory: The Experience of the Holocaust and its Consequences. An Investigation Based on Personal Narratives*, trans. Emma Harris, ed. Gunnar S. Paulsson (London: Leicester University Press, 2001).

EZRAHI, SIDRA DEKOVEN, 'Boundaries of the Present: Two Literary Approaches to the Concentration Camps', in Yisrael Gutman and Avital Saf (eds.), *The Nazi Concentration Camps* (Jerusalem: Yad Vashem, 1984), 649–61.

FALCONER, RACHEL, *Hell in Contemporary Literature: Western Descent Narratives since 1945* (Edinburgh: Edinburgh University Press, 2005).

FEINGOLD, HENRY L., *Bearing Witness: How America and its Jews Responded to the Holocaust* (Syracuse, NY: Syracuse University Press, 1995).

FELMAN, SHOSHANA, and LAUB, DORI, *Testimony: Crises of Witnessing in Literature, Psychoanalysis, and History* (New York: Routledge, 1992).

FÉNELON, FANIA, *Sursis pour l'orchestre* (Paris: Stock, 1976); published in the USA (with MARCELLE ROUTIER) as *Playing for Time*, trans. Judith Landry (New York: Atheneum, 1977); and in the UK (with MARCELLE ROUTIER) as *The Musicians of Auschwitz*, trans. Judith Landry (London: Sphere, 1977).

FINK, IDA, *The Journey*, trans. Joanna Weschler and Francine Prose (London: Farrar, Straus & Giroux, 1992).

FINKELSTEIN, NORMAN G., *The Holocaust Industry: Reflections on the Exploitation of Jewish Suffering* (London: Verso, 2000).

FOX, THOMAS C., 'The Holocaust under Communism', in Dan Stone (ed.), *The Historiography of the Holocaust* (New York: Palgrave Macmillan, 2004), 420–39.

FRANK, ANNE, *Het Achterhuis* (Amsterdam: Uitgeverij Contact, 1947); published in English as *The Diary of a Young Girl*, trans. B. M. Mooyaart-Doubleday (London: Vallentine Mitchell, 1952); as *The Diary of Anne Frank: The Critical Edition*, trans. Arnold J. Pomerans and B. M. Mooyaart-Doubleday, ed. David Barnouw and Gerrold van der Stroom (New York: Doubleday, 1989); and as *The Diary of a Young Girl: The Definitive Edition*, trans. Susan Massotty, ed. Otto H. Frank and Mirjam Pressler (London: Viking, 1997).

196   *Bibliography*

FRANKL, VIKTOR E., *Ein Pyschologe erlebt das Konzentrationslager* (Vienna: Jugend und Volk, 1946); published in English as *Man's Search for Meaning: An Introduction to Logotherapy*, trans. Ilse Lasch (Boston: Beacon Press, 1959).

FRIEDMAN, PHILIP, 'The Road Back for the DP's: Healing the Psychological Scars of Nazism', *Commentary*, 6 (1948), 502–10.

—— 'European Jewish Research on the Recent Jewish Catastrophe in 1939–1945', *Proceedings of the American Academy for Jewish Research*, 18 (1949), 179–211.

—— 'Some Aspects of Concentration Camp Psychology', *American Journal of Psychiatry*, 105 (1949), 601–5.

—— 'Problems of Research on the European Jewish Catastrophe', *Yad [V]ashem Studies*, 3 (1959), 25–40.

—— (ed.), *Martyrs and Fighters: The Epic of the Warsaw Ghetto* (London: Routledge, 1954).

FRISTER, ROMAN, *The Cap or the Price of a Life*, trans. Hillel Halkin (New York: Continuum, 1999).

GANZFRIED, DANIEL, 'Die Geliehene Holocaust-Biographie—The Purloined Holocaust Biography', trans. Katherine Quimby Johnson, *Die Weltwoche*, 27 August 1998.

GELISSEN, RENA KORNREICH (with HEATHER DUNE MACADAM), *Rena's Promise: A Story of Sisters in Auschwitz* (London: Orion, 1996).

GILBERT, MARTIN, *Auschwitz and the Allies* (London: Michael Joseph, 1981).

—— *The Holocaust: The Jewish Tragedy* (London: Fontana, 1987).

GILBERT, SHIRLI, *Music in the Holocaust: Confronting Life in the Nazi Ghettos and Camps* (Oxford: Oxford University Press, 2005).

GILL, ANTON, *The Journey Back from Hell: Conversations with Concentration Camp Survivors* (London: Routledge, 1994).

GITELMAN, ZVI, 'History, Memory, and Politics: The Holocaust in the Soviet Union', *Holocaust and Genocide Studies*, 5 (1990), 23–37.

—— (ed.), *Bitter Legacy: Confronting the Holocaust in the Soviet Union* (Bloomington, Ind.: Indiana University Press, 1997).

GLAZAR, RICHARD, *Die Falle mit dem Grünen Zaun: Überleben in Treblinka* (Frankfurt: Fischer, 1992).

GOLDSTEIN, BERNARD, *Finf yor in Varshever geto* (New York: Undzer Zeit, 1947); published in English as *The Stars Bear Witness*, trans. Leonard Shatzkin (New York: Viking, 1949).

GORDON, ROBERT, 'Holocaust Writing in Context: Italy 1945–47', in Andrew Leak and George Paizis (eds.), *The Holocaust and the Text: Speaking the Unspeakable* (London: Macmillan, 2000), 32–50.

GOTTESFELD HELLER, FANYA, *Strange and Unexpected Love: A Teenage Girl's Holocaust Memoirs* (Hoboken, NJ: Ktav, 1993).

GOUREVITCH, PHILIP, 'The Memory Thief', *New Yorker*, 14 June 1999, 48–68.

GRADOWSKI, ZAŁMAN, *In harts fun gehenem* (Jerusalem: n.p., 1944).

—— 'Manuscript of a Sonderkommando Member', trans. Krystyna Michalik, in Jadwiga Bezwinska and Danuta Czech (eds.), *Amidst a Nightmare of Crime: Manuscripts of Members of Sonderkommando* (Kraków: State Museum of Oświęcim, 1973), 75–108.

GRAUMANN, SAMUEL, *Deportiert! Ein Wiener Jude Berichtet* (Vienna: Stern, 1947).

GREENAWAY, MARK, 'The Entelechy of Auschwitz' (unpublished MS, 1995).

GREENSPAN, HENRY, *On Listening to Holocaust Survivors: Recounting and Life History* (Westport, Conn.: Praeger, 1998).

GREIF, GIDEON, *Wir weinten tränenlos . . . Augenzeugenberichte der jüdischen 'Sonderkommandos' in Auschwitz* (Cologne: Böhlau, 1995).

—— and KILIAN, ANDREAS, 'Significance, Responsibility, Challenge: Interviewing the Sonderkommando Survivors', *Studies on the Audio-Visual Testimony of Victims of the Nazi Crimes and Genocides*, 9 (June 2003), 75–83.

GROSSMAN, MENDEL, *With a Camera in the Ghetto*, ed. Zvi Szner and Alexander Sened (New York: Schocken, 1977).

GUREWITSCH, BRANA (ed.), *Mothers, Sisters, Resisters: Oral Histories of Women Who Survived the Holocaust* (Tuscaloosa, Ala.: University of Alabama Press, 1998).

GUTMAN, ISRAEL, 'Janusz Korczak—Kavim Lidmuto', *Yalkut Moreshet*, 25 (1978), 7–20 [Hebrew].

—— *The Jews of Warsaw, 1939–1943: Ghetto, Underground, Revolt*, trans. Ina Friedman (Brighton: Harvester Press, 1982).

—— 'Social Stratification in the Concentration Camps', in Yisrael Gutman and Avital Saf (eds.), *The Nazi Concentration Camps* (Jerusalem: Yad Vashem, 1984), 143–76.

GUTMAN, ISRAEL, *Resistance: The Warsaw Ghetto Uprising* (Boston: Houghton Mifflin, 1994).

GUTMAN, ISRAEL, and BERENBAUM, MICHAEL (eds.), *Anatomy of the Auschwitz Death Camp* (Bloomington, Ind.: Indiana University Press, 1994).

HAFFNER, DÉSIRÉ, *Aspects pathologiques du camp de concentration d'Auschwitz-Birkenau* (Tours: Union Coopérative, 1946).

HALBWACHS, MAURICE, *On Collective Memory*, trans. Lewis A. Coser (Chicago: University of Chicago Press, 1992).

HARDMAN, ANNA, *Women and the Holocaust*, Holocaust Educational Trust Research Papers, 1/3 (2000).

HAREVEN, SHULAMITH, *The Vocabulary of Peace: Life, Culture, and Politics in the Middle East* (San Francisco: Mercury, 1995).

HART, KITTY, *I Am Alive* (London: Corgi, 1961).

—— *Return to Auschwitz: The Remarkable Story of a Girl who Survived the Holocaust* (London: Grafton, 1983).

HEIMLER, EUGENE, *Night of the Mist*, trans. André Ungar (New York: Vanguard, 1959).

HERMAN, JUDITH LEWIS, *Trauma and Recovery* (New York: Basic Books, 1992).

HILBERG, RAUL, *The Destruction of the European Jews*, 3 vols. (Chicago: Quadrangle, 1961).

—— 'The Ghetto as a Form of Government: An Analysis of Isaiah Trunk's Judenrat', in Yehuda Bauer and Nathan Rotenstreich (eds.), *The Holocaust as Historical Experience* (New York: Holmes & Meier, 1981), 293–305.

—— *The Politics of Memory: The Journey of a Holocaust Historian* (Chicago: Ivan R. Dee, 1996).

HIRSCH, MARIANNE, 'Past Lives: Postmemories in Exile', *Poetics Today*, 17/4 (Winter 1996), 659–86.

—— *Family Frames: Photography, Narrative, and Postmemory* (Cambridge, Mass.: Harvard University Press, 1997).

—— 'Projected Memory: Holocaust Photographs in Personal and Public Fantasy', in Mieke Bal, Jonathan Crewe, and Leo Spitzer (eds.), *Acts of Memory: Cultural Recall in the Present* (Hanover, NH: Dartmouth College, 1999), 3–23.

HOROWITZ, ROSEMARY, 'Reading and Writing during the Holocaust as Described in *Yisker* Books', in Jonathan Rose (ed.), *The Holocaust and the Book: Destruction and Preservation* (Amherst, Mass.: University of Massachusetts Press, 2001), 128–42.

HUBERBAND, SHIMON, *Kiddush Hashem: ktavim miymey hasho'ah*, ed. Nachman Blumental and Joseph Kermish (Tel Aviv: Zakhor, 1969);

published in English as *Kiddush Hashem: Jewish Religious and Cultural Life in Poland during the Holocaust*, trans. David E. Fishman, ed. Jeffrey S. Gurock and Robert S. Hirt (Hoboken, NJ: Ktav, 1987).

HUKANOVIĆ, REZAK, *The Tenth Circle of Hell: A Memoir of Life in the Death Camps of Bosnia*, trans. Colleen London and Midhat Ridjanović (London: Abacus, 1998).

HUXLEY, ALDOUS, *Brave New World* (London: Chatto & Windus, 1932).

HYMAN, PAULA E., 'Gender and the Jewish Family in Modern Europe', in Dalia Ofer and Lenore J. Weitzman (eds.), *Women in the Holocaust* (New Haven: Yale University Press, 1998), 25–34.

ISAACSON, JUDITH MAGYAR, *Seed of Sarah: Memoirs of a Survivor*, 2nd edn. (Urbana, Ill.: University of Illinois Press, 1991).

Jewish Black Book Committee, *The Black Book: The Nazi Crime Against the Jewish People* (New York: Duell, Sloan & Pearce, 1946).

KAPLAN, CHAIM A., *Megilat yishurin: yoman geto Varshah*, ed. Abraham I. Katsh (Tel Aviv: Am Oved, 1966); published in English as *Scroll of Agony: The Warsaw Diary of Chaim A. Kaplan*, trans. Abraham I. Katsh (Bloomington, Ind.: Indiana University Press, 1999).

KARMEL, ILONA, *An Estate of Memory* (New York: Feminist Press, 1986).

KARPF, ANNE, *The War After: Living with the Holocaust* (London: Heinemann, 1996).

—— 'Let's Pretend Life is Beautiful', *The Guardian, Saturday Review*, 3 April, 1999, 10.

KATZ, ESTHER, and RINGELHEIM, JOAN MIRIAM (eds.), *Proceedings of the Conference on Women Surviving the Holocaust* (New York: Institute for Research in History, 1983).

KATZNELSON, YITZHAK, *Ketavim aharonim, 1940–1944*, ed. Yitzhak Zuckerman and Shlomo Even-Shoshan (Tel Aviv: Hakibbutz Hameuchad, 1956).

—— *Vittel Diary*, trans. Myer Cohen (Tel Aviv: Beit Lohamei Hagheta'ot & Hakibbutz Hameuchad, 1972).

—— *Yidishe ksovim fun Varshe, 1940–1943*, ed. Yechiel Szeintuch (Tel Aviv: Beit Lohamei Hagheta'ot & Hakibbutz Hameuchad, 1980).

KAUTSKY, BENEDIKT, *Teufel und Verdammte: Erfahrungen und Erkenntnisse aus Sieben Jahren in Deutschen Konzentrationslagern* (Zurich: Gutenberg, 1946); published in English as *Devils and the Damned: The Story of Nazi Concentration and Extermination Camps*, trans. Kenneth Case (London: Brown & Watson, 1960).

KERMISH, JOSEPH, 'The Underground Press in the Warsaw Ghetto', *Yad Vashem Studies*, 1 (1957), 104–5.

—— 'The History of the Manuscript', in Ilya Ehrenburg and Vasily Grossman (eds.), *The Black Book: The Ruthless Murder of Jews by German-Fascist Invaders throughout the Temporarily-Occupied Regions of the Soviet Union and in the Death Camps of Poland during the War of 1941–1945*, trans. John Glad and James S. Levene (New York: Schocken, 1981), pp. xix–xxvi.

—— (ed.), *To Live with Honor and Die with Honor! Selected Documents from the Warsaw Ghetto Underground Archives 'O.S.' ['Oneg Shabbath']* (Jerusalem: Yad Vashem, 1986).

—— and BIALOSTOCKI, YISRAEL (eds.), *Itonut-hamahteret hayehudit beVarshah*, 6 vols. (Jerusalem: Yad Vashem, 1979–97).

KESSEL, SIM, *Pendu à Auschwitz* (Paris: Solar, 1970); published in English as *Hanged at Auschwitz*, trans. Melville and Delight Wallace (New York: Stein & Day, 1972).

KLEIN, GERDA WEISSMAN, *All But My Life* (New York: Hill & Wang, 1997).

KLEIN, HILLEL, 'The Survivors Search for Meaning and Identity', in Yisrael Gutman and Avital Saf (eds.), *The Nazi Concentration Camps* (Jerusalem: Yad Vashem, 1984), 543–53.

KLEIN, MORDEHAY, *My Life—Our History* (London: Minerva, 1997).

KLIER, JOHN, 'The Holocaust and the Soviet Union', in Dan Stone (ed.), *The Historiography of the Holocaust* (New York: Palgrave Macmillan, 2004), 276–95.

KOGON, EUGEN, *Der SS-Staat: Das System der Deutschen Konzentrationslager* (Munich: Karl Alber, 1946); published in English as *The Theory and Practice of Hell: The German Concentration Camps and the System Behind Them*, trans. Heinz Norden (New York: Farrar, Straus & Giroux, 1949).

KOHANSKY, MENDEL, 'The Last Days of Adam Czerniakow', *Midstream*, 15 (1969), 61–7.

KON, MENAHEM, 'Fragments of a Diary (August 6, 1942–October 1, 1942)', trans. M. Z. Prives, in Joseph Kermish (ed.), *To Live with Honor and Die with Honor! Selected Documents from the Warsaw Ghetto Underground Archives 'O.S.' ['Oneg Shabbath']* (Jerusalem, 1986), 80–6.

KORCHZAK, RUZHKA, *Lehavot Ba-efer* (Tel Aviv: Hakibbutz Hameuchad, 1946) [Hebrew].

KORCZAK, JANUSZ, *The Ghetto Years: 1939–1942*, trans. Jerzy Bachrach and Barbara Krzywicka (New York: Holocaust Library, 1978).

KORMAN, GERD, 'The Holocaust in American Historical Writing', *Societas—A Review of Social History*, 2/3 (Winter 1972), 251–70.

KORWIN, YALE, *To Tell the Story: Poems of the Holocaust* (New Haven: Yale University Press, 1987).

KRAKOWSKI, SHMUEL, *The War of the Doomed: Jewish Armed Resistance in Poland 1942–1944*, trans. O. Blaustein (New York: Holmes & Meier, 1984).

—— 'Memorial Projects and Memorial Institutions Initiated by She'erit Hapletah', in Yisrael Gutman and Avital Saf (eds.), *She'erit Hapletah, 1944–1948: Rehabilitation and Political Struggle. Proceedings of the Sixth Yad Vashem International Conference, October 1985* (Jerusalem: Yad Vashem, 1990), 388–98.

—— and ALTMAN, ILYA (eds.), 'The Testament of the Last Prisoners of the Chełmno Death Camp', *Yad Vashem Studies*, 21 (1991), 105–23.

KRALL, HANNA, *Shielding the Flame: An Intimate Conversation with Dr. Marek Edelman, the Last Surviving Leader of the Warsaw Ghetto Uprising*, trans. Joanna Stasinska and Lawrence Weschler (New York: Henry Holt, 1977).

KRAUS, OTA, and KULKA, ERICH, *Továrna na smrt: dokument o Osvetimi* (Prague: Nase vojsko, 1946); published in English as *The Death Factory: Documents on Auschwitz*, trans. Stephen Jolly (Oxford: Pergamon, 1966).

KUSHNER, TONY, 'The British and the Shoah', *Patterns of Prejudice*, 23/3 (1989), 3–16.

—— 'The Impact of the Holocaust on British Society and Culture', *Contemporary Record*, 5/2 (1991), 349–75.

—— *The Holocaust and the Liberal Imagination: A Social and Cultural History* (Oxford: Blackwell, 1994).

—— 'Holocaust Survivors in Britain: An Overview and Research Agenda', *Journal of Holocaust Education*, 4/2 (1995), 147–66.

LACOUE-LABARTHE, PHILIPPE, *Heidegger, Art and Politics: The Fiction of the Political*, trans. Chris Turner (Oxford: Blackwell, 1990).

LAGERWEY, MARY D., *Reading Auschwitz* (London: Sage, 1998).

LAKS, SZYMON, *Music of Another World*, trans. Chester A. Kisiel (Evanston, Ill.: Northwestern University Press, 1989); translation of the French original with Coudy, René, *Musique d'un autre monde* (Paris: Mercure de France, 1948).

LANG, BEREL, 'Holocaust Memory and Revenge: The Presence of the Past', *Jewish Social Studies: History, Culture, and Society*, 2/2 (Winter 1996), 1–20.

LANGBEIN, HERMANN, *Die Stärkeren: Ein Bericht aus Auschwitz und anderen Konzentrationslagern* (Vienna: Stern, 1949).

LANGER, LAWRENCE, *The Holocaust and the Literary Imagination* (New Haven: Yale University Press, 1975).

—— *The Age of Atrocity: Death in Modern Literature* (Boston: Beacon Press, 1978).

—— *Versions of Survival: The Holocaust and the Human Spirit* (Albany, NY: State University of New York Press, 1982).

—— *Art from the Ashes* (New York: William Morrow, 1991).

—— *Holocaust Testimonies: The Ruins of Memory* (New Haven: Yale University Press, 1991).

—— 'The Literature of Auschwitz', in Yisrael Gutman and Michael Berenbaum (eds.), *Anatomy of the Auschwitz Death Camp* (Bloomington, Ind.: Indiana University Press, 1994), 601–19.

—— *Admitting the Holocaust: Collected Essays* (Oxford: Oxford University Press, 1995).

—— *Preempting the Holocaust* (New Haven: Yale University Press, 1998).

—— 'Gendered Suffering? Women in Holocaust Testimonies', in Dalia Ofer and Lenore J. Weitzman (eds.), *Women in the Holocaust* (New Haven: Yale University Press, 1998), 351–63.

LANZMANN, CLAUDE, *Shoah: An Oral History of the Holocaust. The Complete Text of the Film* (New York: Pantheon, 1985).

LAPPIN, ELENA, 'The Man with Two Heads', *Granta*, 66 (Summer 1999), 7–65.

LAQUEUR, WALTER, *The Terrible Secret: An Investigation into the Suppression of Information about Hitler's 'Final Solution'* (London: Weidenfeld & Nicolson, 1980).

LAQUEUR WEISS, RENATA, *Bergen-Belsen Tagebuch 1944/45*, trans. Peter Wiebke (Hannover: Fackelträger, 1983).

—— *Schreiben im KZ: Tagebücher 1940–1945* (Bremen: Donat, 1991).

LASKER-WALLFISCH, ANITA, *Inherit the Truth 1939–1945: The Documented Experiences of a Survivor of Auschwitz and Belsen* (London: Giles de la Mare, 1996).

LAUB, DORI, 'Bearing Witness, or the Vicissitudes of Listening', in Shoshanna Felman and Dori Laub, *Testimony: Crises of Witnessing in Literature, Psychoanalysis and History* (New York: Routledge, 1992), 57–74.

—— 'An Event without a Witness: Truth, Testimony and Survival', in Shoshanna Felman and Dori Laub, *Testimony* (New York: Routledge, 1992), 75–92.

LEHRER, SHELOMOH ZALMAN, and STRASSMAN, LEIZER, *The Vanished City of Tsanz* (Southfield, Mich.: Targum, 1997).

LEITNER, ISABELLA, *Fragments of Isabella: A Memoir of Auschwitz* (New York: Thomas Y. Crowell, 1978).

LENGYEL, OLGA, *Souvenirs de l'au-delà* (Paris: Éditions du Bateau Ivere, 1946); published in English as *Five Chimneys: The Story of Auschwitz*, trans. Clifford Coch and Paul P. Weiss (Chicago: Ziff-Davis, 1947), and later as *Five Chimneys: A Woman Survivor's True Story of Auschwitz* (Chicago: Academy Chicago Publishers, 1995).

LETTICH, ANDRÉ ABRAHAM DAVID, *Trente-quatre mois dans les camps de concentration* (Tours: Union Coopérative, 1946).

LEVI, PRIMO, *Se questo è un uomo* (Turin: De Silva, 1947; repr. Turin: Einaudi, 1958; published in the UK as *If This is a Man*, trans. Stuart Woolf (London: Abacus, 1987), and in the USA as *Survival in Auschwitz: The Nazi Assault on Humanity*, trans. Stuart Woolf (New York: Collier, 1961).

—— *La tregua* (Turin: Einaudi, 1963); published in the UK as *The Truce*, trans. Stuart Woolf (London: The Bodley Head, 1965), and in the USA as *The Reawakening*, trans. Stuart Woolf (New York: Collier, 1965).

—— *L'altrui mestiere* (Turin: Einaudi, 1985); published in English as *Other People's Trades*, trans. Raymond Rosenthal (London: Michael Joseph, 1995).

—— *I sommersi è i salvati* (Turin: Einaudi, 1986); published in English as *The Drowned and the Saved*, trans. Raymond Rosenthal (London: Abacus, 1988).

—— 'Afterword: The Author's Answers to His Readers' Questions', trans. Ruth Feldman, in *If This is a Man* and *The Truce*, trans. Stuart Woolf (London: Abacus, 1987), 381–98.

—— 'Revisiting the Camps', in James E. Young (ed.), *The Art of Memory: Holocaust Memorials in History* (Munich: Prestel, 1994), 185.

LEVI, TRUDI, *A Cat Called Adolf* (London: Vallentine Mitchell, 1995).

LEVIN, NORA, *The Holocaust: The Destruction of European Jewry 1933–1945* (New York: Schocken, 1973).

LEVINAS, EMMANUEL, 'Ethics as First Philosophy', in Sean Hand (ed.), *The Levinas Reader* (Oxford: Blackwell, 1989), 75–87.

LÉVY-HASS, HANNA, *Vielleicht war das alles erst der Anfang: Tagebuch aus dem KZ Bergen Belsen 1944–1945*, ed. E. Geisel (Berlin: Rotbuch, 1969); published in English as *Inside Belsen*, trans. Ronald Taylor (Brighton: Harvester Press, 1982).

LEWENTAL, SALMEN [ZAŁMEN], 'Manuscript of Sonderkommando Member', trans. Krystyna Michalik, in Jadwiga Bezwinska and Danuta Czech (eds.), *Amidst a Nightmare of Crime* (Kraków: State Museum of Oświęcim, 1973), 130–78.

LEWIN [LEVIN], ABRAHAM, *Mipinkaso shel hamoreh miyehudia*, ed. Zvi Szner (Tel Aviv: Beit Lohamei Hagheta'ot & Hakibbutz Hameuchad, 1969); published in English as *A Cup of Tears: A Diary of the Warsaw Ghetto*, trans. Christopher Hutton, ed. Antony Polonsky (Oxford: Oxford University Press, 1988).

LEWIS, HELEN, *A Time to Speak* (Belfast: Blackstaff, 1992).

LIFTON, BETTY JEAN, *The King of Children: The Life and Death of Janusz Korczak* (New York: Schocken, 1988).

LINDWER, WILLY, *The Last Seven Months of Anne Frank*, trans. Alison Meersschaert (New York: Pantheon, 1991).

LINGENS-REINER, ELLA, *Prisoners of Fear* (London: Gollancz, 1948).

LIPSTADT, DEBORAH, *Beyond Belief: The American Press and the Coming of the Holocaust 1933–1945* (New York: Free Press, 1986).

LUBETKIN, ZIVIA, *The Last on the Wall* (Tel Aviv: Hakibbutz Hameuchad, 1947) [Hebrew].

—— *Die Letzen Tage des Warschauer Ghetto* (Berlin: VVN, 1949); published in English as *In the Days of Destruction and Revolt*, trans. Ishai Tubbin (Tel Aviv: Beit Lohamei Hagheta'ot, 1981).

LUPTON, DEBORAH, *The Emotional Self* (London: Sage, 1998).

LYOTARD, JEAN-FRANÇOIS, *The Différend: Phrases in Dispute*, trans. Georges van den Abbeele (Manchester: Manchester University Press, 1988).

MAECHLER, STEFAN, *The Wilkomirski Affair: A Study in Biographical Truth*, trans. John E. Woods (New York: Schocken, 2001).

MANKOWITZ, ZEEV, 'The Affirmation of Life in She'erit Hapleita', *Holocaust and Genocide Studies*, 5 (1990), 13–21.

—— 'The Formation of *She'erit Hapleita*: November 1944–July 1945', *Yad Vashem Studies*, 20 (1990), 337–70.

—— *Life between Memory and Hope: The Survivors of the Holocaust in Occupied Germany* (Cambridge: Cambridge University Press, 2002).

MARCUS, JOSEPH, *Social and Political History of the Jews in Poland, 1919–1939* (Berlin: Mouton, 1983).

MARCUSE, GÜNTHER, 'The Diary of Günther Marcuse (The Last Days of the Gross-Bressen Training Centre)', trans. Joseph Walk, *Yad Vashem Studies*, 8 (1970), 159–81.

MARK, BER (ed.), *Megilas Oyshvits* (Tel Aviv: Israel Book, 1977); published in English as *The Scrolls of Auschwitz* (Tel Aviv: Am Oved, 1985).

MARKS, JANE, *The Hidden Children: The Secret Survivors of the Holocaust* (London: Piatkus, 1993).

MARRUS, MICHAEL, *The Holocaust in History* (Harmondsworth: Penguin, 1993).

—— 'The Holocaust at Nuremberg', *Yad Vashem Studies*, 26 (1998), 5–41.

MARSHALL, ROBERT, *In the Sewers of Lvov: The Last Sanctuary from the Holocaust* (London: Fontana, 1991).

MEED, VLADKA, *Fun beyde zaytn geto-moyer* (New York: Workmen's Circle, 1948); published in English as *On Both Sides of the Wall*, trans. Benjamin Meed (Tel Aviv: Hakibbutz Hameuchad, 1973).

MENASCHE, ALBERT, *Birkenau (Auschwitz II): (Memoirs of an Eye-witness). How 72,000 Greek Jews Perished*, trans. Isaac Saltiel (New York: Albert Martin, 1947).

MENDES-FLOHR, PAUL, and REINHARZ, JEHUDA (eds.), *The Jew in the Modern World* (Oxford: Oxford University Press, 1995).

MICHELSON, FRIDA, *Ya perezhila Rumbulu* (Tel Aviv: Beit Lohamei Hagheta'ot, 1973); published in English as *I Survived Rumbuli*, trans. Wolf Goodman (New York: Holocaust Library, 1979).

MÜLLER, FILIP, *Sonderbehandlung: Drei Jahre in den Krematorien und Gaskammern von Auschwitz* (Munich: Steinhausen, 1979); published in the USA as *Eyewitness Auschwitz: Three Years in the Gas Chambers*, trans. Susanne Flatauer (Chicago: Ivan R. Dee, 1979), and in the UK as *Auschwitz Inferno: The Testimony of a Sonderkommando*, trans. Susanne Flatauer (London: Routledge, 1979).

NANCY, JEAN-LUC, 'Our History', *Diacritics*, 20/3 (Fall 1999), 97–115.

NEWMAN, JUDITH STERNBERG, *In the Hell of Auschwitz: The Wartime Memoirs of J. S. Newman* (New York: Exposition, 1963).

NIEWYK, DONALD (ed.), *Fresh Wounds: Early Narratives of Holocaust Survival* (Chapel Hill, NC: University of North Carolina Press, 1998).

NOAKES, JEREMY (ed.), *Nazism 1919–1945*, iv: *The German Home Front in World II*, 4 vols. (Exeter: Exeter University Press, 1998).

NOMBERG-PRZYTYK, SARA, *Auschwitz: True Tales from a Grotesque Land*, trans. Roslyn Hirsch, ed. Eli Pfefferkorn and David H. Hirsch (Chapel Hill, NC: University of North Carolina Press, 1985).

NOVAC, ANA, *Die Schönen Tage meiner Jugend* (Hamburg: Rowohlt, 1967); published in English as *The Beautiful Days of My Youth: My Six Months in Auschwitz and Plaszow*, trans. George L. Newman (New York: Henry Holt, 1997).

NOVICK, PETER, *The Holocaust in American Life* (New York: Houghton Mifflin, 1999); published in England as *The Holocaust and Collective Memory: The American Experience* (London: Bloomsbury, 2000).

NYISZLI, MIKLOS, Dr. *Mengele boncolóorvosa voltam az Auschwitzi krematóriumban* (Nagyvarad: Oradea, 1946); published in English as *Auschwitz: A Doctor's Eyewitness Account*, trans. Tibère Kremer and Richard Seaver (New York: Fawcett, 1960).

OFER, DALIA, 'Israel and the Holocaust: The Shaping of Remembrance in the First Decade', *Legacy*, 1/2 (Summer 1997), 4–8.

—— and WEITZMAN, LENORE J. (eds.), *Women in the Holocaust* (New Haven: Yale University Press, 1998).

PAT, JACOB, *Ash un fayer* (New York: Cyco, 1946); published in English as *Ashes and Fire: Through the Ruins of Poland*, trans. Leo Steinberg (New York: International Universities Press, 1947).

PATTERSON, DAVID, *Sun Turned to Darkness: Memory and Recovery in the Holocaust Memoir* (New York: Syracuse University Press, 1998).

—— *Along the Edge of Annihilation: The Collapse and Recovery of Life in the Holocaust Diary* (Seattle: University of Washington Press, 1999).

PAULSSON, GUNNAR S., 'The Demography of Jews in Hiding in Warsaw, 1943–1945', in Antony Polonsky (ed.), *Polin. Studies in Polish Jewry*, xiii: *Focusing on the Holocaust and its Aftermath* (London: Littman Library, 2000), 78–103.

—— *Secret City: The Hidden Jews of Warsaw 1940–1945* (New Haven: Yale University Press, 2002).

PENTLIN, SUSAN L., 'Holocaust Victims of Privilege', in Harry James Cargas (ed.), *Problems Unique to the Holocaust* (Lexington, Ky.: University of Kentucky Press, 1999), 25–42.

PERECHODNIK, CALEL, *Czy Ja Jestem Mordercą?*, ed. Pawl Szapiro (Warsaw: KARTA, 1993); published in English as *Am I a Murderer? Testament of a Jewish Ghetto Policeman*, ed. Frank Fox (New York: Westview, 1996).

PERL, GISELLA, *I Was a Doctor in Auschwitz* (New York: International Universities Press, 1948).

PETRIE, JON, 'The Secular Word HOLOCAUST: Scholarly Myths, History, and 20th Century Meanings', *Journal of Genocide Research*, 2/1 (March 2000), 31–63.

PIPER, FRANCISZEK, 'The Number of Victims', in Wacław Długoborski and Franciszek Piper (eds.), *Auschwitz 1940–1945: Central Issues in the History of the Camp*, trans. William Brand, iii (Oświęcm: Auschwitz–Birkenau State Museum, 2000), 205–31.

POLIAKOV, LÉON, *Brévaire de la haine: la IIIe Reich et les juifs* (Paris: Calmann-Lévy, 1951); published in English as *Harvest of Hate: The Nazi Program for the Destruction of the Jews of Europe*, trans. Albert J. George (Syracuse, NY: Syracuse University Press, 1954).

RAPPORT, HENRY, *Is There Truth in Art?* (Ithaca, NY: Cornell University Press, 1997).

RAWICZ, PIOTR, *Blood from the Sky*, trans. Peter Wiles (New York: Harcourt, Brace & World, 1964).

REDER, RUDOLF, 'Bełżec', in Antony Polonsky (ed.), *Polin. Studies in Polish Jewry*, xiii: *Focusing on the Holocaust and its Aftermath* (London: Littman Library, 2000), 270–89.

REILLY, JOANNE, *Belsen: The Liberation of a Concentration Camp* (London: Routledge, 1998).

REITLINGER, GERALD, *The Final Solution: The Attempt to Exterminate the Jews of Europe 1939–1945* (London: Vallentine Mitchell, 1953).

RINGELBLUM, EMMANUEL, *Notitsen fun Varshever geto* (Warsaw: Yiddish-Bukh, 1952); published in English as *Notes from the Warsaw Ghetto: The Journal of Emmanuel Ringelblum*, trans. Jacob Sloan (New York: McGraw-Hill, 1958).

—— *Polish–Jewish Relations during the Second World War*, ed. Joseph Kermish and Shmuel Krakowski (Jerusalem: Yad Vashem, 1974).

—— 'O.S.', in Joseph Kermish (ed.), *To Live with Honor and Die with Honor!* (Jerusalem: Yad Vashem, 1986), 2–21.

—— *Ketavim aharonim: Yanuar 1943–April 1944* (Jerusalem: Yad Vashem, 1994).

RINGELHEIM, JOAN, 'The Split between Gender and the Holocaust', in Dalia Ofer and Lenore J. Weitzman (eds.), *Women in the Holocaust* (New Haven: Yale University Press, 1998), 340–50.

RINGELHEIM, JOAN, 'Thoughts about Women and the Holocaust', in Roger S. Gottlieb (ed.), *Thinking the Unthinkable: Meanings of the Holocaust* (New York: Paulist, 1990), 141–9.

RITTNER, CAROL, and ROTH, JOHN K. (eds.), *Different Voices: Women and the Holocaust* (New York: Paragon, 1993).

ROBINSON, JACOB, *And the Crooked Shall Be Made Straight: The Eichmann Trial, the Jewish Catastrophe, and Hannah Arendt's Narrative* (New York: Macmillan, 1965).

ROGERS, ANNIE G., *et al.*, 'An Interpretative Poetics of Languages of the Unsayable', in Ruthellen Josselson and Amia Lieblich (eds.), *Making Meaning of Narratives* (London: Sage, 1999), 77–106.

ROLAND, CHARLES G., 'An Underground Medical School in the Warsaw Ghetto', *Medical History*, 33 (1989), 399–419.

—— *Courage under Siege: Starvation, Disease and Death in the Warsaw Ghetto* (Oxford: Oxford University Press, 1992).

ROSE, GILLIAN, 'Beginnings of the Day: Fascism and Representation', in *idem, Mourning Becomes the Law: Philosophy and Representation* (Cambridge: Cambridge University Press, 1996), 41–62.

ROSEMAN, MARK, *The Villa, the Lake, the Meeting: Wannsee and the Final Solution* (London: Allen Lane, 2002).

ROSKIES, DAVID G., 'The Holocaust According to the Literary Critics', *Prooftexts*, 1/2 (May 1981), 209–16.

—— *Against the Apocalypse: Responses to Catastrophe in Modern Jewish Culture* (Cambridge, Mass.: Harvard University Press, 1984).

—— *The Jewish Search for a Usable Past* (Bloomington, Ind.: Indiana University Press, 1999).

—— (ed.), *The Literature of Destruction: Jewish Responses to Catastrophe* (Philadelphia: Jewish Publication Society, 1989).

ROTEM, SIMCHA [KAZIK], *Memoirs of a Warsaw Ghetto Fighter: The Past within Me*, trans. Barbara Harshav (New Haven: Yale University Press, 1994).

ROTH, MICHAEL, 'Trauma, Representation, and Historical Consciousness', *Common Knowledge*, 7/2 (Fall 1998), 99–111.

ROUSSET, DAVID, *L'Univers concentrationnaire* (Paris: Pavois, 1946); published in English as *The Other Kingdom*, trans. Ramon Gutherie (New York: Reynal & Hitchcock, 1947).

ROZETT, ROBERT, 'Jewish Resistance', in Dan Stone (ed.), *The Historiography of the Holocaust* (New York: Palgrave Macmillan, 2004), 341–63.

RÜCKERL, ADALBERT, *Die Strafverfolgung von NS-Verbrechen 1945–1978* (Heidelberg: Karlsruhe, 1979).

SANDBERG, MOSHE, *Shanah l'ayn kayts* (Jerusalem: Yad Vashem, 1967); published in English as *My Long Year in the Hungarian Labor Service and in the Nazi Camps*, trans. S. C. Hyman (Jerusalem: Yad Vashem, 1968).

SCARRY, ELAINE, *The Body in Pain: The Making and the Unmaking of the World* (Oxford: Oxford University Press, 1985).

SCHOLEM, GERSHOM, *On Jews and Judaism in Crisis: Selected Essays*, ed. Werner J. Dannhauser (New York: Schocken, 1976).

SEGALMAN, RALPH, 'The Psychology of Jewish Displaced Persons', *Jewish Social Service Quarterly*, 23/4 (1947), 363–5.

SEGEV, TOM, *The Seventh Million: The Israelis and the Holocaust*, trans. Haim Watzman (New York: Hill & Wang, 1993).

SEIDMAN, NAOMI, 'Elie Wiesel and the Scandal of Jewish Rage', *Jewish Social Studies: History, Culture, and Society*, 3/1 (Fall 1996), 1–19.

SELVER-URBACH, SARA, *Mi-ba'ad le-ohalon beti* (Jerusalem: Yad Vashem, 1964); published in English as *Through the Window of My Home: Memories from the Ghetto Lodz*, trans. Siona Bodansky (Jerusalem: Yad Vashem, 1971).

SICHER, EFRAIM (ed.), *Breaking Crystal: Writing and Memory after Auschwitz* (Urbana: University of Illinois Press, 1998).

SIEGAL, ARANKA, *Grace in the Wilderness: After the Liberation 1945–1948* (New York: Signet, 1986).

SIERAKOWIAK, DAWID, *Dziennik Dawida Sierakowiaka* (Warsaw: Iskry, 1960); published in English as *The Diary of Dawid Sierakowiak: Five Notebooks from the Łódź Ghetto*, trans. Kamil Turowski, ed. Alan Adelson (London: Bloomsbury, 1997).

SMOLAR, HIRSCH [HERSH], *Fun Minsker geto* (Moscow: Melukhe, 1946); published in English as *The Minsk Ghetto: Soviet–Jewish Partisans against the Nazis*, trans. Max Rosenfeld (New York: Holocaust Library, 1989).

SOFSKY, WOLFGANG, *Die Ordnung des Terrors: Das Konzentrationslager* (Frankfurt: Fischer, 1993).

STARGARDT, NICHOLAS, 'Children's Art of the Holocaust', *Past and Present*, 161 (November 1998), 192–235.

—— *Witnesses of War: Children's Lives under the Nazis* (London: Jonathan Cape, 2005).

STAUBER, RONI, 'Confronting the Jewish Response during the Holocaust: Yad Vashem—A Commemorative and a Research Institute in the 1950s', *Modern Judaism*, 20 (2000), 277–98.

STEINER, GEORGE, *Language and Silence: Essays 1958–1966* (London: Faber & Faber, 1967).

STEINLAUF, MICHAEL, *Bondage to the Dead: Poland and the Memory of the Holocaust* (Syracuse, NY: Syracuse University Press, 1997).

STONE, DAN, 'The Sonderkommando Photographs', *Jewish Social Studies: History, Culture, and Society*, 7/3 (2001), 131–48.

—— *Constructing the Holocaust: A Study in Historiography* (London: Vallentine Mitchell, 2003).

STRZELECKI, ANDRZEJ, 'The Plunder of Victims and their Corpses', in Yisrael Gutman and Michael Berenbaum (eds.), *Anatomy of the Auschwitz Death Camp* (Bloomington, Ind.: Indiana University Press, 1994), 246–66.

SUHL, YURI (ed.), *They Fought Back: The Story of Jewish Resistance in Nazi Europe* (New York: Crown, 1967).

SULEIMAN, SUSAN RUBIN, 'Monuments in a Foreign Tongue: On Reading Holocaust Memoirs by Emigrants', *Poetics Today*, 17/4 (Winter 1996), 639–57.

SZMAGLEWSKA, SEWERYNA, *Dymy nad Birkenau* (Warsaw: Czytelnik, 1945); published in English as *Smoke over Birkenau*, trans. Jadwiga Rynas (New York: Henry Holt, 1947).

SZPILMAN, WŁADYSŁAW, *Śmierć Miasta* (Warsaw: Czytelnik, 1946); later published in English as *The Pianist: The Extraordinary Story of One Man's Survival in Warsaw, 1939–45*, trans. Anthea Bell (London: Gollancz, 1999).

TAGER, MICHAEL, 'Primo Levi and the Language of Witness', *Criticism*, 35 (Spring 1993), 265–88.

TANAY, EMANUEL, 'On Being a Survivor', in Alan Berger (ed.), *Bearing Witness to the Holocaust, 1939–1989* (Lewiston, Me.: Edward Mellen, 1991), 17–31.

TARTAKOWER, ARYEH, 'Adam Czerniakow: The Man and his Supreme Sacrifice', *Yad Vashem Studies*, 6 (1967), 55–67.

TAYLOR, A. J. P., *The Course of German History: A Survey of the Development of Germany since 1815* (London: Routledge, 1945).

TEC, NECHAMA, 'Sex Distinctions and Passing as Christians during the Holocaust', *East European Quarterly*, 18/1 (March 1984), 113–23.

—— *Resilience and Courage: Women, Men, and the Holocaust* (New Haven: Yale University Press, 2003).

TEDESCHI, GUILIANA, *Questo povero corpo* (Milan: Editrice Italiana, 1946); published in English as *There is a Place on Earth: A Woman in Birkenau*, trans. Tim Parks (London: Lime Tree, 1993).

TENENBAUM, JOSEPH, *In Search of a Lost People: The Old and the New Poland* (New York: Beechhurst Press, 1948).

—— *Underground: The Story of a People* (New York: Philosophical Library, 1952).

—— *Race and Reich: The Story of an Epoch* (New York: Twayne, 1956).

TODOROV, TZVETAN, *Facing the Extreme: Moral Life in the Concentration Camps*, trans. Arthur Denner and Abigail Pollak (New York: Henry Holt, 1996).

TORY, AVRAHAM, *Surviving the Holocaust: The Kovno Ghetto Diary*, trans. Jerzy Michalowicz (Cambridge, Mass.: Harvard University Press, 1990).

TREVOR-ROPER, HUGH, *The Last Days of Hitler* (London: Macmillan, 1947).

TRUNK, ISAIAH, 'The Organizational Structure of the Jewish Councils in Eastern Europe', *Yad Vashem Studies*, 7 (1968), 147–64.

—— *Judenrat: The Jewish Councils in Eastern Europe under Nazi Occupation* (New York: Macmillan, 1972).

TURKOW, JONAS, *Azoy iz es geven: khurbn Varshe* (Buenos Aires: Tsentral-Farband Fun Poylishe Yidn, 1948).

VALENT, PAUL, *Child Survivors: Adults Living with Childhood Trauma* (Port Melbourne, Victoria: William Heinemann, 1994).

VAN ALPEN, ERNST, 'Symptoms of Discursivity: Experience, Memory, and Trauma', in Mieke Bal, Jonathan Crewe, and Leo Spitzer (eds.), *Acts of Memory: Cultural Recall in the Present* (Hanover, NH: University Press of New England, 1999), 24–38.

VOLAVKOVÁ, HANA (ed.), *I Never Saw Another Butterfly: Children's Drawings and Poems from Terezín Concentration Camp, 1942–44*, trans. Jeanne Nemcova (New York: Schocken, 1964).

VRBA, RUDOLF, and BESTIC, ALAN, *I Cannot Forgive* (London: Sidgwick & Jackson, 1963).

WARHAFTIG, ZORACH, *Uprooted: Jewish Refugees and Displaced Persons after Liberation, from War to Peace* (New York: Institute for Jewish Affairs for the American Jewish Congress & World Jewish Congress, 1946).

212   *Bibliography*

WAXMAN, ZOË, 'Unheard Stories: Reading Women's Holocaust Testimonies', *Jewish Quarterly: A Magazine of Contemporary Writing and Culture*, 177 (Spring 2000), 53–8.

—— 'Unheard Testimony, Untold Stories: The Representation of Women's Holocaust Experiences', *Women's History Review*, 12/4 (2003), 661–77.

WEBBER, JONATHAN, *The Future of Auschwitz: Some Personal Reflections* (Oxford: Oxford Centre for Postgraduate Hebrew Studies, 1992).

—— 'Jewish Identities in the Holocaust: Martyrdom as a Representative Category', in Antony Polonsky (ed.), *Polin. Studies in Polish Jewry*, xiii: *Focusing on the Holocaust and its Aftermath* (London: Littman Library, 2000), 128–46.

WEIN, ABRAHAM, ' "Memorial Books" as a Source for Research into the History of Jewish Communities in Europe', *Yad Vashem Studies*, 9 (1973), 255–72.

WEINBERG, WERNER, *Self-Portrait of a Holocaust Survivor* (Jefferson, NC: McFarland, 1985).

WEISBLUM, GIZA, 'The Escape and Death of the "Runner" Mala Zimmetbaum', in Yuri Suhl (ed.), *They Fought Back* (New York: Crown, 1967), 182–281.

WEITZMAN, LENORE J., 'Living on the Aryan Side in Poland: Gender, Passing, and the Nature of Resistance', in Dalia Ofer and Lenore J. Weitzman (eds.), *Women in the Holocaust* (New Haven: Yale University Press, 1998), 187–222.

WELLERS, GEORGES, *De Drancy à Auschwitz* (Paris: Éditions du Centre, 1946).

WERMUTH, HENRY, *Breathe Deeply My Son* (London: Vallentine Mitchell, 1993).

WIERNIK, YANKEL, *A yor in Treblinke* (New York: American Representation of the General Jewish Workers' Union of Poland, 1944); published in English as *A Year in Treblinka* (New York: American Representation of the General Jewish Workers' Union of Poland, 1945).

WIESEL, ELIE, *Un di velt hot geshvign* (Buenos Aires: Tsentral-Farband Fun Poylishe Yidn, 1956).

—— *La Nuit* (Paris: Éditions de Minuit, 1958); published in English as *Night*, trans. Stella Rodway (New York: Hill & Wang, 1960).

—— 'Words from a Witness', *Comparative Judaism*, 21 (Spring 1967), 40–8.

—— *One Generation After*, trans. Lily Edelman and Elie Wiesel (New York: Random House, 1970).

—— 'Art and Culture after the Holocaust', in Eva Fleischner (ed.), *Auschwitz: Beginnings of a New Era?* (Hoboken, NJ: Ktav, 1977), 403–15.

—— *A Jew Today*, trans. Marion Wiesel (New York: Random House, 1978).

—— 'Trivialising the Holocaust: Semi-Fact and Semi-Fiction', *The New York Times*, 2/1 (16 April 1978), 29.

—— *Legends of Our Time* (New York: Schocken, 1982).

—— 'Questions that Remain Unanswered', in *Papers for Research on the Holocaust*, 7 (Haifa University, 1989).

—— *From the Kingdom of Memory: Reminiscences*, trans. Marion Wiesel (New York: Summit, 1990).

—— 'Twentieth Anniversary Keynote', in F. H. Little, A. L. Berger, and H. G. Locke (eds.), *What Have We Learned? Telling the Story and Teaching the Lessons of the Holocaust: Papers of the Twentieth Anniversary Scholars' Conference* (Lewiston, Me.: Edward Mellen, 1993), 7–8.

—— *All Rivers Run to the Sea: Memoirs* (New York: Knopf, 1995).

—— *And the Sea is Never Full*, trans. Marion Wiesel (New York: Knopf, 1999).

WIEVIORKA, ANNETTE, 'On Testimony', trans. Kathy Aschheim in Geoffrey H. Hartman (ed.), *Holocaust Remembrance: The Shapes of Memory* (Oxford: Blackwell, 1994), 23–32.

WILKOMIRSKI, BINJAMIN, *Bruchstücke: Aus einer Kindheit 1939–1948* (Frankfurt: Jüdischer Verlag, 1995); published in English as *Fragments: Memories of a Childhood, 1939–1948*, trans. Carol Brown Janeway (London: Picador, 1996).

WILLENBERG, SAMUEL, *Surviving Treblinka*, trans. Naftali Greenwood, ed. Władysław Bartoszewski (Oxford: Blackwell, 1989).

WOLLASTON, ISABEL, *A War against Memory? The Future of Holocaust Remembrance* (London: SPCK, 1996).

—— ' "Memory and Monument": Holocaust Testimony as Sacred Text', in Jon Davies and Isabel Wollaston (eds.), *The Sociology of Sacred Texts* (Sheffield: Sheffield Academic Press, 1993), 37–44.

WYMAN, DAVID, *The Abandonment of the Jews: America and the Holocaust, 1941–1945* (New York: Pantheon, 1984).

YABLONKA, HANNA, 'The Nazis and Nazi Collaborators (Punishment) Law: An Additional Aspect of the Question of Israelis, Survivors and the Holocaust', *Katedra*, 82 (1996), 132–52 [Hebrew].

YABLONKA, HANNA, 'The Formation of Holocaust Consciousness in the State of Israel: The Early Days', in Efraim Sicher (ed.), *Breaking Crystal: Writing and Memory after Auschwitz* (Urbana: University of Illinois Press, 1998), 119–36.

—— *Survivors of the Holocaust: Israel after the War* (London: Macmillan, 1999).

YOUNG, JAMES E., 'Interpreting Literary Testimony: A Preface to Rereading Holocaust Diaries and Memoirs', *New Literary History*, 18/2 (Winter 1987), 403–23.

YOUNG, JAMES E., *Writing and Rewriting the Holocaust: Narrative and the Consequences of Interpretation* (Bloomington: Indiana University Press, 1988).

—— 'When a Day Remembers: A Performative History of "Yom ha-Shoah"', *History and Memory*, 2/2 (Winter 1990), 54–75.

—— *The Texture of Memory: Holocaust Memorials and Meanings* (New Haven: Yale University Press, 1993).

ZSOLT, BÉLA, *Kilenc Koffer* (Budapest: Magveto, 1980); published in English as *Nine Suitcases*, trans. Ladislaus Löb (London: Jonathan Cape, 2004).

ZUCKERMAN, YITZHAK, *Sheva hashanim hahen: 1939–1946* (Tel Aviv: Beit Lohamei Hagheta'ot, 1990); published in English as *A Surplus of Memory: Chronicle of the Warsaw Ghetto Uprising*, trans. Barbara Harshav (Berkeley: University of California Press, 1993).

ZYSKIND, SARA, *Ha'atarah sh'avah* (Tel Aviv: Hakibbutz Hameuchad, 1978); published in English as *Stolen Years*, trans. Marganit Insar (New York: Signet, 1981).

Index